A GIFT OF LIFE

A
GIFT OF LIFE

❖❖❖❖❖

by

Alfred W. Beckler

❖❖❖❖❖

RAWSON ASSOCIATES
New York

Library of Congress Cataloging in Publication Data

Beckler, Alfred W.
  A gift of life.

  1. Diabetics—United States—Biography. 2. Beckler,
Alfred W. I. Title.
RC660.B37   1983   362.1'96462'00924 [B]   82-42688
ISBN 0-89256-233-1

Published simultaneously in Canada by McClelland and Stewart Ltd.
Composition by Westchester Book Composition, Inc.
Yorktown Heights, New York
Manufactured by Fairfield Graphics
Fairfield, Pennsylvania
Designed by Jacques Chazaud
First Edition

To Kevin, Scott, and Russell

Our doubts are traitors,
And make us lose the good we oft might win,
By fearing to attempt.

Measure for Measure
Shakespeare

Give, and it will be given to you; good measure, pressed down, shaken together, running over, will be put into your lap. For the measure you give will be the measure you get back.

Luke 6:38

Contents

ototo

Acknowledgments

I would like to thank Allen F. Schmahl, editor of the *Grand Island Daily Independent*, for his help in planning and editing this book. Al has spent thirty-six years in journalism, nineteen as a managing editor, and his assistance has been invaluable to me. I presented the first chapter to him one hot summer afternoon in July of 1981 and since then, he has given unselfishly of his time. I am appreciative of his enthusiasm and encouragement, especially during those periods when I, as a writer, suffered through days and weeks of accomplishing nothing.

I do not know how other blind authors produce the manuscripts they turn over to their publishers. For me the best solution was to use the Dictaphone for the entire book. That meant a lot of typing, because in the course of preparing the final manuscript, the book was retyped three times, not including isolated revisions. Three people who at different stages served as typists also doubled as readers, and I want to thank them.

Karen Gross, my secretary when I started the book, cheerfully accepted the added duties of typist. She also assisted in the basic research, proofread, and helped type the final manuscript. She became a close friend through our association at the business office.

Irene Boehnke has spent many hours working with me. She has a fine sense of humor and always answered my questions about the book with complete candor and honesty. She has remained a close friend in spite of the fact that for the last fifteen years she has sat directly in front of me in choir. Only a really good friend could endure that. She and her husband, Cliff, are enjoying their retirement years in Grand Island.

My wife, Judy, has also spent many hours at the typewriter and has read the manuscript to me so many times she knows it as well as I do. She accomplished this while holding a job in the Grand Island public school system and managing our active household. I appreciate her help very much.

A GIFT OF LIFE

Prologue

❖❖❖❖

How do people react to pain and suffering? Some bend with ill wind, harvest some inner store of strength, and spring back stronger and better for having suffered. Others break.

I've known much pain and suffering in my life. I've had diabetes since I was fifteen, and the disease cost me my sight when I was thirty-three. I've undergone a kidney transplant and two pancreas transplants, the latter in an attempt to cure diabetes. I've faced death more than once—not at some unforeseen, future date but close at hand, when I was brought up short against the fact of my mortality. As one friend told me, "You've had one foot in the grave."

During these times I've tried to bend, to be resilient. Many things helped me through those bleak days and long nights, but the two anchors to which I clung, which made survival possible, were the love of my family and my faith in God's promise that He will never allow anything to enter my life that I cannot bear.

Gold must pass through the fire of a refiner's furnace to become pure, to burn away unwanted metals. And like gold, some lives must also pass through the heat of a refiner's furnace. I was in that fire. I was not consumed, and I know that God's promise is true. Like countless others, I was able to bear it. But I know it is only at my death when, by grace, I will stand before Him completely free of the alien alloys that now flaw the metal of my soul.

Now, in the fall of 1982, my health is excellent. The transplanted kidney maintains perfect renal function and the pancreas exhibits excellent control over my diabetic condition. I'm optimistic about the future. I watch myself closely and monitor at regular intervals those tests that reveal the state of my health. We stand at the threshhold of the development of advanced immunosuppresant drugs and these advances, coupled with other medical discoveries, bolster my feelings of optimism for the future.

My wife, Judy, is also optimistic about the future. Her soft blue eyes flash warm as we plan our life together with our three sons. Her presence was a real strength for the boys when I had to be away, and she has made our home a safe, warm, enjoyable haven.

My family has helped make it possible for me to look forward to the future. I have five brothers and two sisters and they, along with my mother, have helped, supported, and encouraged me during those times when I wondered if there was a light at the end of the tunnel. My brother Victor and my sister Sarah, because of their love for me, and because we share biological similarities, literally gave of themselves to me. But the rest of my family would have done the same.

Friends have also been with me in good times and bad. Duane Obermier and I go back ten years; we met through mutual involvement in church activities. Dr. William J. Landis and I met in Omaha when he was completing his residency. Bill, an internist, became my physician when he opened his practice in Grand Island, and our friendship has deepened over the years. Dr. David Sutherland, another good friend, is a surgeon at the University of Minnesota and heads the pancreas-transplant program at that institution.

Other friends helped bring this book into reality. I think, first of all, of the many who spend time with me in easy, cordial informality, who are always present when help is needed, and whose concern is apparent through all of the many large and small things they do for me. They have watched me almost lose my life on several occasions, have been with me in spirit during three organ transplants, agonized with me over the loss of my sight, encouraged me when I started my business, laughed with me when I laughed, and triumphed with me when I achieved some success. They are aware of what I do, the challenges I accept, the goals I make for myself. They know me as cheerful and smiling in the face of tragedy. That is the face I've chosen to portray. It is a defense mechanism I use to protect myself from the tears. Most of my friends haven't seen or heard the dark side of me—the fears, the anger, the depression. But reveal it I must, for it is a part of this story. And I want these people to know that their friendship has pulled me through some very bad times.

I have never felt discriminated against because of my physical handicap. In fact, I once refused to accept a handicapped-person award for the very reason that, had I accepted it, I would have had to admit that I was handicapped. But I know that other handicapped persons have experienced second-class citizenship. Perhaps this story of someone physically handicapped who attempts things, sometimes failing and sometimes succeeding, who laughs and cries and hurts and rejoices, can help remove some of the barriers that exist between the handicapped and non-handicapped.

The National Kidney Foundation's slogan, "A Gift of Life," is the title of this book. I have received not one but three gifts of life. One gift was needed to save my life; two others were given in an attempt to prolong it and improve its quality. If this book can persuade people to donate an organ to a relative or sign the universal organ-donor card, it will have been worth all of the effort. Tremendous strides have been made in all areas of organ transplantation, and the next few years should bring even more revolutionary advances. I am committed to this program, and I want other people to be aware of it also.

I am a member of the Lutheran Church, Missouri Synod, the church that my father served as pastor for over fifty years, a church staunchly conservative in its doctrinal approach, only slightly ecumenical in its dealings with other denominations, proud, sometimes too stubborn, given to bickering, but always generous and open in her mission outreach to people. I love her deeply. I am proud of the role that I play in placing this large denomination squarely in support of an organ-donor program. Missouri is a conservative church, but she saw the need, and I am proud of the way she responded to it.

Three sons occupy my home, live with me, love with me, fight with me, at times carry on in a fashion that is so mature that I am filled with love for them and must walk away lest they see my tears of pride. Yet at other times, they can act so exasperatingly juvenile that I must walk away lest they see my temper.

Kevin, Scott, and Russell are the real reasons for this book. In the last eight years of our lives, I have been absent from them for twenty-three months. I want them to know where I was and what I was about during those times.

The absences that occurred when I underwent a kidney transplant and when I took rehabilitation training after losing my sight are understandable. There was no choice involved.

The later absences occurred when I chose to pursue a course that I hoped would lead to a cure for juvenile-onset diabetes. I want my sons to know why I accepted the risks I did, even in the face of some formidable odds. I want them to understand the reasons that I placed myself in jeopardy in an attempt to be able to live long enough to meet my daughters-in-law and hold my grandchildren on my lap. I want them to know that while we were separated, I was always concerned about them and thinking about them. I leave this book to them as a legacy, not out of any morbid thought that death may occur at any time, but only because I know that in any life it may occur at any time.

And so, Kevin, Scott, and Russell, I am Alfred William Beckler, your father, the youngest son of Edwin and Frieda Beckler and loved well by them; one of eight brothers and sisters in a grand and glorious family and loved well by all of them; and, after you have read this book and come to know me better, loved I hope even more by the three of you.

The Early Years

❖❖❖❖

1942 to 1971

"Sarah," my mother called from the other end of the long table, "put Alfred to bed. He's so tired he's going to fall asleep in his chair."

My sister rose and I took her hand, following her to my bedroom, my short legs shuffling sleepily. I was four years old and completely exhausted from a day spent outdoors playing in the large yard surrounding the parsonage of a rural Lutheran congregation in south central Nebraska. Sarah had performed this task many times. In our large family everyone helped out, and one of her duties was to keep an eye on me.

"Night, Sarah," I said as she kissed me and rumpled my hair.

"Goodnight," she said, and then continued with her familiar bedtime farewell, "sleep tight and don't let the bedbugs bite."

Before I left the table there had been eleven of us eating supper. I was the youngest child. My father, Edwin Beckler, now fifty-five and a Nebraskan, served a country congregation located near Holstein, and it was in this large, rambling two-story parsonage that I had been born August 3, 1942.

My father, a rather stern individual, rarely displayed his humor, so that the few times he did remain clear in my memory. Once, while standing outside the church after services and greeting the parishioners, he was asked, "Pastor Beckler, do you mind living so close to the cemetery?" The parsonage and the church were parallel to each other, with the cemetery lying behind the church.

"No, I don't mind," he said, standing in the heavy, black gown my mother had sewn for him. A smile turned up the corners of his mouth as the thumb pointed toward the cemetery. "Those members of the congregation don't bother me." Then, as his thumb pointed toward the church, he added, "But those members sometimes do."

Those days shortly after the end of World War II—with the memory of the Depression a decade before still haunting them— weren't easy ones for my parents. There had been times during the Depression when my father would stand with the elders of the congregation after the Sunday church service and, with great dignity, remove his hat and gather the offerings of loose coins into it, which helped sustain us. The dull sheen of copper scattered among the bright silver was moot testimony that his parishioners were mostly poor farmers. My parents supplemented that income and fed their family with the produce of a large garden and with the meat, eggs, and milk provided from the animals that inhabited the barn nestled close behind the parsonage.

The garden we tended was a formidable one. When the entire family was at home it was nothing for my mother to can two hundred quarts of one vegetable. That garden had to be cultivated, and, with strong, healthy boys at home, my father knew just how to do it. He walked behind the cultivator, guiding it between the rows of vegetables. In front, straining on the ropes that ran from their shoulders to the shafts of the cultivator, were two of my older brothers. At the end of a row my father would shout "whoa," remove his hat, and mop his sweaty brow with a handkerchief. Then he would align the cultivator in the next row, and with a shout of "giddyap," march back across the garden. When I was still too young to be harnessed in this fashion, I would prance delightedly beside my older brothers, exhorting them to even greater efforts with shouts of "giddyap, horsey," ignoring the baleful glares that came my way. But when the eldest among my brothers and sisters married and left home, it became my turn, and I spent my time in the hot sun, suffering the same ignominious "giddyaps" and "whoas."

The responsibility for the cows, pigs, and chickens we kept also fell to us children. My brother Gene was adept at milking. He would squat on a stool beside the cow, lean his head against her warm flank, and direct the milk into the pail held between his knees. It was a peaceful scene. The cow chewed her cud contentedly and Gene sang to himself with a gusto never heard in church.

It was evidently too peaceful a scene for some of the other members of the family. One night, before milking time, they gathered in the haymow with an old rubber tire. They waited until they could hear the hiss of milk streaming into the pail and Gene's voice lifted in song, and then they rolled the tire down the steps in front of the cow. The tire gained momentum from its rapid descent, richocheted off the wall, and shot past the astonished beast. The effect was electrifying. The cow's head shot up, her long tail whipped about and caught Gene on the back of his head, and then, with a loud bellow of fright, she reared violently backwards. Gene was caught as one large hoof landed directly in the milk pail, and he was sent sprawling. There was a mass exodus from the barn. The culprits fled from the haymow to the safety of the house. The cow bolted out the door and fled to the pasture, her tail upright and her large udder swinging from side to side. Gene exited moments later, milk covering him from head to foot. He cast a despairing glance at the cow, fast disappearing from sight in the pasture, and then looked toward the house in time to see the screen door bang shut behind the heels of his tormentors.

The cow never did get used to the sight of the tire rolling toward her, and her first astonished look would soon turn to absolute terror as she fled, bawling noisily. Not so Gene. At the first sounds of trouble brewing above him, he would whip the milk pail out from under the cow, win the race with her to the door, and give relentless chase to the rest of the family fleeing toward the house.

The pig, too, provided some enjoyment, and it was after one session in the pigpen that Sarah ran away from home, taking me with her.

"Come on, Sarah," my brother Vic said. "We'll play rodeo. I'm going to rope the pig."

The first throw of Vic's rope succeeded only in moving the pig from the mud hole. It stood and eyed Vic, its back close to the fence, where the rest of us stood watching the action.

"Come on, Vic, you can do better than that," someone shouted, and again the rope whistled toward the pig, landing ineffectively on its back.

Vic prepared for another attempt. But his aim hadn't improved, and when the rope hit it, the pig squealed and headed for another corner.

"Here he comes," Vic yelled excitedly. "Head him off. Scare him back."

We all screamed and shouted to no avail, but Sarah was more prepared than the rest of us. She leaned over the fence brandishing a stout piece of wood.

"Get back, pig. Get out of here. Shooo."

The pig came forward at a dead run and Sarah gave a mighty swing, hitting the pig between the eyes. It dropped like a stone. We stood transfixed, rooted to the spot for an eternity, staring at the huge black animal. Finally, Vic nudged it with his toe. When it didn't move he said breathlessly, "Sarah, I think you killed it." As those awful words shattered the silence, we all glanced uneasily at the house behind us. Where were Dad and Mom? And as the awful realization of what had happened came over the group, everyone slunk away until only Vic, Sarah, and I were left standing by the prostrate animal. Vic wanted to flee with the others, but he couldn't—the game had been his idea.

"What are we—," Vic began and then corrected himself quickly, "what are you going to tell Dad?"

"Well, I—I," Sarah said defensively, not relishing the thought of the imminent punishment, "I'm just going to run away. And I'm going to take Alfred with me."

We hadn't gone far down the gravel road that led past our home, perhaps half a mile, when my legs began to tire. "Sarah," I whined, "let's stop. I'm hungry." We sat in the ditch and, as if by magic, she produced a sandwich from the provisions she had packed in a tin syrup pail. There we sat in the ditch, eating our sandwich and hiding as a few cars went past. As the afternoon lengthened and we continued to occupy the ditch, Sarah became disenchanted with her idea.

"We'll have to go back," she said resignedly, sure of the punishment that awaited her.

Mom was frantic when we entered the yard. "Where have you been? I've looked everywhere for you," she asked, relief flooding her voice.

Sarah was contrite and admitted her sin.

"I killed the pig," she sobbed. "I knew Dad would be mad and I'd get a lickin', so I took Alfred and ran away."

"You what?" Mom asked.

"I killed the pig."

Mom walked around the house toward the pigpen, Sarah and I following dejectedly. The pig was in his favorite mud hole, and as we approached, he stood up and grunted amiably.

"You didn't kill the pig. You only knocked it out," Vic said later, rubbing his bottom. "If you wouldn't have said anything, we wouldn't have gotten a spanking."

But we kids weren't mean. We were normal children filled with a healthy streak of orneryness, and we grew up close-knit and loving in the parsonages of the congregations that my father served. Those days when money was scarce and all of us had to pitch in to help with daily chores—those days provided the mortar that has bound us together as an extraordinarily close, supportive family. My mind is filled with memories of times spent with my brothers and sisters. Since I was the youngest, the baby of the family, they spoiled me rotten.

Eventually, my father accepted a call to Zion, a rural congregation near Tobias, Nebraska, and there, in the fall of 1957, I began my sophomore year of high school. I was playing football, and it was at the practices that I first noticed something was wrong. No matter how much water I drank, I was always thirsty, and the exertion of running made my mouth dry as cotton. In an attempt to keep the saliva flowing, I chewed on the tie strings of my shoulder pads. The burning thirst and excessive urination, which sometimes made eight to ten nightly trips to the bathroom necessary, was soon joined by other symptoms. I developed a tremendous appetite. But in spite of eating large amounts of food, I lost weight dramatically. My parents became alarmed and took me to the doctor.

After examining me, the doctor made his diagnosis. "Alfred's blood sugar is much too high, and he's spilling sugar into his urine. He has the classic symptoms of juvenile-onset diabetes."

He went on to explain. "In people who have diabetes, the pancreas loses the ability to produce a hormone called insulin. Insulin is used by the body to help metabolize sugar. When there isn't enough insulin present, the sugar levels begin to build up in the blood, finally reaching a point where they are so high that the kidneys excrete the sugar into the urine. If this condition is left unchecked, ketones are produced, the acidity in the body becomes dangerously high, and a coma may develop."

Mother took my hand in a protective gesture, and I saw the look of alarm in her face.

Now he looked directly at me. "Alfred, this is how we're going to treat your diabetes. Your pancreas isn't producing the insulin you need, so starting tomorrow morning we'll begin giving you insulin. Now we can't give it to you in a pill." He paused, looked at me closely, and continued, "The only way you can take insulin is by taking a shot."

"You mean with a needle," I murmured.

"Yes, that's right."

"Will I have to take them for a long time?"

"You'll have to take them for the rest of your life." He then addressed the three of us. "Taking insulin by injection is only part of the therapy. The other part is to control his diet. We need to give him enough calories to supply the energy he needs to function normally, and also to provide all the basic vitamins and nutrients. What we need to do is balance the amount of insulin he takes with the amount of calories he eats. His insulin must be sufficient to keep the blood-sugar levels from going too high. But he can't be given so much insulin that insulin reactions occur."

"What are insulin reactions?" my father asked.

"Insulin reactions occur when there is too much insulin present, which drives the blood-sugar levels too low. You'll know when you're having one," he said to me. "You'll feel kind of nervous and you'll be weak and flushed, but don't worry. They're easy to handle. All you have to do is eat a piece of candy or drink a glass of orange juice, and that will raise your blood-sugar level. One thing is very important, though. Once you take your insulin in the morning, you have to eat your meals on time, or else insulin reactions will occur. You can't skip a meal. Also, if you exercise strenuously, you'll burn up excess sugar, and if you don't replace it, that can also cause an insulin reaction."

I didn't like any of what the doctor said, but I was most upset about having to give up football. When I asked why I had to give it up, he had only insisted, "You'll do much better if you participate in a non-contact sport." He did not tell me about the possible serious side effects that can complicate a diabetic's life, particularly a juvenile-onset diabetic. But diabetes is an iffy disease. It affects people differently, and he had no way of knowing that I would be one of the unlucky ones.

Being a diabetic affected my life very little at first, and after spending several weeks at home to adjust my diet and insulin intake, I went back to school. The fact that I was a diabetic didn't bother me, and during the balance of that school year and for the next three years, while in high school and college at Concordia in Seward, Nebraska, I neither tried to hide the fact from my classmates nor felt embarrassed if they knew.

I met Judy in early 1962. My father had retired from the ministry, and my parents had moved to Grand Island, Nebraska, a city of approximately thirty-eight thousand located in the center of the state. I hadn't gone back to college the previous fall; instead,

I had taken a job and was living at home. I didn't want my parents to pay for my telephone calls to the girl I was dating, so I made them at the telephone office. After one of those calls, I stopped at the desk to pay, and that's when I met the pretty, blue-eyed, brown-haired service representative. Our courtship didn't set any records for brevity, but it didn't last all that long, either. In the spring when I popped the question, she didn't need time to consider it. She said yes and on September 8, 1962, we were married.

My sister, Sarah, was a model of quiet decorum as she sang at the wedding service, but afterwards she was the one who led the assault of Becklers on my car, leaving it with shoe-polish messages printed on the top and minus a front seat. I tried driving it sitting on a wastebasket turned upside down, but that didn't work. I was finally able to retrieve the front seat but was unable to retrieve my bride from the various Becklers who had "kidnapped" her. It was a very impatient young man who cooled his heels pacing the sidewalk in front of the home of his new in-laws, but at last Judy reappeared. After a brief honeymoon, we took up residence in Denver, Colorado, where Judy continued to work for the telephone company and I went to work for a hospital.

We loved Denver. We didn't have much money, but the things we enjoyed—the walks, the outings to the mountains, and the Sunday-afternoon drives—didn't cost much. Early in 1963 I took a job with a national food company and we moved to Scottsbluff, Nebraska, a city located in the panhandle of the state, close to the Wyoming border.

We were thrilled when Judy became pregnant, and, during the course of her pregnancy, I accompanied her on many of the trips she made to the doctor. "Diabetes can be hereditary," he had told us. Although we had talked about my diabetes before we married, we had only talked about how it affected me. However, the doctor was reassuring. "There's no history of diabetes in your family. And it's possible that your diabetes may have been caused from an injury or some other complication, and, if that's the case, you won't pass it on to your children." Nevertheless, since we were—and are—unsure of what caused my diabetes, we awaited the birth of our first child with great concern.

"I'm going to take the dog for a walk in the park," I told Judy late on Saturday afternoon. "Want to come along?"

"All right," she said, pushing her very pregnant body up from the chair, "but I'm not going to walk very far."

"Maybe a walk is what you need to help things get started," I teased her. "I'll probably have to take you to the hospital tonight."

And that's exactly what I did. The next day, April 26, 1964, at 4:26 P.M., Kevin was born.

As I stood in the hallway, the nurse gave me a peek at my new son. He was squalling mightily, his little fist tucked under his chin; his head showed the marks of the forceps. Judy and Kevin were doing fine. I had a son, and I wasn't surprised by that fact, since I had known, positively and absolutely, that the baby would be a boy.

We moved back to Grand Island in 1965 and I took a job with another national food company. We rented an old farmhouse from Judy's uncle, five miles north of town. It had been in her family since the turn of the century. We papered, painted, and did minor remodeling, and our home acquired a new charm. We loved the quiet of the country, the peace and solitude, the walks down the long lane in the evenings with the sound of the frogs croaking, and the serenity that seems to come with living away from the bustle and noise of a city.

Judy was pregnant during the summer of 1966, and on September 30 I took her to the hospital. I was concerned that Judy and the baby do well. And I positively, absolutely knew that the baby was going to be a girl.

"Congratulations, Mr. Beckler. It's a boy."

"What?" I stammered, unbelieving.

When we got the baby home, I changed Scott's diapers for the first time and confirmed the doctor's diagnosis. He was right— I had another son.

Rusty's arrival, on March 13, 1968, completed our family.

To say that the boys were a constant delight would be stretching the truth. No three boys separated in age by a mere four years would be a constant delight, but even though our days were at times harried, we enjoyed them.

"Al," Judy called from the backyard late one summer evening, "come take a look at this."

I stepped out of the house and watched as my sons, all in their birthday suits, cavorted around the yard, frisky as young colts. Judy had placed a large tub of warm water on the lawn and had just given them a bath.

They were running in wild, joyous circles around trees and were filled with the exuberance of childhood. They were healthy and growing normally.

As Judy and I, now living in our home on Twelfth Street approached our tenth anniversary, I sometimes worried about my health. Although I had regular checkups and everything seemed to be fine, I felt at times a vague uneasiness. Was I really doing all right? At times I didn't feel well, and by now I knew of many complications that diabetes could cause. There were times when I thought about them at length.

Trouble Brewing

❖❖❖❖

Summer 1972 to October 1973

"Look out, Beckler, or I'll hit you," Purdy shouted as he ran past me.

I remembered when Ron had initiated me into the handball court with a soft serve that landed behind me and then drilled into the cheek of my rump. I hadn't been able to sit down for a week.

As I moved to my left, he took the ball off the forward wall and hit it hard with his right hand. It shot past my right side, and I was too far out of position to return it.

"Thanks for the game, fellows," I heard his partner say.

My partner, Dick DeMuth, and I headed toward the trap door at the back of the court.

Earlier, Dick had already challenged the two players on the farthest court to a game, and although I was tired, I had agreed to play.

I shouldn't have been tired. I had played only one game, doubles at that. But I sat down for a minute to catch my breath.

I was twenty-nine. I stood five feet, eleven inches tall and weighed one hundred and fifty pounds, with just the smallest beginnings of a roll around my middle. After deciding to take up handball, I'd also had a physical and everything seemed to be fine. Although my blood pressure was a little high, it wasn't high enough to warrant medication. The doctor had also said, "your kidney's are passing protein into your urine, but that's to be expected in someone who has been a juvenile-onset diabetic for fourteen years."

Yet this summer I began to realize something might be wrong. The fast starts and stops on the handball court were becoming more difficult, and I winded easily. Still I put in the same number of games as the other fellows in my league.

That day, after one more game, Dick and I hit the locker room, and I stretched out on the bench to rest. After a few minutes I sat up, and, removing my shoes and socks, discovered that my ankles were so swollen that the elastic bands of my socks had made a deep indentation into my flesh. I was dumbfounded. I didn't remember hurting my ankles. Yet, even though they were swollen, I had no pain. I was baffled.

When I went to bed that night, they were still swollen. By the next morning, however, my ankles were completely normal.

I promptly forgot the incident, but a week later I was reminded of it. I was wearing short boots with tops that came above the ankles. At the end of the day, my ankles were so swollen that I could not put my finger into the top of the boot, but again by next morning they had returned to normal. Soon hardly a day went by when they weren't swollen by mid-afternoon.

Finally, I made an appointment to see the doctor. The nurse asked for a urine sample and drew some blood. The doctor took my blood pressure. He didn't ask how I felt, or why I was there. Perhaps he had already seen the lab report, I thought. Perhaps he already knew what the problem was.

I told him about the ankles and about being tired. He pressed my ankle with his thumb. A small depression remained.

"Al," he said, "your problem isn't your ankles, it's your kidneys. They are allowing more and more protein to pass through into your urine. At times they also lack the capacity to expel the excess water that your body accumulates. This excess water collects in the lowest parts of your body, causing the swelling. During the day, while you are in an upright position, gravity pulls the water downward. At night the kidneys are able to expel most of the excess water, and the rest of it is dissipated throughout the body."

"How bad are my kidneys, Doctor?" I asked.

"Well, they are still functioning fairly normally, but another function they regulate is beginning to act up. Your blood pressure is high. It's 167 over 92." He checked it again, but it was only slightly lower.

"We're going to have to do something about that pressure. I'm going to give you a prescription, and I want you to start taking it right away."

Two days later I was back in his office.

"I have the test results back from the lab," he said. "They're pretty much what I'd expected. Your serum creatinine and BUN are too high. Your hematocrit is elevated, too."

"Are all of those regulated by the kidneys?" I asked.

He described at length the various functions of the kidneys and how they controlled those blood chemistries.

"If that swelling in your ankles continues, I'll have to put you on a diuretic."

He took my blood pressure.

"It's about the same as two days ago," he said. "I want to keep tabs on it, so see me again in ten days. If anything comes up in the meantime, let me know."

August was a busy month. I was working as a sales broker, selling to wholesale and retail accounts, and was preoccupied with several sales that had to be closed before the month ended. During the first part of August, I stayed away from the handball court and I didn't run or jog as I had in the past. But my next visit to the doctor, my blood pressure was measured as 140 over 80, so I went back to those activities.

By the end of the month however, my ankles were swollen every day, sometimes by noon. And several times in late August I started having severe headaches. Once, the headache was so severe I pulled the car off the road to lie down until it passed. I wondered whether these headaches were related to the kidney problem and high blood pressure.

Then, one morning in mid-September, I felt a sharp pain on the side of my chest, but it lasted only for a second. I didn't pay much attention to it. One day about a week later, however, I started to experience a different feeling in the center of my chest. There was no pain, just a sensation that something was wrong with my heart. The next day it was gone. I tried to put the thought of heart problems out of my mind. After all, I was only thirty, too young for heart trouble. Several days later I again had the funny feeling in my chest, and again it receded. But on the morning of September 24, I could ignore it no longer. I was driving downtown and at the Third Street intersection, my unvoiced fears took on a new meaning. There was nothing uncertain or obscure about what was happening—my heart was skipping beats. I could feel it fluttering. When the light changed, I turned and headed directly to the doctor's office.

The receptionist, noting that I wasn't expected, asked me what I wanted.

"I think I'm having a heart attack," I told her urgently.

Her manner changed abruptly.

"Sit in that chair nearest the hall," she indicated with a motion of her hand.

I sat down nervously. As I waited for the nurse, the door opened and my brother-in-law's father, Jim Livingston, Sr., entered. He noticed me sitting by the door and came over.

"How are you doing, Al?" he asked cheerfully.

"Fine," I lied.

"Ah," he said, rubbing his big hands together. "That's too bad." It was a joke between us. He was a mortician.

Then the nurse opened the door and said, "Follow me, please."

After an EKG and a chest X-ray the doctor came in and reassured me immediately.

"Don't worry, you haven't had a heart attack and you're not in the process of having one."

What had happened, he explained, was that the fluid that had accumulated in my ankles had now accumulated in the heart and was in the process of stretching the heart. He called it Kimmelstiel-Wilson syndrome.

"Don't worry, Al. Although it's serious, it's fairly simple to treat, and treatment is almost always successful. But I'm going to admit you to the hospital."

Judy arrived at the hospital a short time later. I again explained what the doctor had told me. She saw how distressed I was and tried to reassure me.

Later, the doctor came in and entered something on the chart. Looking up he said, "The medication I've ordered for you is a diuretic called Lasix. It will help the kidneys get rid of excess fluid, especially the fluid that's in your heart. I'm also starting you on digitalis. It's a medicine that will help the heart work more efficiently."

Again he assured me that there was nothing to worry about. He was confident that within a few days, my heart would return to normal size. Two days later the X-ray showed that my heart was normal, but I remained in the hospital another five days. When I left, he told me to avoid all strenuous activity. "If you want to, you can drive the car for short periods of time."

This episode had really jolted me. I worried about the possible consequences of all this. How long would it be before other parts of my body became affected?

The rest of the year passed uneventfully. After spending a week at home, I returned to work and was able to cope with the demands of my job.

As the end of the year approached, with all of the family festivities in store, I felt well enough to enter into them whole-heartedly. When Thanksgiving rolled around, Judy and I loaded my mom and the boys in the car (my father had passed away in the fall of 1970). We drove through the night and arrived early in West Bend, Wisconsin. With other family members we had arranged a surprise at my brother Gordon's.

Gordon, a big athletic fellow, two-and-a-half years older than I, was ideally suited for his position as principal of St. John's Lutheran School. His first love is the classroom, and young people are easily drawn to him, but he is also a good administrator and especially strong at motivating people.

Gordon's home had Becklers from wall to wall. The adults took the bedrooms, and the kids spread their sleeping bags in any available spot they could find. Thanksgiving afternoon I agonized through the football game, watching my favorite team, the Nebraska Cornhuskers, take a drubbing from those upstart Sooners from Oklahoma.

December brought a normal holiday season. Lots of parties, preparations for the choir concert, and other festivities kept me busy.

But during the winter months of 1973, my health began to deteriorate. The doctor increased the medication for my blood pressure. The swelling seemed to be more persistent, and I started having headaches again. There were times when I felt sick to my stomach and would spend all day in bed.

On my next visit to the doctor, I listed my symptoms and asked him what was happening to me. He closed my file and turned toward me, eyeing me closely for a long moment. Then he said, "The headaches are probably a combination of high blood pressure and lousy blood chemistries. Your kidneys just aren't functioning normally. Those lousy blood chemistries are also responsible for your upset stomach."

"Isn't there anything we can do to prevent them? They're so bad at times that I can't work."

He continued to watch me closely. His words were slow, measured, and precise, and he considered each word before he spoke.

"Al, we can try to treat those symptoms as they occur, but the real problem is kidney disease. Unfortunately, there isn't anything we can do to reverse the kidney deterioration that's taking place. The best we can hope to do is slow it down."

He paused, his fingers drumming lightly on the top of his desk. "The best advice I can give you is to watch your diabetes like a hawk. Hopefully, the better your control, the slower the deterioration."

I sat frozen in the chair. There was a burning question I was afraid to ask, but I had to.

"Doctor, how long can this, this—deterioration go on?"

"That's hard to say. Every individual is different. You might stabilize and stay at this level for years, or you could deteriorate more rapidly. There's no way we can tell."

In February I picked up a new account, and in March I went to Memphis for a three-week training program. But I found it increasingly difficult to maintain my normal sales routine. I spent more days home sick than at work. In May, I made a sales trip to Rapid City, and, when I reached the motel after the four-hundred-mile trip, I had to go straight to bed. I remained in the motel for the next two days, returning on the third day without having made a single call.

By this time, my blood pressure had become so elevated that two other medications were added in an attempt to lower it. My cholesterol level was also high, and the doctor added a medicine to try to take care of that. And he increased the diuretic. I was now taking twenty pills a day, but none seemed to be doing any good. I was coming into the busiest season of the year, and sales were down. I knew I was in trouble with several accounts. Something had to be done.

Increasingly alarmed at my failing health, Judy suggested, "Why don't you get a complete checkup at a larger medical center? Maybe there are some new medical advances that would help you."

I considered what she said. "Maybe you're right. I just feel lousy."

I made arrangements to enter the University of Nebraska Medical Center in Omaha. After I was admitted, I met Dr. Tom Gallagher. We discussed my problems, and he ordered a battery of tests to be run over the next several days.

"When you're back in your room, one of the residents will visit with you," he said.

I lay down for a nap. I had just started to doze off when the door opened.

"Hi," a booming voice said, "I'm Dr. Bill Landis."

We surveyed each other for a moment. The voice belonged to a short, stocky man about my age. He stood at the foot of the bed with a chart in one hand and a cigar in the other. His light-brown hair was straight and rather long. His white medical jacket was rumpled, and from one pocket his stethoscope protruded.

His jacket was not buttoned, nor could he button it. His stomach betrayed the fact that an occasional beer may have been on this man's diet.

Hardly the picture of a saintly Doctor Schweitzer, I thought.

He pulled a chair up beside the bed and we began to talk. I didn't quite know what to make of him, but within five minutes I had realized that he was extremely intelligent. He shared his knowledge easily with me, and I quickly decided that I liked Dr. Bill Landis. When our conversation was finished, he greeted the patient in the other bed and, putting the unlit cigar in his mouth, left the room.

The next morning the tests started. Before breakfast a phlebotomist drew what seemed to be a large amount of blood. When he finished, there were nine vials of blood lying beside my leg.

"Any left?" I asked.

"You bet," he laughed. "I'll get the rest tomorrow morning."

After breakfast other tests were started. Between X-rays, EKG tests, and laboratory tests, I visited with a variety of doctors. I spent time with a dietician, who, along with Dr. Gallagher, talked about my diet, the amount of calories and the amount of insulin. All of this information was compiled on my chart.

I had seen Dr. Landis several times during the past few days, and by now we were on a first-name basis. He told me that this was his last year of residency, and that he would soon start his own practice.

"I'm considering Grand Island," he said.

I made a mental note of that.

Late on the fourth day I had a chance to talk to Bill and Dr. Gallagher about the results of all the tests. The picture they presented was rather bleak. My kidneys were in poor condition. The tests showed that I was very anemic. On top of that, my blood pressure was continuing to rise. One positive note, however, was that my heart appeared normal. The EKG showed an excellent reading. They changed some of the medicines, and Dr. Gallagher talked to me about the problems that can occur in an uncontrolled diabetic, or, more typically, in a juvenile-onset diabetic. The list of maladies read like a horror story—strokes, heart attacks, high blood pressure, kidney failure, blindness, loss of limbs—it seemed to go on and on.

Dr. Gallagher eased his large frame into the chair by my bed. "Al, I wish I could be more positive about the outlook, but your kidneys aren't working properly, and, because they aren't you've got some real problems. Let's hope that things begin to stabilize for you."

The three of us finished our conversation and Dr. Gallagher left. Bill stayed for a minute.

"It's really been a pleasure to meet you," he said.

"Bill, I feel the same about you, and I want to thank you for all the time you spent explaining what's going on with me."

"That's okay. I was glad to do it for you. Good luck from here on."

"And good luck to you, too, in your medical practice, wherever you finally decide to set up shop."

We shook hands and he left.

I thought about the complications Dr. Gallagher had described. I had spent the last two years of high school and college years away from home, and had ignored dietary restrictions. After we were married, Judy did her best to keep me on a diet, but there were many times when I didn't follow it. Were all of those indiscretions to blame for the problems I was having now, I wondered. During those years had I lit the fuse of a time bomb now due to explode?

I thought about death and the possibility of dying young, but I never framed those thoughts in terms of a specific number of months or years. There were so many things to be done. I had the responsibility of a wife and family, and they needed to be taken care of. In addition there were personal goals that I wanted to accomplish.

No, better not think about death too seriously, I reflected. Just think positively and do your best, and hopefully everything will turn out all right.

For a few weeks, I thought they might. When my condition

seemed improved, I suggested to Judy that we rent a camper and drive to the annual Beckler reunion, this year scheduled in northern Wisconsin.

Reluctantly, Judy agreed to the trip.

But I hadn't told her the real reason. I didn't really want to admit it, but the thought had flashed through my mind that it might be the last Beckler reunion I would attend.

The trip was a mistake. Much of the time I felt lousy. But I enjoyed being around this outgoing, fun-loving bunch. My family was scattered from California to Illinois, from Minnesota to Tennessee, and all except my brother Gene came to this reunion. It was a typical Beckler gathering full of fun activities—water-skiing, volleyball, evening campfires, and songfests. There was even a snipe hunt, with several nieces left waiting in the dark Wisconsin woods for snipes that never came.

Late one evening I sat warming my feet by the fire, surrounded by members of the family reminiscing about other antic-filled reunions, particularly one held several years ago in Grand Island.

On that occasion, several of us had gone out on Kuester's Lake in a large pontoon boat. The late summer night had been warm and balmy, and the moonlight cast an iridescent glow on the still waters of the lake. As Dick Cavenee, our host, eased the boat into a narrow channel, a wooden footbridge loomed ahead, bathed in the glow of the moonlight.

I saw a movement that moments later materialized into a tall figure dressed in a long topcoat. The man lurched toward the bridge, stepped back drunkenly, and then wobbled onto the bridge, holding the rail with both hands. In the middle of the bridge, he turned to face us, lurching and weaving from side to side.

"That guy's drunk," my sister Priscilla exclaimed.

As we all watched the tall figure, we suddenly realized what was coming. Slowly, inexorably, the pontoon glided toward its inevitable rendezvous with the figure. Dick had cut the motor, but it did no good. Slowly—ever so slowly—the boat continued on its course toward an obvious sprinkling.

My sister, Sarah, had accepted the inevitable and giggled. Her giggle was infectious, and I laughed so hard I held my sides.

Others on the boat were hotly indignant, hurling angry words at the figure. Repeated shouts at the man had no effect. His range and trajectory were perfect, and the confines of the boat prevented escape. My brother Gene was laughing, but the smile froze on his face as he dug in his back pocket for a handkerchief to mop his bald head.

As we joined the rest of the family, everyone was laughing uproariously. Then, from behind a tree stepped the tall figure with the long topcoat—the drunk on the bridge. It was Gordon. Completely sober, he had played the drunk to perfection, spraying us repeatedly with tap water from a large syringe. The rest of the family members had lined the bank of the channel, had witnessed all and heard all, and now were reliving each delicious moment of a prank that was vintage Beckler family reunion, and that had been pulled off beautifully.

Although I was glad we had come to this reunion, my participation was limited. I tried to water-ski, but my legs weren't strong enough. I settled for long walks. After one walk, Gordon asked, with concern in his voice, "Al you look awfully pale. Are you feeling all right?"

I lied a little. "I'm okay, just a little tired." I wasn't, and I knew it. Several times I'd developed splitting headaches and had had to lie down. I was tired most of the time and on a couple of occasions, nauseated.

When we headed home, we made another mistake by driving straight from Vic's home in Wausaw, Wisconsin, to Grand Island—seven hundred miles. I paid for it by spending the next two days in bed.

During the following months, my business began to suffer. Sales were down. I just wasn't making the calls. My work day grew shorter and shorter. Often, while waiting in line to see a buyer, I would become sick and have to leave. Driving for any length of time became impossible. My territory outside a two-hour driving radius of Grand Island was not covered except by telephone. During the first part of September I lost two accounts, and later that month I lost my largest account. I resigned my remaining small accounts. The commission I received from these accounts was not significant, and in any event I couldn't bear the humiliation of being fired. I worried constantly about how I was going to bring in some money. Our small savings were almost gone.

I took a job at an office-equipment store in town and pushed myself hard to get to work on time and to make it through the day. When I became sick I would excuse myself and dash to the bathroom, where I stayed much longer than normal. Occasionally I would have to go home and lie down when I was supposed to be making sales calls. The job lasted exactly one month.

I took another job for a company that sold hand tools and my accounts were spread out over a one-hundred-mile radius of Grand Island. By this time I was so weak I could hardly carry the sample-tool case. While training with the sales manager, I became so sick on two occasions that I had to stop the car, get out, and vomit. Around noon the headaches would start. I took large amounts of aspirin, but even when I could keep them down, they did not help. This job lasted two weeks.

By now I was seeing the doctor every ten days, and when I saw him in October, I was anxious to discuss something with him.

He entered the examining room, accompanied by his nurse, who placed the thermometer in my mouth and took my blood pressure. "Two-hundred-twenty-five over one-hundred-and-five," she said. The doctor frowned and looked at her quizzically.

"What was that?" he asked.

The nurse repeated, "Two-hundred-twenty-five over one-hundred-and-five, I checked it twice."

It was the highest reading I'd ever had. The doctor frowned and shook his head and then asked, "How have you been feeling, Al?"

"Same old thing," I said, "stomach's upset all the time, and I just feel sick. Headaches are a problem."

Then I asked the question that had been on my mind for the last two days.

"Doctor, I know that all my problems are with my kidneys. I was reading an article the other night about the kidney transplants being done in Omaha. Wouldn't something like that help me?"

"Al," he said gently, "I don't want you to get your hopes up. They don't transplant kidneys into diabetics."

"Why not?" I asked, dejected.

"Generally, when a diabetic's kidneys are in bad shape, there are a lot of other things wrong with him, too. Kidneys are in very short supply. When you transplant a kidney into someone, you want to be sure that's the only problem they have. Otherwise, that kidney is wasted."

"Wasted!" I cried.

"Wasted is a harsh word," he said. "That's not exactly what I meant, but you can see the point. There are lots of people waiting to receive a kidney. There's not much sense in giving a kidney to someone when the chances are that he might die shortly afterward from some other cause.

"Al." The doctor's voice was softer and more gentle than it had been before. "You know things aren't going very well for you, don't you? All the recent tests haven't been good, and I don't think they're going to improve, either."

I sat back and looked at him. He paused for what seemed an extraordinarily long time.

He fiddled with something on his desk, straightened out a stack of papers, and then said, "Al, if I were you, I'd begin to get my affairs in order."

I felt numb, and the beginnings of cold panic gripped my stomach.

"How much longer?" I asked.

"That's hard to say. Perhaps as early as six months, maybe a little longer," he answered.

I leaned back in the chair, my head resting against the wall behind me. My thoughts whirled as I tried to register what he had told me.

He stood up and said, "I'm sorry. If you want to sit here for a while, you're sure welcome to."

"No," I said, standing up.

I wanted desperately to get out of there. I made no conscious decision to drive home; yet I found myself in front of my house. But I couldn't bring myself to go in. I started walking down Twelfth Street and came to Trinity Lutheran Church in the next block. The fading light made the stained-glass windows dark. I looked up at the cross on the tall steeple. This was my church. I was deeply involved in its activities, and most of my friends were members there. My children attended its school. I stood in front of the church, staring at its wooden doors.

Then I wanted to run, run as long and as hard as I could to get away from what the doctor had said, but I couldn't. Instead I walked and finally, headed home. On a corner, someone was raking leaves and I greeted him mechanically. As I walked, I prayed for strength to cope with what was happening to me. I considered what to do and resolved not to tell anyone about it—not even Judy, at least not yet. I headed across the school playground. Some children were playing a game. As the ball they were throwing bounced toward me, I instinctively picked it up. The face of the little girl who came to retrieve it was bright and full of laughter.

I held out the ball to her, but she did not take it. She stood a few feet from me. Her expression changed to confusion and bewilderment. She saw I was crying. Fear came into her face—the fear any child would feel when they see an adult weep.

She backed slowly away from me, turned, and ran to the others. I tossed the ball toward them and went home.

Facing Death

❖❖❖❖

October 1973 to February 1974

During the next few weeks there were times when I felt almost total despair. The prospect of death did not seem as terrible as the actual act of dying. Once past death, I would be safe. I was certain of my life after death with God, and this thought held no fear for me. But trying to prepare myself mentally to face those last moments was extremely difficult. I protested the unfairness of it all. I was a young man, with a wife and family who needed me. I cried out to God but never against Him.

The doctor had told me six months or more. Practical considerations forced me to think of the "or more" part of his statement. I was without a job, and my family would have to be kept together. There wasn't enough money to last even six months. Although I rebelled at it, I had to consider the idea of going on welfare. I tried to reason that this was why I had paid taxes all these years: now, when I was in need, I should be able to collect from that same system without feeling shame or embarrassment. But despite all my inner wrestling, the fact remained that the idea was repulsive to me.

Those were bleak, bleak days. I tried to get out of the house each day, if only to take a short drive. But there were some days when I never made it out of bed.

Without having told Judy, I became aware that she knew I was facing death. She had seen my health deteriorate rapidly over the past year. And although we never spoke of what was coming and never used the words death or dying, we both mentally prepared ourselves for what we knew lay ahead. We drew closer to one another, each drawing strength from the other.

"How are the boys handling all this?" I asked her late one night.

Judy answered slowly. "They know that you're sick."

"What do you say to them?"

"When they ask why you're home all the time, I tell them that you're sick. They ask me all the time if they can help you."

"Have you told them how sick I really am?"

"No. Have you?"

"No," I said.

"They're frightened—they're so young."

My stomach was upset. My blood chemistries were so far out of line that the taste of ammonia was in my mouth. I stood up and walked slowly about the room trying to ease the discomfort.

"Judy, I want to fight what's happening to me." I breathed in and out deeply, and my stomach began to settle down.

"But the doctor here and the doctors in Omaha told me that it's just going to get worse."

I couched my words carefully.

"I have to be realistic, but damn it," my anger and frustration now spilling out, "I hate to give up."

"Another doctor might know of a medical advance or new medicine that would help you. I want you to find someone who can help you," Judy pleaded.

One evening I became violently ill at the dinner table. I went to the half-bath off the kitchen and was sick for some time. The dry heaves had set in, and I was on the floor on my hands and knees. I didn't have the strength to stand up, so I pushed open the bathroom door and crawled into the den.

As I did, I looked back into the kitchen. Rusty, my five-year-old son, sat at the dinner table, watching me. He sat perfectly still; his hand holding his fork was suspended in mid-air, his face was white and his expression frozen. His frightened blue eyes stared into mine. Fear had paralyzed him. I put my hand on the door and tried to stand up, but couldn't. It took all the strength I had to crawl over to the couch.

Something had to be done. Judy was right. Maybe another doctor would handle my situation differently. The next day I called the Grand Island clinic. The receptionist said that they had a new doctor specializing in internal medicine. He had just graduated from medical school and set up practice during the summer. His name was Dr. Bill Landis.

I remembered him immediately as the resident who had treated me at the University of Nebraska Medical Center in Omaha six months ago. I also remembered the confidence I had had in him.

The examination he gave me on my first visit was quite extensive. After taking blood-pressure readings and listening to my heart, he sent me to the lab for a chest x-ray and some blood tests. When I returned, Bill asked me for a brief history of what had occurred over the past six months. Then he asked for the names and amounts of medicines I was taking.

"Do you have a calculator handy?" I joked.

"That many?" he asked. I listed all the different medications that had been prescribed for me—forty-six pills per day. When I finished, he leaned back and whistled softly.

"Well," he said, "let's see what we can do."

He told me that my heart was enlarged, but that that was to be expected. It was working against a terrific burden. Not only was my blood pressure extremely high, but there was a tremendous amount of fluid in my body. Both of these affected the heart. I was taking a large amount of diuretics, and even though they were helping remove excess fluid, the amount that I was taking could in itself be making me sick. He explained the interaction that these medications could have.

"The basic problem is kidney failure," Bill said. "I'm going to stop two of the medications," he added. He also changed the time of day that I took two others. Then he explained why and what he hoped to accomplish. He was calm, but there was compassion in his voice. Although neither one of us had spoken about it, we both knew the shape I was in, and we both knew that ahead lay a very difficult road. When he was finished, he pushed his chair back, crossed his legs, and folded his arms behind his head. "Got any questions?" he asked.

He seemed to be in no hurry. I considered telling him what the other doctor had said about getting my affairs in order, but decided against it. I didn't have any more questions; he had explained everything in detail.

As I drove home, I thought about our visit. Although Bill had deleted some medicines and altered the way I was taking others, nothing had materially changed. It was apparent that he was very concerned about my case and would do his level best to help in any way he could. He would know the latest techniques and procedures that could help a diabetic suffering from kidney failure. I felt that I had made a good decision in going to see him, and I had confidence in his ability as a physician.

During the next few days, as I considered my financial situation, I realized that I couldn't put off applying for help. I learned that Social Security disability was available for people physically unable to work and went to the local office, only to discover that there was a six-month waiting period before those benefits could be expected. Which meant, once again, that welfare was my only real option for immediate help.

The prospect of going to the welfare office still galled me, but it had to be done. The question uppermost in my mind was, how does one dress when applying for welfare? Do you need to look down and out in order to convince them that you are really needy? Or do you dress so they will see you at your best?

It was a stupid question, and I fretted over it much too long. Finally I decided to dress as though I were going to work.

The welfare office was downtown. As I pulled into a parking spot, I saw two of my salesmen friends near the car. They hadn't seen me park. Immediately, I started the car and pulled out. When I was sure they were gone, I parked the car in the same location. I gripped the steering wheel hard. This thing had to be done, but I didn't want to do it. I gritted my teeth and walked toward the welfare office.

The whole interview process took about two hours. I explained the situation in detail and the interviewer assured me that there would be no problem with my application. All I had to do was have a medical certificate signed by my physician. My heart sank. I would have to go back to see Bill; he would know that I was applying for welfare.

I called the clinic early the next day, explaining to the receptionist that I had a medical form requiring Dr. Landis's signature. I asked if I could stop in before noon, and I told her that I didn't have to see the doctor. The truth was that I didn't want to face Bill. I arrived at eleven and handed the forms to the receptionist. As she glanced at the welfare form, I wondered if it was my imagination that she looked at me a little more coolly than she had two days before. As she directed me to a chair, Bill walked by.

He greeted me. "Hi, Al. I thought I just saw you a couple of days ago. Has something come up?"

"No," I said. "All I need is a form signed. The receptionist has it."

"All right. Go on back to my office and I'll bring it."

Dejected, I walked into his office. He had the form when he came into the room. He looked at it briefly, recognizing it immediately. I started to explain the situation, but he stopped me in mid-sentence.

"That's all right, Al, I've done this before. I'll be glad to sign it for you."

Bill signed the form and handed it to me. Silence filled the room for a moment, and then Bill said, "You're lucky you caught me. Usually, I make my rounds at both hospitals in the mornings. Today was a light day and I finished early. I'm not an early riser—the hardest work I do all day is getting out of bed." He laughed. There was nothing in his manner that indicated he thought less of me. But I felt worthless. He held the door open for me and I faced him for an instant. He started to say something but then smiled, and I left the room. He understood what I was going through and did not want to offend me. This morning he couldn't get through to me. No one could have.

I knew most of the grocers in town, and I resolved not to go to one of their stores and spend the food stamps. I didn't want them to know that I had sunk this low. So late one Friday afternoon, we drove to Hastings for groceries. When the clerk finished totaling our purchases, she turned to me for payment. Just then I heard a voice behind me.

"Why hello, Al, what are you doing here?" someone asked.

I turned and, to my horror, saw a salesman friend. I greeted him and we talked for several minutes. The people in line behind us were becoming impatient. I couldn't put off paying for the groceries any longer. I was caught. Reaching into my pocket, I paid for the groceries with the food stamps. When I turned to say goodbye to my friend, I saw a look of astonishment on his face.

On the drive home I tried to come to grips with our situation. I was on welfare, and even though I didn't like it, I'd have to accept it. Driving to other towns in order not to be recognized was utter stupidity, and it was a mistake I was not going to repeat. It was a tough situation, but I was making it tougher on myself and Judy.

As the holidays approached, I could not bring myself to enter into the spirit of the season. At times, I was filled with such utter despair that I found it hard to go on. The thought that this would be my last Christmas with my family haunted me. I tried to prepare myself for death. I had been blessed with a strong faith in God, and I clung desperately to it. That faith sustained me through those rough times.

When I finally told Judy what the doctor had said, we cried bitterly. I thought constantly of the passage "Now we see through a glass darkly, but then face to face."

I tried to explain to Judy. "Right now we don't understand why things happen the way they do, but one day we will see God's plan and our purpose in this life."

But it seemed small comfort to offer her, and we ached for each other. During those bad days, the bonds of love that had brought us together grew even stronger.

In the middle of December, I checked into the hospital so that Bill could monitor and make adjustments in my medications. He suggested that I include more protein-rich foods in my diet.

"You're losing a tremendous amount of protein, and it has to be replaced," he told me.

While I was in the hospital, the Rev. Eldor Meyer, the administrative pastor of Trinity, came to visit, and for the first time, I told someone other than Judy that I had only a short time to live.

I also told the Rev. Otto Hussmann, who had preceded Pastor Meyer. I had served as chairman of the board of education while Hussmann was at Trinity, and our friendship had grown strong.

As he sat beside my bed, he took my hand in his, and in words quiet but strong, he talked to me of death and of God's sure promise of life after death. His voice held only strength and an unquenchable faith as he led me in the Twenty-third Psalm.

The new year came, and my condition slowly worsened. During January, I was hospitalized twice for short periods. I was very anemic and during the last stay, had to be given whole blood. It was then that I asked Bill about the possibility of going on dialysis.

Bill leaned against the window ledge and put his unlit cigar in the ashtray.

"We've given you whole bood because you are anemic. It's possible that you may be a bleeder, and, if so, dialysis wouldn't work."

"How do we find out if I'm a bleeder?"

"We'd send you to Omaha to run those tests. But let's hold off for a while."

I could tell that he did not hold out much hope. By now it was apparent to family and friends that something was radically wrong with me. I had lost weight and my skin had a pale, sickly look. Word got around that I was out of work and hadn't worked for quite a while. One afternoon, the chairman of the board of elders of Trinity came over with a check. "It's been given by some of your friends," he said.

Then my mother-in-law brought us a hundred-dollar bill. "It's from someone who knows you," she said. "But they want to remain anonymous. They want you to use it however you need it."

My health continued to deteriorate. None of the results of the blood tests were within normal range.

On a Sunday in mid-February, I became acutely ill. Bill said, "Get to the emergency room as quickly as you can."

I was so weak that I had difficulty dressing. I was experiencing sharp pains through my stomach and rib cage. Bill arrived with the results of the tests. My white count had skyrocketed to 26,000; a normal white blood count is between 5,000 and 10,000. I had an infection somewhere. Before leaving, Bill told the nurse to call him immediately if my condition worsened. A few minutes later Pastor Hussmann's wife entered the room. She was the nurse on duty that afternoon.

"I've got a shot for you," she said, and obediently I rolled over on my side.

She stood by the bed and offered a short prayer for me. I was very moved that in the middle of her busy day she took time for my spiritual needs.

My own prayers now were that the end of my life would be peaceful and blessed. Judy's grandfather had died several weeks before. He had chosen not to die in the hospital, but had stayed with Judy's mother. Early on the morning he died, he called out and said it was time, time for the Lord's Prayer, and then he died—calm, peaceful, and dignified.

I hoped that my death would be like that—peaceful for my sake and those who would be with me. I shared those thoughts with Pastor Meyer.

"When I die, I don't want it to be a last, frantic struggle for life. I don't want to cry out and scream. I want to accept it calmly."

"You seem to have given up all hope, Al."

"Yes, I guess I have. What I'm trying to do is reconcile myself to death and to leaving Judy and the boys behind. I read that when a person prepares for death, he goes through different stages and that the last stage is acceptance, but I haven't come to that yet."

"You know that through all this, God is by your side, don't you?"

"Yes, of course," I said, "but I don't understand the 'why' of all of this. I've had to suffer a lot, and it just seems unfair."

I was choking back tears.

Pastor Meyer continued. "Whom the Lord loveth he chasteneth. He'll give you all the strength that's necessary to see you through this. Al, nothing is impossible with God. If it's His will that you die, His promise is sure that He'll be with you. But it's also possible for Him to provide a cure for you. Do you remember the story of King Hezekiah?"

I searched my memory for the story of the Old Testament Israelite king.

"No, not all of it," I said.

"Hezekiah was a king of the Israelites during the period when Isaiah was the prophet. The king was very, very sick, and he prayed to the Lord to save him. The Lord instructed the prophet Isaiah to go to the king. When the prophet entered the king's bedchambers, he told the king that the Lord had heard his prayers, but that he had been sent to tell the king that his sickness was unto death. Then the prophet turned and left the king. When the prophet had gone, the king prayed again to the Lord, this time even more earnestly. Again, the prophet was sent back to the king. He told him that this time the Lord had heard his prayers, and that He would add fifteen years to his life.

"Al, I tell you this story because even though it's wise to prepare for death, we don't know what God has in store for us. It may be that soon He will call you to Himself, but it's also entirely possible for His healing hand to come upon you so you'll be restored again to health."

We talked for a while longer and prayed together before he left.

I lay thinking about what he had said, but my faith was not

strong enough to believe that God would cure me. I knew the course of my illness and its inevitable end. That day, I only prayed that I be granted strength to accept what was happening to me, and that my death be a calm, peaceful, dignified ending to life.

A Glimmer of Hope

❖❖❖❖

February to March 8, 1974

I improved slightly during the next two days. My white blood count dropped, and my temperature returned to normal. The intense pain in my stomach was also gone.

I had finished my lunch Wednesday when Bill came back.

We had grown closer during the past few months, and I knew that Bill had contacted medical centers as far away as California, in an effort to find something that might help me. He didn't waste any time getting to the point.

"What you need, and you need it desperately, is a kidney transplant."

"Got one handy?" I said jokingly.

"I'm serious," he said. "Do you know that they transplant kidneys in Omaha? They've just initiated a new program," he continued. "They will now consider a diabetic as a potential candidate for a kidney transplant."

I felt a tremendous surge of hope as Bill continued to explain what was involved. There might be problems. If I was bleeding internally, that ruled out all possibility not only of dialysis, but a transplant as well. He talked of all the possibilities that might prevent a kidney transplant for me.

"But, I think you ought to give it a try. What do you think?"

"Of course, what have I got to lose?" I replied.

"Great," he said. "I'll make the arrangements to transfer you to Bishop Clarkson in Omaha. It'll probably take a couple of weeks. Meantime, we'll see if we can get you home for a little while."

I listened to the sound of his cheerful voice as it receded down the hallway. The smell of his cigar lingered in the room. I thought about how much I owed him. We had become friends, but more than that, he was a dedicated physician. He didn't throw in the towel. If it were not for his persistence, I would never have been made aware of the new program at Bishop Clarkson.

Later that afternoon Judy visited me, and I told her about the possibility of having a kidney transplant.

"How do you feel about it?" she asked excitedly, pulling her chair up to the bed.

"I don't have a choice; I've got to take the chance," I said.

"Al, this is just what we've been praying for," she said gripping my hand.

We talked about all the things that would have to be done.

"I want to be with you in Omaha," she said. "I can stay with Bob and Linda. I'll talk to my folks about keeping the boys. I'm sure they'll want to help."

After Judy left, my eyes fell on the *Portals of Prayer* booklet Pastor Meyer had left me.

I sat, stunned as a cold, eerie feeling swept over me. I remembered about the Israelite king who had prayed to the Lord and been granted another fifteen years of life. Was I being offered the same opportunity? Was this God's way of showing me that He was still in control of my life? I had been praying for a peaceful end to my life, but only He knew how best to answer that prayer. Did He have something else in store for me, other than an early grave?

My prayers that night were for God's will to be done. For the first time in months, my sleep was sound and restful. A few days later, however, I became very sick again. This time Bill said that we couldn't wait any longer, and he made the necessary arrangements for my transfer to Bishop Clarkson. On Tuesday I made the three-hour journey to Omaha, lying in the back seat of the car.

Bill had given me the name of the transplant surgeon—Dr.

Richard Steenburg. At four o'clock that afternoon he entered my room.

He was a tall, athletic man in his late forties. A pipe was planted firmly in one corner of his mouth and his glasses were pushed a little forward on his nose. His handshake was firm and his manner one of complete assurance. He read the information on my medical chart, lowered his head, and peered over the top of his glasses.

"Well, let's start from the beginning. You first," he said.

I filled him in on the last two years, pausing occasionally to answer his questions. When I had finished, he asked for a list of medications.

"What's your blood pressure like?" he asked.

"Pretty high," I said.

After taking the reading, he looked at me and said, "You're right. It is high. How's the diabetes doing?"

"Lately, not so good. I seem to be having a lot of insulin reactions."

"The next couple of days are going to be full of tests. I'll want to have a lot of blood drawn, some x-rays and other tests run. We should know something by the end of the week."

I looked hard at him.

"Dr. Steenburg, from the tests run in Grand Island, I know what's wrong with me. I'm in real rough shape and if something isn't done, I know how this is going to end up. The odds against you being able to help me are really formidable. I wish they weren't, but I know they are. All I want is a chance—just a chance."

He stood at the foot of the bed, one foot resting on the lower rail. He peered at me over his glasses, tapped me on the foot with the chart, and said, "We'll get the tests started in the morning."

During the next two days, every conceivable test designed to measure kidney functions was run. My diabetic condition also came under close scrutiny. Slowly, my medical profile was emerging in the charts for Dr. Steenburg, and it was not very encouraging.

Judy's parents, Forrest and Irma Pollard, had agreed to keep the boys as long as necessary.

It would be quite a change in their routine, but they were capable, loving people and Judy and I were secure in the knowledge that the boys would be safe and happy with their grandparents.

During the week Judy would stay with her brother, Bob, and his wife, Linda, who lived about twenty minutes from the hospital. On Friday afternoon she would go home to spend the weekend with the boys, returning to the hospital Monday morning.

Shortly after Judy left, my brother Vic and his wife, Gret, walked into the room. I was completely surprised, since I had not been expecting them. We only had a chance to visit for a few minutes before Dr. Steenburg came in. I introduced them, and Vic and Gret sat in the chairs by the window. Dr. Steenburg stood at the foot of my bed, looked at my chart briefly, and then, in a manner that I soon found to be typical of him, came straight to the point.

"Al, we've found that you're not bleeding internally, but the tests show that your kidney function is less than 5 percent of normal. In fact, all the test results are terrible. You're in such poor shape, we'll have to get your strength built up before we can even attempt surgery. Another thing—your kidneys are doing you more harm than good. They'll have to come out. I'm really reluctant to do that until we have a kidney for you."

I thought for a moment and then asked, "How long will it take to get a kidney?"

"A cadaver kidney," he said, "could be available in two days or two years, but you just don't have the luxury of being able to wait too much longer. You're going to have to go on dialysis until one becomes available. Most people tolerate dialysis well, but a few don't. If you're one of the unlucky ones, that would present a real problem."

Vic rose from his chair and stood by the bed. He looked at Dr. Steenburg and asked, "Couldn't one of the family donate?"

Dr. Steenburg looked at him appraisingly.

"Yes, in fact, the chances of success are highest when a family member donates. In Al's case, where time is important, that should be a consideration. And from the number of brothers and sisters Al has listed on the medical-history forms, the chances are very good that one of them would have tissue types that closely match his. You see, you receive two antigens from each of your parents. Antigens are tissue types. Sometimes, members of families will have only two antigens that match, but the likelihood exists that someone in your family has the same four antigens that Al has. In that case, the chances of a successful transplant are around 90 percent," he concluded.

I looked at Vic, who was obviously considering the doctor's words.

"Al, you think about it. It will be a long, hard road if we try it, but you know what the alternatives are if you don't. But you're a fighter, and if you decide to try it, I want you to know I'll help you all I can."

When he left, Vic and Gret stood by my bed. Vic, who stands a shade over six feet, has a muscular build. He's fun-loving, and things always liven up when he's around, yet he's capable of displaying a serious side, too. He is genuinely concerned about people and compassionate in his dealings with them.

Seven years older than I, a great athlete, he had been my boyhood idol. It was a thrill just to tag along behind him. He had met Gret, his wife of eighteen years, while both were in college. Gret is quiet and reserved. When Vic is teasing or kidding around, Gret would say with mock severity, "I just don't know what's come over him." They are an ideal couple and complement each other well.

"What do you think?" Vic asked.

Although Dr. Steenburg hadn't said it in so many words, I didn't have the time to wait for a cadaver kidney. That had not occurred to me before. I pulled the sheet up to my chin and folded it back. My fingers formed a crease in the sheet.

"I think I'm going to go ahead and try for the transplant, but—"

"But what, Al?" Vic persisted.

"Vic," I blurted out, "I can't ask any of you to give me a kidney."

"Why not?" he persisted.

When I didn't answer, he continued, "If the rest of the family knew you needed a kidney to save your life, I know that every one of them would volunteer to give one. Besides, you shouldn't be the one to make that decision for others. They should be free to make that decision themselves.

"Look, Al, if I were lying in that bed and needed a kidney, and you were able to give me one, you would, wouldn't you?"

There was no way I could answer that question except with a yes.

Instead I countered humorously, "Do you remember that time when I was a little kid and you were going hunting? I wanted to go along, but you didn't want to take me. I bawled for so long that you finally told me if I ate a whole bowl of cold spinach, you'd take me. You didn't think I'd do it, but I ate all that crap, and you still didn't take me. Heck, if you needed a kidney, I'd probably walk right out of here."

But he had made his point. Were our roles reversed, I would do everything I could to help him. The ties that bound us together as brothers were strong, as strong as the ties that knit the whole family together. Confused about my feelings, I changed the subject. And Vic, sensing that I didn't want to talk about it any more, let it drop, too.

My dinner tray arrived, and they left to have their dinner. I was not hungry and so pushed the tray away and tried to sort out my feelings. What if one of my family donated a kidney, and my body rejected it? Would they feel that it had been a waste of their sacrifice? Worse yet, what if something were to happen to one of them? I knew that surgery to remove a kidney was a major operation. Did I have the right to ask one of them to take the risk? Everyone had responsibilities of spouse, children, home and job.

About half-past three the next day I was awakened by the sound of Vic tiptoeing around the room. He pulled a chair over to the bed and sat down.

"I've talked to Dr. Steenburg," he said.

"What about?" I asked.

"About the transplant. Actually, what I talked to him about was the possibility of me donating."

Seeing that I was about to object, he hurried on.

"He told me what was involved for you and whoever donated. If someone in the family is a good match, then the chances of success are really high. Dr. Steenburg said that once a good match was found, he would put a fistula in your arm, and then you'd be able to go on dialysis. After that, he'd take out your kidneys, and when you regained your strength from that operation, the kidney transplant would take place."

"Now wait a minute, Vic," I said, "I haven't decided anything yet."

"That's tough, buddy," he said, "because I've already decided to donate mine. In fact, they've already drawn my blood for the tissue-typing test."

I was astonished.

Vic brought his chair closer to the bed and began to talk compellingly.

"I talked to Don last week, and he mentioned that he felt a kidney transplant was the only thing that could save you. Since then I've known that if I were chosen, I would donate. And once I made that decision, I had the feeling I'd be the one chosen. I don't know why, I just had that feeling. Dr. Steenburg did say he would consider all members of the family except those with any kind of health problems. Don and Howard both have mild cases of high blood pressure, so they won't be eligible. But as far as I know, the rest of us don't have any problems, so we should all be suitable candidates."

Vic had been talking in low, hurried tones. Now he sat back and relaxed.

Vic had seen the need and had responded. He was willing to give of himself in an attempt to save my life. He'd also seen my hesitancy, my unwillingness to ask any of the family to donate. He would be the one to approach everyone else, to explain the situation to them. I felt a deep surge of love for him. I fumbled for words to express what I felt, but nothing came. I turned my head toward the wall. When I faced him again, he was relaxed and calm, and his deep blue eyes were steady on my face. Tears flowed down my face as I reached for his hand and gripped it hard.

Two days later the results of Vic's tests were ready. All four of the antigens matched mine exactly. Dr. Steenburg called it a "full-house match." And because our tissues were identical, he was very optimistic.

But Dr. Steenburg also urged that the other members of the family be tissue-tyed. Although it was highly improbable that a better match would be found, he felt it wise to proceed in this manner.

Vic and Gret left early Monday for their home in Wausau. They planned to return later in the week, at which time Vic would be hospitalized to ascertain the general state of his health and verify that his kidneys were functioning properly. He would have specific tests to determine whether he had any tendencies toward diabetes.

Vic and I visited briefly on his return to the hospital. All of the family had called and expressed a willingness to donate— even Don and Howard. Gene would have his blood test in Berkley; Gordon would go to Milwaukee for his, and Priscilla would travel to Chicago. Sarah planned to come to Omaha. All of them were going to have their tests performed the following week.

The operation to install the fistula was scheduled for March 8, also Vic's thirty-ninth birthday. It would be done with a local anesthetic. A small incision would be made on the underside of my wrist, and openings would be made in an artery and an adjoining vein. These two openings would then be joined. Since the pressure in the artery was greater than that in the vein, blood would flow into the vein. A large-diameter needle could then be inserted into the enlarged vein, and enough blood could be obtained for the dialysis machine.

The anesthesiologist gave me a shot in the shoulder, close to the armpit, and my arm became completely numb and ready for surgery. A drape was placed across my chest so that I would not see what Dr. Steenburg was doing.

About two hours later, I was back in my room with my wrist bandaged. Dr. Steenburg said that it would take about ten days for the fistula to mature. My first dialysis was set for March 20, and the date for the removal of my kidneys was scheduled for March 22.

Late Friday, the day the fistula was installed, Vic came in the room.

"So far, the results of all of my tests are positive, and it appears that I will be a very suitable donor," he said. "I even had to talk to the shrink," he added wryly. "Evidently that's standard procedure for anyone who donates a kidney. They want to make certain that you don't get cold feet after it's all said and done."

"What did he say?"

"Well, he wanted to make sure that I knew what I was getting into. I told him I knew what I was doing, and that I was convinced that it was the right thing to do. He said he felt there wouldn't be any problem with me."

"Good," I said, and meant it.

The First Dialysis

❖❖❖❖

March 20, 1974

During the next weeks, the doctors concentrated on building up my strength. I was put on an extremely strict diet—absolutely no salt was allowed. My fluid intake was reduced, and I was put on diuretics to help reduce the amount of fluid that my body was retaining. I forced myself to get up for an hour in the morning and two hours or more in the afternoon. Judy and I went for short walks around the hospital. We spent time in the lounge across from the elevators, while Judy read the cards and letters that I had been receiving. I was retaining so much fluid that even the retinas of my eyes were swollen, and my vision was so blurred I could not read.

All of the students in the boys' classes at Trinity had made cards, and Judy taped them to the wall beside my bed. The messages varied from the terribly poignant to the outrageously funny. Some cards had drawings of stick figures as doctors, nurses carrying bedpans, and patients lying in beds.

Miss Brandt, Kevin's fourth-grade teacher, sent a copy of a coupon book she had given him. She knew that Kevin was upset about my illness, so each coupon was for a special privilege. Interspersed were coupons for a moment of prayer for his father.

Bill Chandler, the principal of the school, sent copies of the board of education minutes and several documents requiring my signature. One paper was to permit a school event in June, and

I prayed that I would be alive to attend it. The letters that I received from my mother were especially enjoyable, full of neighborhood news. And they were also testimonials to her faith in God and her certainty that He would continue to see me through all that lay ahead.

My first dialysis session was set for Wednesday, March 20. By this time, the results of all the tests were in. Gordon, Gene, and Priscilla were two-antigen matches, but Sarah, like Vic, was a "full-house match," which meant that she could donate with an equal chance of success. And although Sarah was every bit as willing, it was decided that Vic should donate the kidney.

Sarah spent the weekend with me the week before the first dialysis was to begin. Hers was a spirit of continued encouragement and support. Sarah, sixteen months older than Vic, is just as fun-loving and extroverted.

On Sunday afternoon she decided that my hair needed shampooing. Against my protests, she rounded up all the necessary equipment, laying extra towels on the bed and draping several around my shoulders. A basin of water was placed on a table across my knees, and I leaned over it as best I could while Sarah scrubbed vigorously. Soon, water was everywhere—down my back, up my nose, and across most of the bed. My scalp tingled as she dried my hair with the rough hospital towels. When she was through, she looked at me and said, "I haven't gotten you this wet since I dropped you into the tank."

The remark recalled an incident from my childhood. We had had a windmill with a pipe running to the tank that supplied water for our milk cows. The pipe extended several feet over the water in the tank. I had wanted a drink from the pipe, and so Sarah held me while I stretched over to take a sip. But she lost her grip and I fell in the tank. I climbed out completely drenched.

Before she left, she sat on the bed and took one of my hands in hers and, with the other hand, brushed my forehead. My hair, once wavy, now lay straight and lifeless.

"You've lost your curl," she said quietly.

"My protein levels are all screwed up. That's probably the reason."

I watched her studying my hair, and tears were in her eyes. For an instant she looked sad; then she bent over and held me close for a long time.

"I've got to go," she said hoarsely. "But I'll be back. Call me when you want to—or when you need to."

I was extremely nervous on Wednesday morning as I walked to the dialysis center. It was a long room located behind the lounge area and the nurses' station. Against one wall were some beds and reclining chairs. Between each of these was a dialysis machine. The beds were used for those patients who were not tolerating dialysis, or who had recently undergone surgery. The chairs were for persons who tolerated dialysis and were ambulatory. Some of the old-timers who came two or three times a week as outpatients would use these chairs.

By now the fistula had matured; it was distended and large. The sound of the blood pulsing through it was so loud that I could hear it through my pillow.

Dr. Frederick Ware, who was in charge of the dialysis unit, greeted me and explained the procedures I would be using.

"You will be connected to the machine by a tube inserted in the fistula in your arm; the tube will conduct your blood into the machine and over one side of a plastic filter. After it's cleansed, your blood is routed back to a vein in your arm by another tube. During the entire treatment, the blood flows through the machine, back through your body, back through the machine, making the round trip about twice an hour. Each trip, some impurities are filtered out. You are scheduled for dialysis three times a week, and it will last approximately five to seven hours."

It was common practice for a patient being dialyzed for the first time to be given Demerol, a painkiller.

"It'll make you sleepy," he said. "You won't be too aware of what is going on. This first time, we'll give you a free trip."

He asked if I preferred a bed or the chair for the next five hours, and I opted for the chair. Char, my nurse, greeted me cheerfully and busied herself getting the machine ready. By this time the shot was beginning to make me drowsy. But I became fully awake when she took my arm and began to probe on the fistula.

"I'm going to inject a little novocaine on the spot where I will insert the first dialysis needle," she explained. Then she injected more novocaine in my arm, slightly above the elbow.

"That's where we'll have to inject the needle into the vein," she said.

The dialysis needle was huge. It had to be in order to ensure an adequate flow of blood into the machine. She had no difficulty inserting the needle into the fistula, which was grossly distended and an easy target.

The second needle was placed above the elbow and taped in place. While she was working, Char explained each procedure to me.

"We're all set now. Are you ready?" she asked.

"I guess so," I replied, "nothing I can do about it now."

She laughed. The dialysis machine was started, and I watched the flow of blood leave my arm and travel down the long tube to the machine. It took a long time for the blood to reach the machine, but I was not alarmed. However, an eternity passed before the blood appeared in the second tube coming back to me. At the rate the blood was flowing in the second tube, I felt I would be drained before any of it reached me.

Char, sensing my alarm, said, "Don't worry. The amount of blood that is out of the body at one time is not significant."

I tried to stay awake as long as I could, but the Demerol was beginning to take effect. I was surprised when Char woke me and said that the session was almost over. Almost five hours had passed.

I sat forward in the chair cautiously. Char helped me stand up and I gingerly took a few steps. I was still dizzy and weak from the effects of the hypo. We walked to the scales where I had been weighed before the dialysis began. Char adjusted the weights of the scale. "Not bad, not bad at all. I wish I could lose weight that easily.

"Things really went well for you today. Pretty soon you'll be an old pro at this," she said.

Neither one of us realized then that the dialysis sessions would be pure hell after my kidneys had been removed.

As I turned to leave the room, Judy, anxiously standing by, took my arm and slipped hers around my waist.

"Let's go for a walk," I said.

"A walk?" she asked, amazed.

"You're not going to believe this, but this is the best I've felt for six months. I can't believe that one dialysis session could make such a difference. I really feel good. Do you know how much water they took off? Five-and-a-half pounds. Five-and-a-half pounds!" I reached down and felt my ankles. They were still swollen from sitting in the chair for five hours. "Boy, I must still have an awful lot of water on board. My ankles are as tight as a drum."

My mother came in the room and asked, "How's Alfred?"

"He says he feels just fine. In fact, he wants to take a walk," Judy answered.

They both looked at me a little dubiously.

"Now Alfred," my mother said, "you shouldn't overdo."

"Yes, Mother," I replied with mock severity.

I was thirty-one years old and the apron strings had been snipped a long time ago. But to my mother, I was still the baby of the family, and a little maternal advice, judiciously applied, couldn't do any harm.

Close Brush with Death

✿┼✿┼✿

March 21 to April 16, 1974

On Thursday, various members of my family came for the surgery, scheduled the next day. Priscilla and her husband Gene Kruse drove from Peoria. Married young and the mother of a large family, Priscilla has kept her family close. She's capable and strong, with a sense of humor that lies close to the surface.

Sarah drove the 275 miles to Omaha by herself. Vic, Gordon, and Howard arrived at various times during the day.

Howard, my third-oldest brother, has the kinkiest, curliest hair in existence. Brushed tightly back straight across his head, it never seems to be out of place. Not as impulsive as the rest of us—certainly not as impulsive as I—he thinks and plans to the nth degree. Once while I was visiting his home, a tube went out on the TV. I was dumbfounded to find that he had records on every tube he had put in that set during the previous seven years. He seems ideally suited to be an electrical engineer who designs computers.

That evening we all gathered in the lounge. With that many Becklers in one place, something was bound to happen. Gordon started by teasing Howard about the little paunch he was developing. Howard, hotly disputing the statement, stood up and sucked in his stomach. Vic started the countdown. Howard's face was beet red when he finally gave up and took a long, deep breath. The stories that were told whenever the family was together were recounted. The laughter was infectious, and soon some of the nurses were stopping by to join in the fun. The other patients and their families in the lounge were caught up also, and the atmosphere became lively. While this was going on, different members of the family would join Judy and me on the couch, sharing their feelings of love and concern. My mother, too, joined us on the couch. The matriarch of the Beckler clan, she was proud of her antic-filled, close-knit offspring, even though at times she pretended indignation at their pranks. The prayer she offered for my safety and for the success of the surgery was again a demonstration of her deep, abiding faith.

A young nurse's aide came toward us. She asked in a barely audible voice, "Is Mr. Beckler here?"

Almost in unison my three brothers answered yes. Not knowing what to make of the situation, she looked from one to the other.

Then gathering a bit of courage, she announced, "Well, one of you is going to get an enema."

Howard quickly seized the opportunity.

"That's him over there," he said, pointing an accusing finger at Gordon.

Vic joined in. "He does best with an ice-water enema."

"No, no!" someone exclaimed. "Give him the old 3-H enema— high and hot as hell."

In the face of the uproar following that statement, the young aide fled, but not before announcing, "The real Mr. Beckler had better show up in five minutes."

Vic accompanied me to my room, where we had a chance to talk alone about my surgery the following morning. While I was scheduled to have both my kidneys removed, he faced the same type of surgery to remove one of his in two weeks. We both knew the operation was a major one.

"Al, I know what I'm doing is right. I've got the strongest feeling that everything is going to turn out all right. I don't know why, but I knew that I was going to be the one to donate, and it's funny how all the tests have confirmed that. I'm sure your surgery tomorrow morning will go well, and I'm sure my surgery will go just as well."

That night I asked for a sleeping pill, and after settling down for the night, I had a chance to really think about my surgery. Dr. Steenburg called it a bilateral nephrectomy. A fourteen-inch incision would be made on my side, slightly below the rib cage. The kidney on that side would be removed, the incision closed, and then I would be turned over so the process could be repeated on the other side. It was major surgery, and I would be awfully sore for a long time. Several weeks ago when he had first explained the procedure it had not seemed so frightening. Now that surgery was about to take place, the prospect was upsetting. I prayed that I would have the strength to handle it, and it was a long time before I fell into a fitful sleep.

I was awakened at five by the night nurse, who weighed me and took blood-pressure and temperature readings. At six, she began to explain what to expect. Since the surgery would cut through muscles and it would be extremely painful for me to move afterward, shots would be ordered for the pain. She explained that I would have an IV in one arm and a tube through my nose into my stomach. She also said that I would have a catheter; then, remembering the type of surgery I was having, she explained with a laugh that since I had no kidneys to produce urine, there would be no need for a catheter.

Judy arrived before the other members of the family. We had a prayer together and talked about the procedure. The surgical orderly and the rest of my family arrived almost simultaneously. Judy hugged and kissed me.

The family offered words of encouragement and then everyone left as the orderly helped me onto the cart. I looked at the faces of those I loved as I was wheeled down the corridor toward the elevators.

I had a difficult time coming out of the anesthetic. During one period of consciousness, I was aware of people standing in the room, dressed in green. Then I faded back into unconsciousness. I awoke again as the nurse was removing the artificial air passageway from my throat. It was a hollow plastic tube with a flange that fit around my lips. The end of the tube extended down my throat. Without it, I found that I could not breathe at all, and I panicked, rolling my head violently from side to side to attract the nurse's attention. She saw the difficulty I was having and reinserted the tube, and again I slipped into unconsciousness.

When I awoke next I was in my room, Priscilla was encouraging me in a loud voice to cough.

"Cough, Al," she said. "You've got to get the anesthetic out of your lungs."

I tried a feeble cough, and my body was racked with spasms of pain. I felt as if I were split open along both sides. I lay still, again succumbing to the effect of the anesthetic, but Priscilla persisted in her attempts to have me cough. The pain was excruciating.

A nurse came in to check my blood pressure, and she also encouraged me to cough. I became aware of Judy on the other side of the bed. There was a worried look on her face as she stroked my forehead and smiled bravely. The nurse brought in a pillow and placed it gently over my stomach.

"Al, can you hear me?" she asked.

I grunted an acknowledgment. "When you cough, take your hands and press down on the pillow. It'll lessen the pain, but we want you to cough. It'll help clear your lungs."

The next few days remain a blur in my memory. Dr. Steenburg had prescribed Demerol every four hours if needed. He came often during those days, and I remember being awake when he changed the dressing on the incisions. Although his bedside manner was precise and professional, his concern was obvious.

"How did the surgery go?" I asked him late Sunday afternoon.

"It was a tough one, but we expected it. You're doing fine."

The next morning at half-past five, the dialysis team entered the room and rolled me into the dialysis room. The session was terrible. I developed a tremendous headache, and although my stomach was empty, I had dry heaves. The retching aggravated the incisions. My blood pressure skyrocketed, and medication was given in an attempt to lower it. The seven hour session seemed to last forever. The rest of that day and evening I was sick and completely exhausted.

Tuesday evening the telephone rang, and Judy answered it.

Sarah was calling to see how things were going. I hadn't been feeling well, but I couldn't put my finger on what was wrong. I told Sarah what I was experiencing.

"I don't know how to explain it. If I close my eyes, it's as if I cartwheel up to the ceiling, but when I open my eyes, I'm back in bed. It's the funniest feeling."

"Have you told Dr. Steenburg about it?" she asked.

"No," I said, "it's probably nothing. Maybe it's just something that goes along with this type of surgery."

After Judy left, I again experienced a sensation of cartwheeling out of bed whenever I closed my eyes. It was well past midnight when sleep finally claimed me.

Sometime during the night, the tube that went through my nose into my stomach began to bother me. I fidgeted with the tape holding the tube and pulled it loose, extracting a portion of the tube. I felt it move in my stomach, and in a dream-like, foggy state, I withdrew the entire tube. It lay there on the bed beside me.

When a nurse came in to check my vital signs, she exclaimed in horror, "My God, Al, what did you do?"

I don't remember offering an explanation. She took my vital signs and hastily left the room, returning with the night-charge nurse. They were concerned and more than a little angry.

"What are we going to do?" the junior nurse asked worriedly.

"We'll have to call his doctor. Is he one of Dr. Steenburg's patients?"

"Yes," the other nurse groaned.

"I hate to wake him up at this time of the morning," the charge nurse said, "but it can't be helped."

Ten minutes later she was back.

"Al," she said, not at all cheerfully, "guess what Dr. Steenburg said? He said to put the damn thing back in."

I looked at her, not caring what she had said. From the way she picked up the end of the tube, I could tell that the job was distasteful to her. She raised my bed to a semi-sitting position.

"All right, Al," she said, "here goes."

She inserted the tube down my nostril and pushed it back. I

gagged as the tube became caught in my throat. She handed me a glass of water.

"Here, when I tell you, take a sip," she said.

I took a swallow, and, as I did, she inserted the tube down my throat and into my stomach. After taping it to the bridge of my nose and cautioning me not to touch it, she left the room. She returned a few minutes later, carrying several long strips of cloth. She wrapped them around both my wrists and tied the other ends to the bedrail.

"I'm sorry, Al," she said, "but we just can't have you fiddling with that tube. It's got to stay down."

I spent the rest of the night drifting in and out of a shallow slumber and was awakened at five-thirty by the dialysis team. This time I was transferred to a cart, where I was weighed before dialysis started. Movements seemed to hurt more today than on Monday, particularly on my left side.

The dialysis session was a repeat of Monday's—absolutely terrible. The headaches were so bad that I saw red spots in front of my eyes. My blood pressure again rose, and medication had to be administered. Judy arrived about eight o'clock and spent the rest of the session wringing out cold washrags and placing them on my forehead. At times I was so hot that I took off all the blankets covering me. At other times I was so cold that no amount of blankets could warm me. The session dragged on interminably. When it was finally over, I was transferred from the bed to the cart and weighed. They had removed seven pounds of fluid. Without any kidneys to flush out my system, I was allowed only 60 cc of water every hour, but still the fluid accumulated.

After the weighing was completed, Dr. Ware examined me.

"Why is he having so much trouble with dialysis now?" Judy asked him. "The first time went so well."

"I don't know, Mrs. Beckler. Generally, it doesn't make any difference if a person has his kidneys or not. He may be having problems because of his recent surgery. Or he may just be one of those few who have trouble with dialysis. I just don't know, but we'll certainly do everything we can to make these sessions comfortable for him."

I dozed fitfully after returning to my room. I awoke to see Dr. Steenburg standing at the foot of the bed, with one foot resting on the end of it as usual. He was looking very intent. As I looked back at him, he suddenly split into three identical images. I stared at him, not comprehending what was happening. I turned and glanced around the room, but everything remained the same. Then I looked at the patient in the other bed, and he, too, assumed a triple image. Something was desperately wrong, and I tried vainly to communicate that to Dr. Steenburg, but I couldn't even manage a sentence. I slipped into a world full of horrifying hallucinations. I was forced headfirst into a hole, the bottom of which was full of snakes. The sides of the hole constricted me so I could not move my arms, and I hung upside down, suspended over them. Then, gloved hands with the fingers of the gloves worn away would reach down, pick me up, and toss me into the air. At other times I would be flying in a plane and the centrifugal force of the plane diving, twisting, and turning was absolutely real to me. One time I hallucinated being on the moon, floating silently by rocky crags. As I turned the corner by one of the crags, I saw a huge owl perched on a rock. Then someone held my hand in a viselike grip and ran my fingers through a sewing machine. The needle stitched through the flesh of my fingers, and my hand became a web.

On Saturday morning I returned to reality for a brief instant. I was on dialysis when I looked up to see my brothers, Vic and Don, standing by the bed. Their faces looked grim and drawn.

"What are you guys doing here?" I greeted them and immediately slipped back into another world.

Later, I learned that I had developed a staph infection deep in the incision where my left kidney had been removed. The site of the infection was so deep that it could not drain to the surface. As a consequence, my body had picked up the infection and transferred it into the bloodstream. From there it had traveled to the brain, causing the hallucinations.

Judy told me that she had first noticed something wrong early Wednesday afternoon. As she stood by the bed, a nurse entered the room and I attempted to introduce the nurse to my brother Don, who was not present. Later I began to type on an imaginary typewriter. My language toward Judy was vulgar and abusive. I sang at the top of my lungs. At first, some of the doctors thought I had suffered a nervous breakdown, and Judy was asked if there was any mental illness in the family. She answered negatively.

Dr. Steenburg then noted that my temperature had risen to an alarming 104 degrees. He discounted the idea of a nervous breakdown, and he started searching to isolate the problem. My fever remained alarmingly high all through Wednesday and Thursday. Dr. Steenburg ordered every conceivable test in an attempt to find out what was going on.

I had another dialysis session scheduled for Thursday morning, and it was after this session that another doctor told Judy that he could not hold out much hope for my recovery. He also mentioned that with the sustained high temperature, it was probable that even if I survived, I would suffer irreparable brain damage.

Judy called Vic immediately. "Your brother needs you. Can you come right away?"

Vic called Don and Howard. Don flew to Omaha to be with Judy and spent Thursday night with her in my hospital room. It was not a pleasant night for them. I was completely delirious and could not be kept still. I was given tremendous amounts of sedatives, but they did no good.

Friday morning Vic and Howard arrived on an early flight. Judy and Don had been up all night with me, and they both needed some rest. Vic and Howard spelled them while they rested in the lounge.

Meanwhile, Dr. Steenburg's persistent search for the cause of the staph infection had borne fruit. Having identifed the source of the infection, he had the left incision opened and the infection drained. I was given derivatives of penicillin intravenously. I owe my life to Dr. Steenburg.

Judy was having a rough time coping with everything, and

my brothers decided that Howard would take her home to Grand Island Friday. Vic and Don remained by my bed until one A.M. By then the sedatives had taken hold, and I was quiet, although not out of danger. No one knew whether the high fever had caused any brain damage. Vic and Don didn't know what to expect when they came to dialysis Saturday morning. Vic told me later that they had experienced immense relief when I opened my eyes and was able to greet them.

My first clear recollections of any conversation were from Sunday morning when Don stood by the bed.

"How you doin', buddy?" he asked, his gruff voice filled with emotion.

Don is over six feet tall and heavy of frame. His broad face matches his voice and gives the appearance of gruffness until a twinkle lights his eye and the corner of his mouth curls up in a slow, sly, ornery grin. When that happens, the fun begins. Don has spent more time beside my hospital bed than any brother should be expected to. Hospitals seem to scare him and upset him, but he is always there when I need him. When he leaves my room, I do not resent it. Sometimes, he can't stand to see me suffer.

My mind registered the fact that I had been close to death, but specific events and dates were still foggy. During the day I gradually became aware of my surroundings and what had taken place. I began to think about the transplant.

The transplant surgery was scheduled for April 10, and I was concerned that I would not be able to tolerate it that soon. I tried to tell Dr. Steenburg of my concerns, but I was unable to form the words into sentences that made any sense.

He understood what I was trying to say.

"Al," he said, with one of his rare smiles, "when you can talk straight, we'll talk about the transplant."

He tapped me on the toes with the medical chart and left the room.

Vic had told me of Dr. Steenburg's tremendous efforts during the last few days. Without him the course of the infection would have been fatal. Even though he worked hard on my behalf, his relationship with his patients was never a close one. His dealings with me had been honest and professional, but also distant. His manner suggested a person who was very sure of himself and his abilities. I liked that. I didn't want a doctor who was unsure of himself and overly cautious. But I also wanted to feel that Dr. Steenburg regarded me as a person rather than just another statistic, just another patient. The smile he gave me when he left the room pleased me very much.

It was not until Wednesday that I felt completely clearheaded. I was very weak, but I would not allow myself to remain in bed. With assistance, I took short walks in the mornings and afternoons. The original date for the transplant had been scrubbed because I was just not strong enough to tolerate surgery. It was rescheduled for a week later, and I was determined to use the time to regain my lost strength.

Dialysis remained an agony. I was now being dialyzed on Monday, Wednesday, and Friday mornings. After the session on Monday, I would need most of the afternoon and evening to recuperate. By late evening I would be feeling better and the next day would be able to move around the room and hallways.

The following day, however, dialysis would roll around again and the whole process would be repeated. The weekends offered a break from the routine. I would have Saturday and Sunday to enjoy. But I paid for it in dialysis on Monday morning. More fluid had to be removed, and it was a longer run on the machine.

One Sunday afternoon was very memorable. Judy's parents had brought the boys to the hospital to visit me. Since they were unable to come to my fifth-floor room, I journeyed to the play area in a wheelchair. We had a very happy reunion.

Kevin, who has his mother's soft blue eyes and brown hair, leaned over the wheelchair and hugged me close. Full of nervous energy, he paced in front of the chair as he asked me, "Do your sides hurt, Dad?"

"A little bit, but not too bad."

He continued his pacing. "Are the meals any good?"

I laughed as I thought about my bland, tasteless diet.

"Well, they're not as good as the ones your mother cooks."

His pacing stopped, and he stood close to me, a hand on each of my knees.

"Dad, at school we pray for you each morning."

I looked closely at my oldest son. He was making a brave attempt to be strong, but in his eyes I saw fear, the questioning, the groping attempt to understand what was happening to his father.

"I pray for you every night, too, Dad."

I reached out and pulled him close. "I pray for you all the time, too, Kevin. When the transplant's over we'll have lots of time together. This summer we'll spend some time at Johnson's Lake. Would you like that?"

He smiled when he looked at me, and his eyes sparkled.

"Gosh, Dad, maybe Grandpa Pollard will take all of us water-skiing."

"You can water-ski, Kevin," I grinned at him. "I'll settle for a boat ride."

Rusty's investigation of the toys spread throughout the room was punctuated by frequent stops at the wheelchair. When he heard the words "boat ride," he came over and held my thumb tightly and patted my forearm and shoulder. It was as if I could become real to him by touching. Active—like his oldest brother— he has the same blue eyes and my dark-brown hair. He seemed to miss me and asked when could I please come home. His five-year-old world was disrupted by his father's absence.

"What's that stuff?" he asked, pointing to the IV-bottle hanging above my head.

"That's medicine, Rusty. That's medicine."

"What's this?" he said, running his finger over the fistula.

"That's where they stick the needle when I have dialysis."

"Does it hurt?" he asked, a frown on his face.

"It only hurts for a little bit, Rusty."

Scott was busy hammering on a pegboard.

"What have you got there?" I asked him.

"I've been pounding these things down," he said as he gave a final rap to one of the pegs. He leaned against the chair. He was heavier than his brothers, also quieter.

"I wish you could come home," he said.

"Maybe when school's out I'll be home."

"Gee, that's a long time." For him, two months seemed forever.

"I like it when you call us at Grandma and Grandpa's. That's fun." He smiled.

Judy entered the room, carrying three sodas for the boys. She handed the boys a drink. I watched her with them, always calm with quiet tones. She was strong and loving and the boys responded to her.

"Isn't it great to be together again?" she asked, her fingers squeezing my shoulder gently. "I can't wait for you to come home."

And as I watched them, I realized that if the transplant were successful, I would live to see the boys grow up. I was filled with a great surge of hope and resolved again to see this thing through to a successful end.

Getting Ready

❂✛❂✛❂

April 17 to April 25, 1974

After what seemed an eternity, April 17 finally came. Vic and his family arrived a few days early, and he checked into the hospital. It had been almost two weeks since I had had an opportunity to talk to Vic in person.

"There's still time to back out," I said. "Steenburg can't operate on you if he can't find you."

"Too late for that. He already knows I'm here," he laughed.

I put my hand on his arm, and in a more serious tone I said, "Vic, there's still time to change your mind."

"I know," he replied. His eyes were steady on my face as he continued, "But I'm not going to. I know what I'm doing, and I'm confident that it's the right thing."

Sarah and Howard also arrived on Tuesday to be with us for the surgery.

The next morning the nurse took my temperature and blood-pressure readings. After sufficient time elapsed for the thermometer to register, she looked at it and said, "Let's try this again."

Frowning, she shook it and put it into my mouth. This time, she made absolutely certain of the reading.

Alarmed, I asked, "What's the matter?"

"Your temperature is 100.8°. I'll have to call the doctor."

Minutes later Dr. Steenburg came in the room.

"We'll have to postpone the surgery today, Al," he said. "I

don't know what's going on, but we don't dare operate when you have a temperature that high."

He asked me to roll over on my right side and then examined the incision, which had now begun to heal. "There's our problem." He opened the incision, let it drain and cleaned it, and inserted a small tube into the opening to allow the incision to drain.

I was bitterly disappointed. I was not looking forward to the surgery, but to the expected results. And now I had to wait.

Vic wasn't feeling much of anything. He had already been given a shot and was awake only enough to be informed that the surgery was postponed.

Later Sarah came to my room. Sensing my disappointment, she tried to cheer me up. She said, laughing, "You should have seen Vic. They sent his breakfast up to him, and before he started to eat, he tried to tuck a napkin in the top of his gown. Only he wasn't wearing one."

That afternoon Dr. Steenburg visited with both Vic and me. He explained that it would have been foolhardy to go ahead with the surgery that morning.

"There's an infection at work in Al's body," he said, "and we don't dare give immunosuppressant drugs to someone with an infection. We'll have to postpone the surgery for a week at least, possibly ten days."

I dreaded the thought of continued dialysis. The constant discomfort of those sessions was beginning to take its toll. I was mentally and physically apprehensive, and many times the breakfast and lunch I had while being dialyzed would not stay down. I was so weak that at times I was not able to stay on the scales long enough to be weighed.

Vic decided to remain in Omaha. The weather during those spring days was balmy and beautiful, and occasionally, late in the afternoon on the days I was dialyzed, Vic and I would take a ride in his van. On the alternate days, we would make excursions all over Omaha. On one of these afternoons Vic stopped to get us each a malt. Since I was allowed only 60 cc of fluid per hour, I calculated the amount of fluid in the malt and realized that I couldn't have anything else for six hours. I drained mine in a few minutes, and Vic handed me his while he made an adjustment on the seat of the van. When he wasn't looking, I stole a few sips and handed it back. At an intersection a few blocks later, he again handed me the malt while he made another adjustment. This time it was too tempting. I drained it.

"Why, you piker!" he said, looking at me in exasperation.

He had been thirsty, too, and the malt had tasted good. I felt guilty, not only because I had taken his malt but also because I knew that I had exceeded by a huge amount my allowed fluid intake. That indiscretion cost me the next day on dialysis—more fluid than usual had to be removed.

Early the following week, it became apparent that the drainage had stopped in my left side. The transplant was scheduled for Friday. I kept a watchful eye on my side, not wanting a repeat performance of the last episode, when surgery had had to be postponed.

On Wednesday the dialysis team took special measures to make sure that my blood values would be acceptable for surgery. I learned later that the team did a superb job of preparing me for surgery. All of the blood values were within the range needed for a successful operation.

Wednesday evening the phone never stopped ringing. Gene called from California and talked for forty-five minutes. He is quieter than the rest of us, but his feelings run deep and strong, and although he is sometimes hesitant to express them, we know that they are there. He called me so often that his phone bill must have resembled the national debt.

Gene also spent a long time talking with Vic. Priscilla, who could not be with us, called and wished us both well. I had calls from Judy's family and from many friends back home.

On Thursday Vic was admitted to the hospital. After lunch Sarah arrived. "My car knows the way to Omaha by heart," she said cheerfully as she gave me a big kiss. Gordon and Howard arrived that afternoon, and my mother joined the clan that evening.

After dinner, the family congregated in the lounge. Someone

said that after tomorrow's surgery, there would only be one spare kidney among the three of us who shared identical tissue, and that would be Sarah's. Vic then decided Sarah was not to exert herself, and he even refused to allow her to pick up a magazine. When she prepared to sit down, Vic would rush to hold the chair for her and ease her gently into it. When she passed through a doorway, he would exhort her to be careful not to bump that kidney. Although everyone was laughing at Vic's antics, I could not help thinking that behind it was a truth. If Vic's remaining kidney were to be impaired, Sarah would be the logical choice to give him one of hers. Again, as I had so often in the past two months, I thought of the immensity of Vic's love for me. During our drives and walks through Omaha, we had developed an even closer bond than the one we had had before. Only rarely was that love mentioned, but expressing it verbally wasn't necessary. His actions indicated it.

All of the surgical preparations were made that evening. Then I called Judy's parents and talked to my sons.

"Tomorrow is a big day for you, isn't it Kevin?" I asked.

"Yes, Dad. We've got a track meet, and I'm entered in seven events. I can hardly wait," he said excitedly.

"But tomorrow you're having a birthday, too. You'll be ten years old. I wish I could be there."

Kevin suddenly became more subdued. "You're going to have the transplant tomorrow, aren't you?"

"Yes."

"Will it hurt much?"

"It'll hurt some, Kevin, but it has to be done. I need this operation to make me feel better."

"I know," he said, "but—," and his voice trailed off.

"It would be nice if I didn't have to, but I do," I said, reading his thoughts. "You say a prayer for Uncle Vic and me tonight, will you?"

"Okay, Dad."

Scott was not too excited about the track meet, but looked forward to spending the day outside.

"I'm going to eat at the carnival at school tomorrow night,

Dad," he said. "Grandpa and Grandma are going to take us. When do you have your operation?"

"When you eat your lunch the operation will be over."

There was a long silence at the other end of the line. Finally Scott said, "I'll pray for you, Dad."

When Rusty got on the phone he was able to speak only a few words before he started to cry.

"I'm scared," he sobbed.

"I know you are, Rusty. That's all right." I talked to him for a while, reassuring him as much as I could. We finished our conversation and my heart went out to him as I heard his small, quiet voice.

"Bye, Daddy. I love you," he said unhappily.

Judy sat close to the bed, her finger tracing the outline of the distended fistula on my wrist. We talked of the surgery and of the prospect of a normal summer with the boys. She was confident about the surgery, and I could physically feel this confidence as I held her hand.

My brothers and sisters stopped in and talked for a long while. They were also cheerful and confident. After surgery I would be in isolation for three to four days, and it would be hard to visit then. They wanted to spend all the time they could with me before we were separated. By ten-thirty everyone had left, and I was alone with my thoughts.

Although I was nervous about the surgery, my strongest feeling was of anticipation, of having a task to do and wanting to be about it. I was concerned about Vic, who was lying in his bed at the end of the hall, and sleep did not come easily that evening.

The Kidney Transplant

❖❖❖❖❖

April 26 to May 12, 1974

As I watched the day break, my thoughts turned homeward. Today was Kevin's tenth birthday. My sons were growing up, and I felt bad that during the past year and a half, my illness had prevented me from doing the things that most fathers do with their sons. As well as developing physically, they were developing distinct personalities. I loved them very much and missed them deeply.

I thought of the transplant surgery scheduled this morning. Dr. Steenburg had said, "Al, this transplant, if successful, could give you a complete new lease on life."

He explained that this operation, although major, would not be nearly as traumatic as the previous surgery to remove my kidneys. Donating a kidney—the operation Vic faced this morning—was the tough one. I shuddered at the thought of the pain that I had experienced when mine were removed, and I hoped that when Vic woke up, he would not regret being a donor. But then, I knew he would not.

"I'm expecting pain and I'm prepared to meet it," he had told me.

Judy arrived early, looking calm and steady. We talked of things other than the surgery—we had talked about that enough.

Sarah was next to arrive. Were it not for Vic, she would be in the hospital getting ready for surgery.

We were soon joined by Gordon, Howard, and my mother.

A tall dignified woman, only slightly rounded shoulders betrayed her seventy-five years. Everyone was laughing about some high jinks that had occurred around the breakfast table in the cafeteria.

"I just don't know what's gotten into you kids," my mother said. "I brought you up to behave better than that in public. I just don't know what's come over you." We all knew she was kidding.

Then everyone trooped out except my mother. She sat in the chair and took my hand in hers and placed it on her knee. I had learned many lessons while kneeling beside those knees, and I had learned just as many bent over them. She was a strong woman in body and mind. She needed to be. Raising eleven children through the Depression years on the salary that her husband made as a Lutheran minister was not easy. She was strong in other ways, too. She had stood beside the graves of three sons and a husband, and through those trials, her faith in God had remained undaunted, her cheerfulness and warmth intact. Her faith had not wavered when I had lain close to death. This morning, when not one but two of her sons faced major surgery, her voice was resolute as she said a prayer for us. When she finished, I told her that she should see Vic before he left for surgery. As she passed the foot of my bed, she paused and that long right forefinger waved at me. "Now you be good, you hear?"

I chuckled to myself. Come on, Mom, there isn't much a person can do in surgery to be ornery.

Judy came back, and soon there was a regular procession of Becklers going between our rooms. Sarah, returning from Vic's room, wanted to be sure that we did not forget to have pictures taken during surgery. So she taped a large piece of paper across my stomach with a message reading "Don't forget to take the pictures." It was a typical Beckler antic.

My eyes brimmed with tears. I wanted to tell them all how much I loved them, but I couldn't express it. Instead, I joined in the joke.

"Just be damned careful where you put that tape, Sarah," I laughed.

A few minutes later the nurse arrived. She gave me a clean

gown and a pre-operative shot. As the shot began to take effect, I felt sleepy. When I heard a noise outside the door and saw the surgery cart, I felt a moment of apprehension and fear. Judy leaned over and held me tight for a minute and whispered, "Honey, I love you. Please don't worry, everything will be all right. We are all praying for you."

As the cart was led to the elevators, I got my last glimpse of love and concern on the faces of my family. The elevator ride was short. The surgical room felt cold. They always do.

Someone stood beside the cart and checked my ID-number and, without saying a word, began an IV. I was becoming very drowsy. I wondered where Vic was. I looked around but couldn't see him. I dozed off.

I was awakened by the sound of laughter. Obviously, someone had uncovered the message printed across my stomach, and I felt the tape being removed. I dozed off again. I awoke again to the feeling of someone dry-shaving me in a vulnerable area. I angrily muttered something about common decency dictating the use of lather if they had to shave that. Then I was wheeled into surgery and moved to the surgical table. I tried to relax; I thought about Vic and what he was doing for me. If there were to be any problems during either surgery, I wanted them to be mine. I prayed that there not be any complications for us.

Dr. Steenburg stood beside me, surveying me. He was at ease in these surroundings, in total command. And I could feel it.

"Doing all right?" he asked.

"Yes," I replied.

The coolness of the room kept me awake. At times I was calm, and at other times, shaking with apprehension. I tried to concentrate on one thing, but I couldn't. Someone brushed my right shoulder, and I turned to see a hand open a valve on the IV-tube. Something seared my brain, and I lost consciousness.

I don't remember anything about the recovery room. My first recollection was of waking up in a private room with the bed in the center. I asked the nurse dazedly what time it was.

"It's 11:50," she said. She was clothed completely in surgical green. Even her hair was covered by an awkward-looking cap. She spoke to me in an unnaturally loud voice.

"Al, can you hear me?"

I nodded assent.

"The surgery is over and you're back in your room. Do you understand?"

Again, I nodded.

"Your new kidney is working perfectly," she said. "Everything went just fine."

"How's Vic?" I asked.

"He's doing fine," she said, patting me reassuringly on the shoulder.

I drifted in and out of unconsciousness for the rest of the day. When I was awake I marveled at how much less pain I felt this time, and I thought of Vic and the pain he must be feeling. When I was awake enough to carry on a coherent conversation, I asked the nurse about the kidney.

"Your kidney is putting out so much urine that it's keeping me very busy just emptying the container," she said. She clipped the end of the catheter and carried it to the bathroom to measure the amount. The container was about the size of a bread pan. I noticed that the urine was pink in color.

"Is that normal?" I asked.

"Oh, yes, bleeding can be expected from the site where they connected the urethra from the kidney to the bladder," she responded.

When I changed position in bed, I complained about the pain in the lower part of my abdominal cavity. The nurse gave me a shot of Demerol.

The shot kept me asleep until three-thirty A.M. Another nurse was on duty, and I asked her how I was doing. She said my blood pressure was the lowest it had been since I had entered the hospital. The kidney was producing copious amounts of urine, and she was kept busy emptying the container.

"In fact," she remarked, "it's removing so much fluid so fast that I have to replace some of it by IV." I didn't understand the logic of that remark, but I was too groggy to care.

On Saturday morning, I saw Sarah standing by the door to the room. I was in isolation, but members of the immediate family could be admitted if they were capped and gowned; Judy had been in earlier.

"Come in," I said.

She seemed reluctant, but donned the cap and gown and came in the room. She exclaimed in a loud voice, "Oh, look at all that pretty urine."

The nurse and I both laughed.

"It's the color of straw now. He's really doing well. I can't believe the amount of urine that he's putting out."

She explained that during one five-hour period the previous night, I had taken in through the IV a total of 650 cc, but had put out a whopping 4,900 cc. The difference was almost a gallon of fluid.

"I can't even sit down to rest," she laughed. "It's just back and forth to the bathroom, back and forth to the bathroom."

"Is Vic having much pain?" I asked Sarah.

"Yes," she said, "but he's been getting shots, and they seem to help a lot."

Judy stood in the doorway, and Sarah, noticing her, bade me goodbye and left. Judy donned another cap and gown and came in.

"I've talked to Dr. Steenburg. He said you and Vic are both doing just great." She looked immensely relieved.

Now Gordon and Howard were standing at the door. Since only one person at a time was admitted, they tried to carry on a conversation while craning their necks to see around the corner of the bathroom.

Dr. Steenburg made frequent visits that day. With gloved hands and sterile instruments, he changed the dressings.

"Al, I want you to be sure that when you roll over, you roll over only on your right side."

"Why?"

"The kidney is on the right side of your abdomen. If you lie on your right side, the pressure on the stitches that hold it in place isn't significant; but if you lie on your left side, the pressure on the stitches could cause them to tear, and I don't want that to happen. So either lie on your right side or on your back."

The pain during Saturday was not great, but I called for an occasional hypo, and the day passed quickly.

On Sunday I was alert enough to take an interest in my surroundings. Several IV's were going at once. I understood why I was getting blood, but I wondered about the other bottle.

"That," Dr. Steenburg explained, "is a medicine called Solu-Medrol. It's a steroid that keeps the inflamation down. It helps to keep your body from rejecting the kidney. Later on you'll be able to take that medicine in pill form, but now I want to give you a massive amount of it. The other medicine you're taking is called Imuran, which is mainly what keeps your body from rejecting the kidney. You'll be on these immunosuppressant drugs for the rest of your life. Your kidney is doing an amazing job. The blood values I'm getting back are almost all normal."

After he changed the dressing, I mentioned that I was hungry.

"Not today. But tomorrow we'll start you on some regular food. What would you like?"

Half joking I said, "How about bacon and eggs?"

"Sounds fine to me," he said. "I'll see that you get it."

I couldn't believe it. Bacon is heavily salted, and I hadn't eaten anything like it for months.

The isolation was lifted on Monday morning, and, true to his word, Dr. Steenburg made sure that bacon and eggs were on my breakfast tray. Judy, entering the room the same time the tray did, was astonished at the sight of all that food. I ate it ravenously. The nurse looked at me dubiously.

"That's awfully rich food for your first meal," she said.

It was apparent by now that both Vic and I were out of danger and were on the road to recovery. Gret, Vic's wife, stopped in my room periodically to keep us posted on Vic's progress.

"He's doing all right," she said, but there was concern in her eyes and voice.

Monday afternoon the scales were wheeled into the room. It was hard to believe, but I now weighed 115 pounds. Shortly before surgery I had weighed 134 pounds. One of the effects of that rapid fluid loss was apparent when I tried to stand up. I became faint immediately, and if I stood in one position too long, I passed out.

The chart that hung on my door indicated that on several occasions the nurse had had difficulty obtaining any blood pressure reading at all while I was standing. The minute that I lay flat on the bed, my pressure returned to within normal. On one occasion I tried to sit up in bed. Sticking one skinny leg over the edge of the bed, I made a "V for victory" with my hand while Judy snapped a picture. I immediately fainted and fell back on the bed.

Vic made his appearance in my room on Tuesday. The tube that had been inserted into his stomach had irritated his throat, and he had a slight cough. With Gret on one side and a nurse on the other, he clutched a pillow against his incision when he had to cough. He looked pale and drawn, but it was the same old Vic. He grinned and sat down gingerly on a chair beside the bed. We gripped each other's hands hard.

"How are you doing?" he whispered to me.

"Great," I said, "how about yourself?"

"Oh, I'm doing okay. I'm doing much better, now that I got that tube out of my nose. When did you get yours out?" he asked.

For the first time I realized that I had not had to put up with that kind of tube during this surgery. When I told him, he surveyed the IV-tubes and the catheter.

"I don't know why you didn't get it, one more wouldn't have hurt."

We both laughed softly. Laughing, coughing, or any sudden movement this soon after surgery hurt too much for either one of us.

The biggest problem I had during that first week was low blood pressure. Whenever I stood up, I fainted. Later that week, I was able to get up and sit in a chair for a short time. These brief excursions three or four times a day did a lot to improve this condition. My appetite had also improved, and I was eating everything in sight and asking for more. The calorie increase was matched with an increase in insulin to keep my blood-sugar levels acceptable. I was gaining strength daily and I felt better than I had any time in the past two years. Vic's progress, too, was exceptional.

Dr. Steenburg told him, "If you continue to do well for the rest of this week, I'll dismiss you on Friday." This would be only a week after the transplant surgery.

The tremendous volume of urine the new kidney had put out immediately after the transplant had lessened considerably and was now more normal. Dr. Steenburg removed the catheter.

"I'll give you till four o'clock to urinate on your own," he said, "or else I'll have to put it back in." I checked my watch; I had slightly over two hours to accomplish this task. At three o'clock, after two unsuccessful attempts, I drank two large glasses of water. But it was to no avail. Four o'clock arrived and so did Dr. Steenburg.

"I just don't have to go," I said. He looked at me and pressed down with his hand on my bladder. "Wanta bet? I'm not going to take a chance on you having a full bladder and it backing up into the kidney."

As he turned on his heel and left the room, I knew what was going to happen next. He came back carrying a small package. Carefully opening it so as not to contaminate its sterile contents, he put on a pair of rubber gloves. All of this seemed to be taking an agonizingly long time.

"Damn it, doctor," I wanted to say, "if you're gonna do it, hurry up and get it over with."

"Now, Al, when I tell you to, take a few quick deep breaths."

Vic had much better luck when they removed his catheter. given the same mandate of two hours, he accomplished his task in the allotted time.

"It wasn't easy though," he told me later. "I tried everything. I drank a lot of water, and that didn't work. Then I went to the bathroom and turned on the faucet, thinking the sound of running water would help. That didn't work either. Finally, I sat on the stool and poured warm water over it, and that did the trick." Vic grinned broadly and Gret nearly died laughing.

Hearing this, I didn't feel too bad. "After all," Vic said, "older brothers are supposed to be a lot smarter."

The next day after the catheter was removed again, I remembered Vic's trick and returned happily to what had been standard procedure until March 22, when my kidneys had been removed. Vic left the hospital Friday. Although he was weaker and walked as if he were on eggs, his color had returned and so had his normal high spirits. Gret said they would call daily to check on my condition. A gentle hug from him and a kiss from Gret, and they were off.

The second week, Dr. Steenburg allowed me to roam the halls at will during the day. He also encouraged me, weather permitting, to go outside. Judy assisted me on walks around the hospital. The first stop we made was at the Storz Pavilion, a beautiful cafeteria connected to the hospital. While I sat at the table, Judy went through the line and picked up a large piece of spice cake a la mode. Although the cake played havoc with my diet, it was a treat that I allowed myself. Unfortunately the cold ice cream bothered my teeth. When I asked one of the doctors about it, he said, "Any person who has been on as many drugs as you have will experience a time when their teeth will be sensitive to hot and cold foods."

Another indication of my recovery was the fact that Judy had never seemed more beautiful, and the nurses on the floor were positively charming. During the time I had been sick, Miss America could have walked by my door, and she wouldn't have rated a second glance.

Returning to normal physical condition after almost two years of failing health was easy to accept. I felt wonderful. I returned to my hospital bed only at night and once or twice during the day for naps. I walked the corridors, making new friends and greeting old ones. The walks with Judy around the hospital grounds were a special delight to me. One time we sat down on the grass and talked. It was a red-letter day for me when I could rise unassisted.

Occasionally, my mental outlook did not keep pace with the improvement in my physical condition. I became moody and depressed for no reason at all. At one point, I called Bill Landis and talked to him about it.

"Give yourself some time, Al," he counseled me. "You've come a long way in an awfully short period of time. It's bound to be hard on anyone. After all, you've made a 180-degree turn from facing death to facing life."

I knew he was right. For a long time, all I had had to look forward to was the certainty of an early grave. Now, new vistas opened to me. I thought of the promise of full health and pondered the type of work I would engage in, the hobbies and sports I could enjoy, and the organizations that I had always wanted to join—but for one trivial reason or another had not. Dr. Steenburg had told me that I would be able to return to work late that fall.

"Just take things one day at a time. Don't rush into anything," Dr. Steenburg cautioned me. "Just get used to living again."

The best therapy for me was to look at the chart on my door and read the daily log of the blood chemistry entered there. Two-and-a-half weeks had passed since the transplant and nothing adverse had occurred. I was encouraged. I decided to try to take the doctor's advice and live one day at a time. The depression and anxiety that had affected me occasionally began to recede.

Back Home

❖❖❖❖

May 13 to August 20, 1974

My release from the hospital had been scheduled for the fifteenth of May, but we beat that date by a few days. The day came finally, and I rose before dawn. I dressed and was walking the halls when Judy arrived. We breakfasted together and waited impatiently for Dr. Steenburg to make his rounds. The transplant coordinator brought in all of the materials that I would need while at home. For the first two months, every Friday would mean a trip to Omaha to be checked at the outpatient clinic. During those first two months, I would also go to the hospital lab in Grand Island every Tuesday for blood tests. These results would be phoned into the transplant office. The key indicator of a possible rejection was the serum creatinine level, and they would monitor that level closely. I felt certain that strict measures would be followed to help ensure a successful transplant.

When Dr. Steenburg arrived for the final checkup, we talked about the do's and don't's of living at home. He impressed upon me how important it was to keep close tabs on the kidney, and that this could only be done through blood work. We went over all the medications. He explained that one medication, Medrol, could give me a puffy appearance and also would make me put on weight, but told me not to be concerned about it.

"As the dosage is decreased, that weight will come off," he said.

I was taking digitalis for my heart, and I was concerned about that. Dr. Steenburg explained, "Your heart's taken a terrific pounding these last couple of years. Of course, you haven't had a heart attack; in fact, all your EKG tests look normal, but the digitalis will help your heart, and I want to keep you on it for a little while longer. Even though the heart does not have regenerative powers, it does have recuperative powers, so there should be nothing to worry about there. But we'll keep an eye on it just the same."

He advised me not to drive a car for at least a month, because my reaction time might be slow.

Gripping my hand firmly, he said, "You've gone through a lot, Al. There were times when I wouldn't have given a plug nickel for your chances, but you kept fighting, and that helped bring you through. Be sure to keep Fridays open for me for a while, will you?" And smiling, he left the room.

The 150-mile journey home was interspersed with frequent stops at the rest areas along the interstate. My bladder had shrunk, and it would be a while before it regained its normal size. As I went in the restroom, Judy would pace nervously outside, waiting for me to reappear.

I was filled with tremendous excitement when at last we pulled in our driveway. I looked around at the trees, now in full bloom, and at the flowers beginning to poke through the ground. Four months ago, I was absolutely convinced that I wouldn't be around to enjoy this spring. Now I was arriving home, and I felt more full of life than ever. I went into the living room. Hung across the fireplace was a large sign that said "Welcome Home." Further investigation of the house revealed a sign hung on the bathroom door—a picture of two kidneys with the inscription "Old kidneys never die, they just peter out." Our friends, aware of my arrival that day, had gotten a key from Judy's folks and had decorated the house.

The reunion with the boys was very poignant. Treasures had been saved for three months to show off to me. Kevin displayed three blue ribbons he had won at the track meet in April and a radio he had won. Scott exhibited the drawings that he had saved from his first-grade art class. Rusty was excited about the prospect of kindergarten graduation the end of the month. My mother walked over from her house a block away and wished me well. There were tears in her eyes, tears of happiness.

When the excitement of being home and seeing the family had gone, I became anxious at the prospect of spending the night away from the hospital. The hospital represented a safe haven. Although I hated being awakened on a hourly basis to have my vital signs read, still it represented stability; and if anything went wrong, there were people immediately at hand to take care of the matter. The boys trooped into the bedroom to say good night. As we said prayers together, a calm, peaceful assurance came over me. My sleep was sound and restful, and I was awakened the next morning by the smell of bacon frying.

I gained strength rapidly. Walks with the boys to school, or to the church office to have coffee with Darlene, the church secretary, and Pastor Meyer helped to build up my endurance. My appetite was enormous. The last thing I did at night was eat a snack, and I would go to bed eager to get up and put my feet under the breakfast table. I put on weight like a steer in a feedlot. By late May I was a somewhat skinny, healthy 127-pounder. The waistbands of my pants had been pinned to keep them up, but now they could gradually be let out.

Summer vacation was imminent, and we sat down with a calendar and blocked out every week with a different activity. Our plans included a week at Johnson's Lake and two weeks at Sarah's farm in Canby. The family reunion was to be there, and everyone looked forward to it. Planning an entire summer and putting it down on paper was a great feeling. I had indeed come back to life.

Under Judy's watchful eye, I resumed mowing the lawn and tackling other odd jobs around the house. One summer evening Duane and Bonnie Obermier, our close friends, invited us to a picnic at Ashley Park north of town. When we arrived, we were amazed to find over a hundred friends gathered for a picnic supper in our honor. On one of the tables was a box with a picture of a cat on top. The inscription above the drawing was "A Kitty

for the Becklers." Judy and I listened with tears in our eyes as
Pastor Meyer in the invocation spoke of the value of friends and
family. We knew how much they had supported us through the
bad times, and now they were with us to celebrate my cure.

The family reunion that year was of special importance to me.
Although I had seen Vic briefly when they had come through
Grand Island on their way to California in June, I was anxious
to see how he was getting along. When we drove to Bern and
Sarah's farm, I was overjoyed to see Vic engaged in a game of
volleyball. Leaving the game, he came toward us. We stood,
gazing at each other for a moment, and then we embraced.

He stepped back, looked me over from head to toe, and said,
"Boy, you're really getting fat."

What he said was true. I couldn't blame all the weight gain
on Medrol.

"I never had this problem before I had your kidney," I said,
grinning.

"How's the kidney doing?" he asked.

I told him in glowing superlatives that the kidney was functioning perfectly.

"It ought to," he laughed. "I gave you my best one."

All during the reunion, when I felt that Vic wasn't watching
me, I was watching him. I wanted reassurance that what he had
done for me hadn't hurt him in any way. A good athlete in college,
he was still trim at thirty-nine. I was glad to see that he engaged
in all the games that week, and that he held his own in all of
them.

He was hot and sweaty after a game of touch football and he
stripped off his shirt. I saw the long, red scar on his side. Once
again I was reminded of what he had done for me.

We stayed on a few days after everyone else left the reunion.
Bern is superintendent of the school system in Canby, and he
and Sarah had purchased the eighty-acre farm that spring. Although they did not farm it themselves, they were hobby farmers
at heart. Our boys had great fun feeding the horse, pigs, and
cows.

Sarah and I took a long walk on the country road one cool

evening. We talked about my diabetes—the disease that had caused all the problems and made the transplant necessary. For the first time, I mentioned my determination to help find a cure for it if at all possible. My diabetes had ruined my kidneys, and I was determined to find a cure before the same disease affected the kidney Vic had given me.

"But, Al," she said, "when Vic gave you his kidney, he didn't want a guarantee that it would last for five or ten years. He gave it to you because you needed it."

"I know that, but if a cure can be found for diabetes, the kidney he gave me will last me the rest of my life."

"Well, I sure hope something will come up," Sarah said, and, taking my arm, we walked down the lane to her house.

New Starts

❖❖❖❖

August 20, 1974 to October 1975

By the end of August, the boys were making preparations to return to school. During the summer, Rusty would come up to me for no reason and hug me. After reassuring himself that I was there, he would return to whatever he had been doing. But a more serious problem began the first day of school.

"Al," Judy said, "I can't get Rusty to go to school. I've tried everything, but he just won't go."

"All right, I'll talk to him."

He evidently felt that I would not be there when he returned. He would only agree to go to school if I went with him. I took his hand and we walked a block to the school door. I walked with him to his room and introduced him to his new teacher. But as I turned to leave the room, he began to cry loudly. I promised to wait for him at recess time, and, with him still crying violently, I left the room. I was there at recess and lunchtime. This went on for a week, and then I began trying to change the schedule gradually. I met him at lunchtime and after school. Over the next couple of weeks, I was able to leave him at the front door of the school, and soon he was able to walk from the corner where I stood to the school by himself. Every fifty feet or so, he would turn to make certain that I was standing there. When he reached the school door, he would wave his cap toward me.

When at last he was able to leave the house alone, I thought the problem had been solved.

Several weeks later, Judy and I decided to go for a walk after dinner. We told the boys we would be gone for only a short while. I took Rusty aside and said, "Mom and I are going for a short walk. We'll be back in a while. You be a big boy and stay here with Kevin and Scott." Rusty seemed a little uncomfortable but didn't cry.

As we left the house, I heard a rapping sound on the big picture-window in our dining room. Rusty had pushed the curtain aside and was rapping loudly in an attempt to get our attention. I waved at him, but his rapping became louder and harder, and then I heard the brittle crack of the glass as it broke. As I rushed back into the house, I was angry at the thought of the cost of replacing that large pane of glass. Tears streamed down his face as he ran to embrace me. I grabbed him by the shoulders and forced him away from me. I was going to punish him for breaking the window, but I noticed a thin trickle of blood on his wrist where he had been cut. It was only a small scratch, but I was sick with revulsion at my anger. My youngest child had seen his father leave on too many occasions and not return. He was frightened and had broken the window to gain my attention.

I put my handkerchief over the cut and held him in my lap, very tightly. Gradually his crying subsided, and he was quiet in my arms. I had suffered a lot in the last year and a half, but now it was clear to me that other people had suffered too, in many ways.

During the early fall months, I began to think seriously about a job. Before becoming sick I had traveled for twelve years, and I was not eager to return to the road. Sales work had always appealed to me. I applied at several companies but was always turned down because of my health record.

It was Forrest, my father-in-law, who suggested that I consider a career in real estate and insurance. He was sales manager of one of the larger real-estate firms in town, and he felt that I would do well. Since real-estate salespeople are considered independent contractors, there would be no problem with my past health record. Selling real estate and insurance was strictly a commission job, and I liked that. Hard work was necessary, but there would be no punching a time clock, and I could arrange my schedule to take care of personal business. After considering it at length, I decided to give it a try. To sell real estate it was necessary to be licensed by the state. The next examination was in November, and I would have to do a lot of studying.

That fall I was busy cracking the books, but I enjoyed it. I was also involved in other activities—the church choir, the Grand Island City Singers, board-of-education meetings, and various school functions. At times, there didn't seem to be enough hours in the day, but it didn't matter. I was so full of being alive, I enjoyed every minute of it.

The real-estate exam was set for the last Wednesday of November, and I presented myself at Lincoln's Pershing Auditorium early that morning. From there I headed to the hospital in Omaha, where a routine checkup showed no problems. The following week I returned to Lincoln for my insurance examinations. Then I went home to sweat out the test results, which arrived in mid-December. The real-estate commission report was marked simply "pass." The results of the insurance examination were just as good. I felt a real sense of accomplishment. I decided to activate my licenses on January 1, 1975. Then I entered wholeheartedly into the festivities of the Christmas season.

The Christmas choir concert was as usual a success. And as usual, the church was overflowing for the children's Christmas Eve service.

I remained in the back of the church after everyone had left. The main lights had been turned out, and a soft glow from the office dimly lit the altar and the cross. I reflected on the difference between this year's service and the last. With a sinking heart I had sat through last year's children's service, ignoring its message of hope. Uncertainty and despair had filled me. Now, I was restored to health and to a full, active life, and I was truly grateful.

A light snow was falling as Judy and I loaded the boys into the car for the short trip to her parents' house on Christmas Eve to exchange gifts. This beautiful holiday season was a fitting climax to a year that had started with little promise but was ending with renewed hope.

January saw me back on the job; I settled into the established routine of the office. I found the work both interesting and exciting, but it was not until early February that I listed my first property. It wasn't much—a small two-bedroom bungalow—but the listing was all mine, and I was very proud of it.

Although most of my strength had returned, I wanted to get into better physical shape. And when Neil Williams, another new salesman and an avid swimmer, learned of my wish, he invited me to join him in his lunch-hour swims.

"Neil, I don't know how to swim a stroke."

He was adamant. "Don't worry about it, I can teach you to swim."

Not one to go through unnecessary preliminaries, he had me jump off the side into the deep end of the pool. After a few lessons, swimming came naturally, and I worked up to swimming at least a half-mile each session. It was tremendous exercise, especially for those muscles in my sides that had been injured during surgery to remove my kidneys. By early summer, I had swum twenty-seven miles toward a goal of membership in the one-hundred-mile swim club.

During February, Judy and I decided to jump into a business venture with our friends Duane and Bonnie. Our personalities are somewhat different—I'm a plunger, Duane is more cautious—but we complement each other well.

I had been trying to get a listing on a piece of property owned by another friend, Dick Cavenee, and now he suggested that I buy it myself. The property was an older home that had been converted into three apartments. Duane and I decided to make Dick an offer that we felt sure he would refuse. To our amazement, he agreed not only to our price but also to our terms. He was being more than generous. I borrowed my half of the down payment and became a landlord.

A name for this new partnership had to be chosen. Obermier-

Beckler Properties was the leading choice for a time, but that was too much of a mouthful for any tenant to handle.

"Why not shorten it?" Judy suggested.

Bonnie agreed, and the search was on. We took the first three letters of Duane's name, OBE, and the first three letters of mine, BEC, which could be combined in the name of OBEC Properties.

Judy and I kept the books. The first of the month, when the rents were due, I loved being a landlord. By the fifth of the month, if tenants hadn't paid, I became a little worried. If the rents were still unpaid by the fifteenth, I would wonder what in the deuce ever had possessed me to buy rental property.

However, the cash flow supplied by the apartment house made a nice balance in our checkbook, and the four of us were itching to get our hands on another piece of property. That opportunity came in late May. On the Tuesday-morning tour, the sales force at Da-ly Realty went through a property that was conveniently located between my house and Duane's. Since it was a fixer-upper and needed a lot of work, it sparked my interest. We took a closer look at it that evening.

"This place needs more time than money," Duane said approvingly.

And since he had the summer free and I could get six weeks off, we had the time.

We figured that we would have to replace the entire bathroom, kitchen, furnace, and hot-water heater. Other items would include carpeting, new interior walls, and exterior siding. Even with the cost of these expenditures, the home could be sold for a tidy profit. Two days later our offer was accepted, and as July approached and we took title to the house, I exchanged the suit and tie of a realtor for the work clothes of a would-be novice carpenter.

Our plan of attack was to tackle the outside first. We began by ripping out the dilapidated porch, saving only the roof, which we propped up with long poles. Footings were dug and forms set so concrete could be poured. After the foundation dried and cured, concrete blocks were set in place and the new porch was formed. The number of beer cans between the concrete blocks and the house grew day by day.

"I wonder how many six-packs it takes to build a house," Duane asked, mopping his brow at the end of a hard day.

The day the chimney was removed, I felt it in my best interest to attend an unimportant sales meeting. I sent Kevin to help Duane with the task. When I saw Kevin and Duane later, they were covered with soot.

"How did the sales meeting go?" Duane asked sarcastically.

"Oh, it was a good one," I lied unconvincingly.

"I'll bet!" Duane said.

It was hard work, but our efforts were rewarded when we put on the new siding. After we had covered the dull green slate on the east side, we stepped back and admired our work. It had transformed an eyesore into a modern-looking house.

A few days later, I got a hint of what lay ahead for me, but at the time, I didn't realize it. As we were finishing the west side of the house, the intense, bright sun beating down on the white siding produced a glare so great that I had trouble focusing my eyes to hit a nail. When Duane handed me the tape to measure to the edge of the house, I handed it back because I couldn't read it.

I developed a headache and saw red spots through the center of my vision. The symptoms lasted a few hours but then faded away, and my vision returned to normal. I thought about it briefly but attached no particular significance to the incident.

Duane and I went to the house one morning to solve what appeared to be a ticklish problem—a header across a doorframe.

"The doggone header has to support the rafters," Duane exclaimed time and time again, "but how are we going to make it do it?"

Finally, we decided to break for coffee, and in exasperation, Duane nailed a piece of wood into place as a temporary measure. And there, with only a very minor change, was our solution. I sawed a piece of wood the required length and Duane nailed it up, both of us laughing all the while.

The thermos of coffee and sack of doughnuts were on the floor in front of the east window of the dining room. Duane and I sat cross-legged on the floor, feeling the warmth of the early morning sun beating on our backs.

Duane was many things to me, more than just a business partner. We had become close friends, confidants, companions, and at that moment I felt all the good qualities about him; the honesty, sincerity, and warmth.

"You know," Duane said speculatively, perhaps thinking about the Bible class we had attended that morning, "do you suppose God was watching us and had Himself a good belly laugh?"

"I suppose He did," I said. "I'm sure He has created better carpenters than you and I."

It was quiet in the room, and I wondered to myself whether God had indeed laughed. I searched my memory for any Bible story that showed God as humorous. And I realized that my image of God was of one who was wrathful, forbidding—loving, certainly—but who sometimes allowed too much disaster to enter a life. But I held to the thought of a humorous God, and the more I thought about it, the better I liked it. My perception of my God needed to be changed, changed to include the side of Him that was more human—the side that could enjoy a joke or a prank. A small grain of faith was added to my belief in God, and I felt very good about it.

My six weeks off from work were just about over. My condition was fine, as the monthly visits to Dr. Steenburg in Omaha confirmed. My kidney function was excellent, blood pressure was normal, and the diabetes seemed to be under control. My heart, which had been enlarged, had returned to its normal size, and the digitalis was discontinued. The only medication I continued to take (besides insulin) was 175 mg of Imuran and 8 mg of Medrol. These last two I would take for the rest of my life in order to keep the kidney from rejecting.

"Eventually we'll get the Medrol down to 4 mg," Dr. Steenburg said.

I was a trim 155 pounds and had never felt better.

Late in the summer during one of my visits to Dr. Steenburg, I asked him about the effects of my diabetes on Vic's kidney.

My own kidneys had lasted roughly fourteen years from the onset of diabetes.

"Will my diabetes have the same effect on Vic's kidney?" I asked.

"Probably, but no one knows for sure. Diabetics haven't been transplanted that long," he replied.

I asked, "If you can transplant a kidney to cure a renal problem, why can't you transplant a pancreas to cure diabetes?"

"The pancreas is a very different organ, and transplanting it would present a whole different set of problems. Perhaps someday I'll be transplanting them, but more research needs to be done. They're doing that type of research at the University of Minnesota."

I made a mental note of the conversation.

The usual fall activities were beginning. School opened, footballs were flying, and there was a nip in the night air. Wednesday nights were reserved for rehearsal with the City Singers and Thursday nights for choir at church.

I was progressing as a realtor, and my income was growing steadily. I liked the idea of investing in real estate. One day, while having lunch with Bill Landis, I shared my optimism with him. He was also interested in purchasing some property, and we decided to buy some rental property together. I told him that I would scout around until I found something suitable for the two of us. Our friendship was deepening and our lunches were a bright spot in my busy routine. An extremely intelligent individual, his wit and humor made our conversations lively and enjoyable.

"Bill, the last time I was in Omaha, Steenburg told me about the University of Minnesota doing research on pancreas transplants. Do you know anything about it?"

"Yes. I read something about it in the medical journal. Pretty experimental at this stage, though. Why?" he asked.

"Just curious."

"Come on, Al, I know you better than that. What are you thinking about?"

I explained my concern about the effects my diabetes might have on the kidney Vic had given me.

Bill chuckled.

"Not only did you want to be one of the first diabetics in Nebraska to receive a kidney transplant, now you want to be one of the first diabetics in the world to receive a pancreas transplant."

"Nothing wrong with that," I shot back at him.

Bill eyed me intently and, seeing that I was serious, said, "All right, I'll go back to the medical journals and find that article."

Hemorrhage

✿✦✿✦✿

October 1975 to March 1976

In early fall I began to notice problems with my vision.

The office where I worked was across town, and as I headed south, I noticed that the morning sun, shining into the corner of my left eye, would blind me on that side. I had to hold up my hand to shade my eye from the sun's rays. About the same time, I noticed that when I held a camera to my right eye to take a picture, I was unable to focus through the viewfinder. Then I started having problems going from the bright sunlight into a building. It seemed to take a long time for my eyes to adjust to the change in light.

Late one Sunday evening, I was alone in the basement, lying on the floor watching football reruns. Suddenly, a dark spot appeared at the bottom of my left eye. The dark spot grew and after several minutes, a thin, black line extended from the bottom of my eye toward the top. A half-hour later, the dark spot and line had disappeared, but my eye remained very cloudy, with tiny bits of black snow scattered throughout my field of vision. My heart sank as I realized that I had suffered a hemorrhage in a blood vessel in my left eye.

I went to Bill's office immediately the next morning. He checked the interior of my eyes for a long time. When he had finished, he placed the ophthalmoscope on his desk and sat back in his chair.

"How long have you been having problems with your eyes?" he asked.

"I had minor hemorrhages in my right eye just before the kidney transplant. They found them when I was in the hospital in Omaha, but they didn't suggest any treatment. When I look through that eye, I can tell it is weaker than the other, but it isn't that bad. At that time they said that my left eye was perfect."

"Have you noticed any other changes lately?"

"Not as far as being able to read or see distances, but I have noticed that my eyes are really sensitive to light, and that they don't adjust quickly to changes in light," I explained.

"What's going on with your eyes is a disease called diabetic retinopathy. Last night you had a large hemorrhage in your left eye. Do you know anything about diabetic retinopathy?" he asked.

"Yes," I said, recalling with a sudden feeling of apprehension what I had been told.

Diabetic retinopathy occurs in some diabetics, particularly juvenile-onset diabetics. The disease affects the very small blood vessels in the eye, weakens them, and causes them to hemorrhage. When hemorrhages occur, blood flows into the vitreous humor—the fluid that fills the eye—and blocks the vision. The eye can cleanse itself of this blood, but repeated hemorrhages severely restrict this capability. Eventually the eye is weakened, and other vision changes occur. In some severe cases, repeated hemorrhages can seriously damage the retina and cause blindness.

Then Bill said, "Evidence now shows that elevated blood-sugar levels over a prolonged period of time are the cause of these changes. In some cases, diabetic retinopathy and kidney failure are parallel. That's why controlling the disease is so important. Al, I hate to tell you this, but the disease process looks pretty far advanced, and now it's affected your left eye as well."

I sat in my chair, stunned.

"What do you suggest we do, Bill?" I asked as calmly as I could.

"I want you to see an eye specialist as fast as you can," he answered. "When you were in Omaha for the transplant, who checked your eyes?"

"An ophthalmologist named Dr. Filkens," I said.

"Okay, I want you to get an appointment with him as soon as possible."

At home I called Dr. Filkens's office. Although he could not see me that week, his associate, Dr. Meissner, could, and I made an appointment for late Thursday morning.

Wednesday evening I was sitting in the recliner listening to the stereo when another hemorrhage occurred in my left eye. The bleeding first appeared as a spot, then as a thin strand of blood extending away from the spot. Ten minutes passed and I couldn't stand it any longer. I called Bill at home.

"Bill, my left eye is bleeding again. For God's sake, isn't there something we can do?" I asked him hoarsely. "My eye is filling up with blood."

There was an anguished note in Bill's voice as he told me that there was nothing he could do.

"I know this doesn't sound like much, but the best thing you can do is to lie down and try to relax. The more agitated and upset you are, the higher your blood pressure will go. The last thing those veins need is a lot of pressure in them."

I thanked Bill and lay down on the couch. In another fifteen minutes the dark spot had gone away. Evidently, the hemorrhage had stopped, but everything I saw through the left eye was covered in a thick, black, speckled fog.

Early the next morning, Judy and I headed for Omaha. Dr. Meissner's office was in the medical complex adjacent to Bishop Clarkson Hospital. The doctor confirmed Bill's diagnosis.

"You've had several large hemorrhages in your left eye," he said, "but there's evidence that hemorrhages have occurred sometime in the past in your right eye also. The right eye is noticeably weaker."

"Couldn't this problem have been spotted before?" I asked.

"Not necessarily. Some diabetics exhibit problems with their eyes while they're still in their teens. Some never do. Some can have problems with their eyes and get along nicely for years and years, but in others, the bottom drops out all at once."

I sat for a while looking at the room through the gray-black specks that clouded my vision.

"Is there anything that can be done to stop the hemorrhages?" I asked.

"We can try photo-coagulation. In this treatment, a bright light is focused through the pupil of the eye and directed to an affected area on the retina. The purpose is to cauterize, or burn, the vein, cutting it off from its blood supply, and thus stopping the hemorrhaging. But I can't begin that treatment until the eye cleanses itself of the blood that's in it. Right now, there's so much blood in the eye, I can't see back to the retina. It will probably take your eye two weeks to get rid of the blood that's accumulated. We can start the treatments then. In the meantime, I'm going to put you on Valium. It'll keep you relaxed and help reduce the chances of further hemorrhaging."

"What next?" I thought bitterly. If my vision were impaired, my life would change dramatically. It seemed so unfair that this was happening just when I felt everything was going my way. Physically, I had never felt better. Everything was going well for the family, and I felt that I had found a niche in real estate and insurance.

During the first part of November, my eyesight began to clear, and I was able to resume driving. Although reading presented some difficulty, I was still able to watch television. After about an hour, my eyesight would improve. My vision would be practically clear after a few hours in front of the TV. I noticed that in the morning my vision would be free of the telltale spots of blood. I asked Bill about it.

He explained, "When your eye is fixed on one object, such as a TV, or when you're asleep, the blood settles to the bottom, and your vision clears. When you move your eye, or when you're active, the blood disperses throughout the vitreous humor in your eye, and your vision becomes cloudy."

In mid-November I drove to Omaha and admitted myself to Bishop Clarkson Hospital. That afternoon I received the first treatment. Before treatment I was given a shot to relax, and then novocaine was injected below the eye to keep it immobile. The treatment itself was painless; at times I felt a warm sensation. An hour later I was back in my room. Although this procedure was usually done on an outpatient basis, the patient is hospitalized over night for the first treatment. The next day I drove back to Grand Island.

The man in charge of the pancreas-transplant program at the University of Minnesota was Dr. David Sutherland. Dave is an associate professor of surgery and besides his teaching duties, he writes and presents papers on transplant procedures to symposiums around the world. I phoned him and expressed an interest in the program, and he explained briefly the research that had taken place. He was interested in my case and said that perhaps I might be a suitable volunteer candidate for the program. We decided that January 5, 1976, I would be admitted to the Clinical Research Center at the University of Minnesota for a series of tests to determine my suitability as a candidate. Not only was I interested in a cure for diabetes to save the kidney; now I also felt that a cure was imperative in order to avert further deterioration of my eyesight.

I arrived in Minneapolis on the morning of January 5. Howard picked me up at the airport and took me to the Clinical Research Center, which accommodates eleven patients. Since it is not an acute-care facility, people were generally admitted there for tests only.

I met Dr. David Sutherland after dinner. A tall man in his mid-thirities, he was dressed casually. He was on the thin side and very energetic, but he looked tired. His rapid speech was sometimes punctuated by movements of his hands.

"The pancreas program has been in the research stage in animals for a number of years," he explained. "In our laboratories, certain rats are made diabetic by artificial means. Then, from the pancreas of a healthy, non-diabetic animal, we remove the insulin-producing cells, which are called beta cells. These cells are then transplanted into a diabetic animal and are lodged in the capillaries of the liver. The cells then have an immediate blood supply available to keep them alive and produce insulin in response to the needs of the animal's body."

"What about rejection episodes?" I asked Dave.

"That's a good point," he replied. "The animals are closely inbred so that they all carry the same genetic strain. Because of that, there is no possibility of rejection, and it isn't necessary to put them on immunosuppressant drugs."

He went on to explain more about the program and its application to humans.

"One of the most important things is that we're looking for candidates who already have had a kidney transplant. Since you've had one, you're already on the drugs that would be needed to keep the body from rejecting the new insulin-producing cells. That's why I think you might be a suitable candidate. At this point in our research, we haven't progressed far enough to try it on diabetics who are not on immunosuppressant drugs."

I was very much interested in the program, and I explained about my eyes and why I hoped that a successful transplant could be done early enough to help save them.

"Unfortunately," Dave said, "the pancreas can only come from a cadaver, and it might be a long time before one is available with a match close enough for a transplant."

We discussed the program in more detail, and Dave outlined the tests that they would run during the next two days. "A glucose-tolerance test will also be run," Dave added. "It will serve as a baseline for comparing your blood sugars as of now to those after a transplant."

As he stood up to leave, I shook his hand; I felt satisfied with our talk. Two days later I checked out of the center. I spent the evening with Howard, and the next morning, in the bone-chilling cold, I returned home.

The following week, as I was sitting at my desk, I felt something happening with my left eye. A shadow covered the lower portion of my vision. Over the next several days, the shadow would come and go, but on the third day, it didn't go away. I called Dr. Meissner in Omaha and made an immediate appointment.

"The retina is detaching," he told me. "So much blood has been in the eye that some of it has congealed into a protein strand. This strand is attached to the retina at different points. Now the protein strand is contracting, and it's peeling the retina off the eye.

"There isn't much that can be done at this time," he continued. "We will have to wait to see how much of the retina detaches before attempting to reattach it."

Although there was no pain with the retinal detachment, there was agonizing mental pain from realizing what was happening to me. And every morning I would notice a larger part of my vision gone. From the shadow that first appeared, there now rose a spiral which curved toward the center. In that area, all vision was gone. On January 19, I was back in Dr. Meissner's office.

After checking the eye, he said, "You've got to have surgery on this eye."

The type of surgery he suggested was a vitrectomy. A small incision would be made in the eye, the blood would be cleansed, and the protein strand severed. Then an attempt would be made to reattach the retina. There were only a few centers in the United States doing this type of surgery. He referred me to Dr. Okun in St. Louis. Before I left his office, he made the necessary arrangements for me to see Dr. Okun on Thursday.

Wednesday afternoon I flew to St. Louis and spent the evening with relatives. I arrived at Dr. Okun's office Thursday morning. After an extensive examination of the eye, he advised surgery for the next morning. That afternoon I checked into Barnes Hospital.

Judy flew to St. Louis for the four-hour surgery Friday morning. That afternoon Dr. Okun came in my room.

"It was a tough surgery, but I think I've been able to reattach at least the top portion of the retina. I'm uncertain about the rest of it."

He said that this was significant, because if the top portion of the retina was reattached, it would help with my mobility, since the top half controlled what I saw in the lower half of my vision.

He had reattached the retina by placing a Teflon strap or buckle on the outside of the top portion of the eye. This buckle would constrict the diameter of the eye, forcing it back against the retina.

Dr. Okun told me that I would be hospitalized for at least a week to ten days. But he was hopeful about the outcome of the surgery, and consequently my spirits were somewhat buoyed. Although I didn't have too much pain, my eye had completely filled with blood as a result of the surgery, and it was impossible for me to see through it. Also, the lens of the eye had been removed.

I left the hospital eight days after surgery and arrived home wearing an aluminum shield over the bandaged eye. When the boys saw it, they knew that their father was having serious eye problems. One Sunday after we returned from church, Rusty asked Judy, "Why doesn't Daddy sing in church anymore?"

"Daddy's eyes aren't strong enough to read the words," she explained to him slowly.

"He can't catch the football anymore either," Scott said, a note of sadness in his voice. "He misses it all the time when I throw it to him."

I had to wait for the incision to heal and the eye to clear itself of blood. After that, a contact lens would be fitted, and with the aid of glasses, sufficient vision could perhaps be restored. In the meantime, I would have to adapt to the restricted vision of the right eye. That eye was too weak to allow me to drive. I was unable to read regular print, so I read large type with the aid of a magnifying glass.

The next few weeks were extremely hard for me. Unable to work, I was also housebound because of inclement weather. The extreme cold hurt my eye. Those were dreary days, and I became very depressed. It was hard for me to make the adjustment to a severely limited field of vision.

Eventually, the pain became extreme in my left eye and I made an appointment with Dr. Meissner. After checking my eye, he was not at all optimistic.

"Two things are happening," he said. "One is a disease called rubiosis. It is a wholesale proliferation of the small blood vessels.

They're growing out of control. The other one is glaucoma. The pressure in the eye is too high, and that's why you feel the pain."

Dr. Meissner wanted me to enter the hospital for two or three days of observation. For several days, I received treatments in an attempt to reduce the pressure. But each day the pressure reading was a little higher than the day before. Dr. Meissner informed me that the pressure and the pain would continue to grow, and that the only way to stop it was with an alcohol block to the optic nerve. But if he administered the alcohol block, it would kill the nerve itself and, with it, all hope of sight in that eye. Although the pain was at times excruciating, I was determined that nothing would force me to give up the eye. In a very cheerless mood Judy and I returned home.

For over two weeks I endured the pain. There was a constant sharp pain in the eye and the area around it throbbed. One Saturday I could stand it no more, and I called Dr. Meissner at home. He made arrangements with his associate to meet me at the outpatient clinic of the hospital where the alcohol block would be administered. Rusty was sick with flu and we had to find a driver, so Judy called Duane and Bonnie, who agreed to take me to the hospital that evening. Once again I made the three-hour journey lying in the back seat of the car.

It was with mixed emotions that I received the alcohol block. The sudden cessation of pain was an immense relief, but my heart sank as I realized that I had lost my eye.

Right Eye Fails

✧✦✧✦✧

April to June 3, 1976

During the next few weeks, I tried to come to grips with the new situation. Although my eyesight was very restricted and might get worse, I wanted to continue working. Of course, Judy or someone else would have to drive for me. I had my real-estate license and I still felt capable of selling. Elsie, our secretary, a very congenial and warm-hearted person, typed all of our listing information in large print. With the aid of a magnifying glass I could handle phone duty and also work with clients. With Judy driving, I set up some appointments and had a few showings. I wanted to keep active and was determined to earn a living for myself and my family.

The first week in April, I began to have problems with the right eye. When the living-room drapes were pulled, the folds made straight lines from ceiling to floor. One evening when I looked at them, some of the lines veered off at a distinct angle. Over the next several days, I checked my vision against the straight lines of the drapes. By the third day, I knew that what had happened to the left eye was now beginning in the right. I immediately went to Dr. Meissner, but because of several recent small hemorrhages in the eye, he was unable to see the retina and identify the problem. I was sure it was serious, however. Although my vision was limited, I was able to see through the eye, and the distorted images I saw frightened me.

A week later I was back at the doctor's office. The area affected was nearly the entire right half of my eye. Although I saw no shadows as I had with the previous retinal detachment, I knew there was something wrong. But again, because of blood in the eye, Dr. Meissner was unable to see back to the retina, and he was reluctant to do anything.

"It's up to you. Your choices are these: do nothing and hope that the eye stabilizes, or go in and have surgery. The eye is very weak and the risks are obvious. You have a tough decision, Al. You have to put your eggs in one basket and choose a course of action—and not blame yourself later if it doesn't turn out right."

While in St. Louis, I had been given the name of Dr. Knobloch, at the University of Minnesota. He was also one of the few surgeons in the country who was doing vitrectomy operations. Late in April, Judy and I drove to Minneapolis. We stayed with Don, and a few days later I had my first appointment with Dr. Knobloch.

He was a tall, slim man in his fifties. His face radiated concern and kindness. His voice was soft, but the instructions he gave his nurses held a hint of authority. His handshake was firm, and his touch on my face was gentle and sure.

"There's an awful lot of blood in your eye, and it's difficult for me to see what's going on. My guess is that the retina is detaching. My suggestion is to hospitalize you for a few days, keep you very still, and let the blood settle to the bottom. With the blood out of the way, we can tell better what's going on."

Although Judy wanted to remain with me during my stay, I encouraged her to return home to the boys. Reluctantly, she agreed.

Since the University of Minnesota hospitals were connected with a teaching institution, residents and interns were everywhere. An intern was sent to admit me and compile a medical history. I gave him information on the insulin dosages and on the medications I was taking, which at this time were only two—Imuran and Medrol. He marveled that I was taking so few medications having had a kidney transplant only two years earlier.

After the intern left, I arranged my clothes in the locker. I had the bed next to the window, and at the end of the bed was the bathroom. The door was mounted in a metal frame and as I looked at it, my partially detached retina distorted the frame into a crazy, abrupt angle. Since it was handy to look at to check on the detachment, the image of the distorted door and frame remain etched in my memory.

At nine P.M. the nurse placed a patch over my right eye.

"The patch will keep you from using your eye, and the blood will settle to the bottom."

This precaution, coupled with complete bed rest, was supposed to give Dr. Knobloch the opportunity he needed to view the retina.

The next morning before breakfast, a nurse put drops in my eye to dilate the pupil and then replaced the patch.

A short while later Dr. Knobloch entered the room. "Good morning, Al. Let's see what we have here." He removed the patch and aimed his ophthalmoscope at the pupil. After several minutes he said, "Still too much blood in it, but I think by tomorrow morning we'll be able to see something. I'm going to put you on complete bed rest for the next twenty-four hours. I've ordered Valium for you so it won't be so hard to lie still in bed."

Before leaving the room, and almost as an afterthought, he again addressed me in his quiet voice.

"I want you to meet somebody. Just stick out your hand. You can take a look at her some other time. This is the head nurse on this floor. Better watch out when she's around." Then laughed.

I extended my hand, and said, "Hi, I'm Al."

A voice, bright, lively, and somewhat embarrassed, said, "Hi, I'm Mugs."

A nurse named Linda arrived with the breakfast tray. Eating while lying supine proved to be quite an adventure. Linda and I were not very synchronized. My mouth opened just as the spoon left the bowl and closed just as she was about to put it in. I felt as if there was more breakfast around me than in me. After breakfast I took the Imuran, Medrol, and Valium. I slept most of the day.

The next morning, I spent several hours in the examining room with Dr. Knobloch. Other tests were performed on the eye, and several doctors, residents, and interns examined it. His report was about what I had expected. The retina was detaching, and there was a lot of blood and scar tissue in the eye.

Dr. Knobloch felt that the retina, if left alone, would become detached. I agreed with him. A vitrectomy, the same surgery that had been done in St. Louis, was scheduled for next Monday morning.

The eye patch was removed until Saturday evening. Then it would be replaced so as to have the eye as settled as possible for surgery. After lunch my pupil had returned to its normal size, and it was easier for me to focus on things. The door opened and a nurse stood by the foot of the bed. She was a tall, slim woman in her late twenties. Her brown hair was short and she was wearing large, square-framed glasses. Her expression seemed somewhat expectant.

Questioningly, I said, "Yes?"

She looked at me blankly for a second and then said, "I'm Mugs."

The moment I heard her voice I remembered.

"Oh," I said, "so you're Mugs."

She asked how I felt about the upcoming surgery. I explained that since the right eye was following the same pattern as the left one, it would be better to go into the eye now rather than let the retina detach.

"I'm not looking forward to it, though," I admitted.

We talked for a while longer about the surgery and the prospect of success.

"Look, I've got to run. I've got all my charts to do before three-thirty. But I'm on duty tomorrow and Sunday. If I get a chance, I'll stop back and we can talk some more."

She smiled and left the room.

The spring night was warm and the windows in the room were open. My roommate and I were talking when we heard a thud and a moan outside the window. I looked out and saw a white form a short distance away, lying between the building and the driveway. Not quite sure, afraid of what it was, I rang for the nurse. A male attendant responded, and I told him what I had heard and seen. He looked out the window.

"Oh, God," he murmured, and ran to the nurses station.

The nurse told me later that a patient who was hospitalized for an attempted suicide had tried again, this time jumping from a upper-floor window.

I was shaken by the incident and was unable to sleep. I was sickened by the thought that anyone would take his own life, and I was angry, too. I was desperately trying to save my eyesight, and someone was deliberately throwing his away.

The moonlight streamed into the room. The metal frame of the bathroom door reflected the moonlight. As I lay awake that night, the image of that metal frame burned itself into my memory.

My first recollection after surgery on Monday was Don standing beside the bed. He leaned over the bedrail and asked, "How you doin', buddy?"

Groggily, I extended my hand toward him and he grasped it. "How'd it go?" I asked.

"Well, Dr. Knobloch said it was pretty rough."

"But how did it go?" I asked again.

"Well, I don't know. He just said there was a lot of stuff in there that they didn't expect. I don't know. You'll have to ask him when he comes in. Do you want me to call Judy?"

"No, I'll call her later," I said. The effects of the anesthetic were beginning to wear off and there was a sudden pain.

Later I called Judy and told her that they would not be sure of the results until the eye cleared. Dr. Knobloch hadn't removed the lens and hadn't put on a buckle either. But once the blood was cleared up, and if the retina was still attached, I would be able to see.

"Al," she said worriedly, after I had explained, "I just hope and pray everything goes all right. I want to come up to see you."

"No," I said, trying to reassure her. "Everything will work

out all right. Just stay with the boys. They need you."

Eye drops were placed in the eye routinely, and after the third day, there was not a great deal of pain. What I saw was blackish-gray. If I looked toward the window, I could see light. If someone moved in front of the window, I saw a shadow. Other than that, I couldn't see anything.

The biggest hurdle was learning to eat by myself, since I preferred not to have the nurses feed me. My plate took on the face of a clock.

"At twelve o'clock is your meat, at three o'clock your vegetables, and six o'clock your potatoes," Mugs said. "On the tray, the milk is at one o'clock, ice cream at eleven, and coffee at three," she continued.

They were simple instructions, but they helped immensely. I coped with eating in this fashion, assuring myself that it was only a temporary inconvenience until the blood in the eye cleared. Deep inside me a cold truth lurked, but I pushed it down and would not listen to it. During those periods I reached out for Judy, and we spent hours on the phone.

I was dismissed from the hospital the following week. Before leaving, Dr. Knobloch said, "You can be up and about, but avoid any strenuous activity. Be sure not to bump the eye. If at any time you notice bright, star-like points of light, get in touch with me right away. Those pinpoints of light could indicate that the retina is detaching."

Don carried my suitcase as we left Station 12. I held onto his right elbow and we walked to the car. Even in the bright sunlight, I saw only blurred images. I groped for the handle of the car door and opened it. As I started to get in, I felt a seat in front of me and realized that I had opened the back door by mistake. Embarrassed, I shut it quickly and fumbled for the front-door handle.

I had seen Don's house, so the layout of the rooms and the yard was familiar. By holding my hands in front of me, I was able slowly to navigate the interior of the house. By keeping a hand on the house, I could trace my steps from the front door, across the garage, along the side of the house, and to the patio in back. I would then find a chair and smoke a cigar.

After I had been at Don's over a week, I began to notice small pinpoints of light in the right side of my vision. I didn't say anything the first day I noticed them. The morning of the second day, I sat on the patio with a cup of coffee. Before going into the house, I moved a lawn chair to step around it. The sun shone on the webbing of the chair and dimly, from one part of my eye, I could see the different colors of the straps. That was the last thing I ever saw.

By the afternoon the pinpoints of light were so strong, I knew that I would have to see Dr. Knobloch. My niece took me to the eye clinic at the hospital. I was scheduled for another vitrectomy.

In the operating room, Dr. Knobloch's associate examined my eye thoroughly.

"The eye seems to be clearing up some," he said. "I feel it would be best to give the eye a few more days to clear up, and perhaps then it will be easier to see where the trouble is."

I could not see anything other than a small area of light that disappeared as he bent over to examine the eye.

Dr. Knobloch informed me several days later that a scleral buckle would have to be placed on the outside of the eye to try to force the eye back in contact with the retina. That surgery was performed the next day. Afterward, I tried to prepare myself for the results. I had to face possible blindness.

Waiting for the outcome of the second surgery became unbearable. The thought of permanent blindness preoccupied me, and I was depressed. My emotions were at their lowest a week later. I was transferred to a four-bed ward, where I occupied the bed in the corner. I wanted nothing to do with anyone, only to be left alone. I pulled the curtains tightly around my bed in an attempt to shut out everything and everyone. I ate so little that my insulin dosage had to be dramatically reduced. I was angry at everything.

On the third day of self-imposed seclusion, the nurse's aide brought my lunch and set it on the tray beside the bed. I was not talking to anyone.

"I've got your lunch, Al," she said as she pushed the tray

across the bed. "Come on now, you've got to eat some of this."
She unfolded the napkin and placed it across my lap.

"Do you want me to help you?"

"No," I muttered angrily.

She stood beside the bed for a minute, and then, when I hadn't
moved, she said in exasperation and anger, "You're not eating is
just plain stupid."

"I don't want it, so take it away."

"No, you're going to have to eat something," she shot back.

By now I was coldly furious. I took hold of the tray, held it
over the edge of the bed, and deliberately let the tray fall to the
floor. The sound of the tray and dishes breaking brought another
nurse running. She took in the situation at a glance and, without
saying a word, both nurses began cleaning up the mess. When
they had completed the chore, they left the room, closing the
curtain behind them.

I sat still in bed as the anger flowed out of me. I was ashamed
and embarrassed at what I had done. Despair came over me, and
I wrapped the pillow around my face. The tears flowed freely
and afterward I felt weak. I prayed for strength to see this thing
through and fell asleep.

I was awakened by voices in the room. The shift had changed
and the nurses were charting vital signs. Calmer now, I resolved
to face whatever lay ahead. I got up, grabbed the curtain, and
pushed it around the bed and back against the wall. It was the
last time that I closed myself inside.

Several days later I asked Dr. Knobloch to explain what would
be done if the retina was still detached.

"Al, it's kind of a last-ditch effort we'd have to use. I have to
tell you right now that the chances of success are around 5 percent. If the buckle surgery isn't successful, then we will go in
and replace the fluid of the eye with a clear silicone solution.
The solution is heavy, and with it we would hope to press the
retina back against the eye."

The dots of light around the side of my vision continued. Too
much blood remained for Dr. Knobloch to see the retina. After

several more days passed, it became evident that, when I looked at the light of the instrument shining in my eye, only the left half saw the light. A few days later, Dr. Knobloch confirmed that the retina was detached in a large part of the eye. The silicone implant would be scheduled for Friday, June 4. With a very heavy heart, I called Judy and told her the news.

Blindness

❖✦❖✦❖

June 4, 1976

I was awake when a doctor and Mugs entered the room. Mugs squeezed my toe. "Good morning," she said as she walked past the bed. The doctor stood at the foot of my roommate's bed, and I could hear him flip through the chart. My roommate had had a cataract removed a few days earlier.

"You're doing just fine," he told him. "You'll be able to go home in a few days." Cheerfully he added, "In six weeks, we'll fix you up with a contact lens, and you'll be doing everything you used to do."

Then he stopped by my bed. "How are you getting along?" he asked.

"I'm having eye surgery later this morning."

"What kind?" he asked.

"I'm having a silicone implant in my right eye."

"Oh! Well, good luck," was his reply.

I could tell by the tone in his voice that he knew the full implications of the surgery.

I lay there thinking about the surgery. Dr. Knobloch had been very blunt when he told me that today's surgery had only a 5-percent chance of success. But I could not give up hope. Somehow a miracle would have to happen. If it didn't, I'd be blind, and I couldn't face that.

I tried not to think about the surgery. I thought about my roommate, about how well his surgery had gone and how fortunate he was. I was angry and resentful because of his good fortune. He had everything to look forward to, and probably all I had to look forward to was blindness. Nevertheless I still clung to the slim, slim hope that this last surgery would be successful. But with all of my previous surgeries, nothing had gone right, and this last one could prove to be even worse.

Mugs came back into the room.

"I've got a shot for you to make you drowsy. Which side do you want it in?"

"It doesn't make any difference," I said. "They're both sore." I rolled over to one side and felt the sting of the needle a few seconds later.

"How do you feel?" she asked.

"Scared." I said.

She stood there a few moments. Then without saying anything, she patted me on the leg and left the room.

The shot didn't seem to have any effect. I was wide awake when the orderly rolled the surgical cart next to the bed.

I heard voices at the nurses' station as we rolled by; then the voices became quiet. The orderly stopped by the desk and asked the secretary for my charts, which he put under the pillow. No one spoke.

Mugs came and stood by the cart. She took my hand and pressed it gently.

"I hope everything goes all right in surgery. I'll be praying for you."

Other nurses came by too, nurses whom I had gotten to know well in the last six weeks. Some were lighthearted, some more serious, and some said they'd pray for me. They all wished me well. Hands touched my shoulders and arms. The pressure of those hands told me that these people knew what I was going through, and that they hurt for me.

Mugs said jokingly, "I've got to quit holding your hand and get to some people who are really sick. You'll be back in about two hours and I'll see you then." She squeezed my hand once more, tightly, and then I heard her footsteps going down the hall.

The orderly pushed the cart through the halls to the elevator. As we entered someone inquired, "Surgical floor?"

"Yes," the orderly replied.

The surgery room felt cold, and I shivered although I was covered by several blankets. I prayed earnest, desperate prayers.

"Oh, God, Oh, God—if it is Your will, let this operation be a success. Let me keep my sight, even if it is only a small portion."

I prayed over and over.

Fear and apprehension built—fear of the surgery, fear of the surgical knife entering my eye, and a deep fear of the possible outcome. By then the shot was taking effect; I was slightly drowsy. Another person said, "We're ready for you now." They moved the cart through a doorway and positioned it by the surgical table. People were talking and laughing—talking of ordinary everyday things, their children, the plans they had made for the evening. Somewhere in the room a radio was playing.

A nurse undid the strap that was across my knees and unfolded the blanket.

"Put out your left hand, Mr. Beckler, and you'll feel the table."

I did. It felt hard and cold.

"On the count of three, we'll help you slide across onto it."

When I was on the table, someone buckled a strap across my knees and tucked blankets around me again.

"I'm going to start an IV," one nurse said. Another nurse wrapped sterile cloths around my head and face, and across my chest and the arm that was tucked against my side.

I heard Dr. Knobloch's quiet voice coming from the other side of the room. He came to the table, put his hand on my shoulder, and asked, "How are you doing, Al?"

"So-so," I said.

"Are you feeling drowsy?"

"Yes, sort of."

"Are you sure you want to stay awake for this surgery?" he asked. "You know we can put you out if you want us to."

"No, I'd rather be awake, and then I'll know right away," I said.

"All right, it's up to you. We'll be ready to start in just a few minutes."

One of the assistants said, "Al, I'm giving you a shot under your eye so that you won't feel any pain, and also one in front of your ear, which will also help deaden the pain. Are you ready?" he asked.

I was.

As I lay on the table, the bright lights beat down on me and I could feel the heat from their glare. A dark shadow moved across my right eye. I felt the sharp sting of the needles as the assistant gave me the shots. He waited a minute and then asked if I could move my eye. I tried, but could not.

He said, "We'll wait a little longer and then start."

Dr. Knobloch stood by me again.

I didn't feel the incision or any pain, only movements. Time seemed to pass slowly. There was some conversation between the doctors. I heard them asking for different instruments and then the slap as they were placed in the hand.

More time passed and then Dr. Knobloch said, "We're ready to start injecting the silicone now."

This had to work; it was the final act that could save an eye ravaged by the effects of diabetes.

I was tense and lay rigid on the table. "Oh, God," I said to myself. "Oh, God, oh, God, oh, God—"

Time passed. It seemed to take forever.

"How much silicone is left?" Dr. Knobloch asked his assistant.

"Not much" was the reply.

"Hold up a minute while I check the eye." I felt his face close to mine. "Give me the rest of it," he said.

"That's it, doctor," the assistant said.

It was very quiet for what seemed an eternity. Again, Dr. Knobloch's hand was on my shoulder. "It didn't work, Al. I'm sorry."

Then to his assistant, in a tone that conveyed his anger, frustration, and sense of failure, he said curtly, "Close up that eye," and walked away.

I heard the click of the instruments as they sutured the incision. No one had spoken since Dr. Knobloch had walked away. The voices that had talked of everyday things were now silent; the only noise in the room was the radio. The cloths were removed and a hand gently held my shoulders. The cart was brought to the table, and I tried to move over to it but couldn't. I laughed and made a joke of it and tried again. This time, gentle, caring hands helped me. I could feel their anguish for me.

The orderly rolled the cart into the hall and told me that in a while, someone would take me back to my room on Station 12.

I was alone in the hall. I put my left hand in front of my face and moved it. I could see nothing. I moved my fingers to see if I could see movement. Nothing but blackness.

I was alone with my thoughts. A part of me knew what had happened; another part of me had not accepted it. I lay very quiet, not moving. Somewhere in a far distant place, I heard someone sobbing deeply.

It was me.

Trying to Adjust

❖❀❖❀❖

June 1976

M y niece Tammy took me to the airport Monday. My eye was swollen and inflamed, and the pain made me restless and agitated. I was uneasy for other reasons. Getting on the plane was awkward, and my inability to explain to the stewardess how she could help me only underscored my feelings of fear and helplessness. My movements were uncoordinated. As I sat down, my head struck the baggage rack. Feeling as if the eyes of everyone in the cabin were on me, I sunk gratefully into the safety of the seat.

Over the last two months, the hospital had represented safety and security. Now I was alone and felt helpless and entirely dependent on others. I heard the stewardess taking beverage orders.

"Would you like something to drink?" she asked.

Suddenly the realization of my blindness hit me. I didn't know if her question had been directed at me or to the person on my left—or the people sitting across the aisle.

The plane arrived in Grand Island late in the evening. Judy and friends and family were there to meet me. I was nervous as I descended from the plane. I had been able to see when Judy and I had been together last. Now I was blind. I wondered how she would react. I wondered how I would react.

My hand was on the elbow of the cabin attendant as we walked toward the passenger area. We walked through a steel gate as we approached the door. The attendant misjudged my proximity to the post and I struck it with my side. She murmured an embarrassed apology as we entered the passenger area.

Inside the doorway, I heard my brother Gordon's voice. The incision hurt terribly, and the Darvon I had taken before I left Minneapolis hadn't helped. Neither had the drink I had had in Omaha. My eye was watering incessantly and I wiped at it, not so much to remove the water as to show that I was not crying.

An arm slipped around my waist, and I felt a brush of hair against my cheek.

"Hello, honey," Judy said softly.

"How are you doing?" I greeted her quietly.

We stood close, our arms around each other. We could not, dared not, say more. I was terribly wounded at heart. I ached. I hurt to the very center of my being, and Judy stood close beside me, feeling my anguish. She trembled slightly and her arm tightened around my waist. The crush of other passengers was around us.

Time seemed disjointed during the first week home. I felt as though I were living outside the normal pattern of past, present, and future. The disease process had been going on since I had become a diabetic, but it had been only seven months from the first massive hemorrhage until I lost my sight. The uncertainty of these past months was over. No longer would I lie awake nights worrying whether or not I would be blind. Blindness was now a fact, but the finality of the situation had not yet hit me. I was in a daze, unable to make the simplest decisions, unwilling to search for the path that would lead back to a normal life. I was tentative in my actions and speech, and for the first week, I did not venture outside the house.

During the second week, I was aware of the unnatural attitudes of Judy and the boys. They were quiet, almost as if a death had occurred. They were nearby and always ready to help in any way they could, but it wasn't normal for the boys to be so quiet around the house. Judy—always willing to help—was even more solicitous of my welfare. It wasn't natural; things had to get back to normal and I knew it.

I then made my first attempts to do more for myself and to teach the family how they could be helpful. I explained how they could tell me where my food was located on the plate, referring to it as the face of a clock. Eating became more manageable. The boys learned to pick up their toys and not to leave doors halfway open.

We rearranged the furniture in the living room so that I could get around more easily. We also redid my closet and dresser drawers, separating some items by color. I commandeered two drawers in the bathroom vanity and put my toothbrush and other articles where I could find them.

Moving about the house didn't present any problems because I knew the house well and could move through familiar areas by touching the furniture or trailing my hand along the wall of the hallway. When I hit an open space, I walked tentatively with my hands extended in front of me. Although this method was fine in the house, it was totally unsatisfactory outside. I couldn't expect Judy or the boys to drop whatever they were doing to walk with me. Something had to be done, and so on Thursday, I called the Department for the Visually Impaired in Lincoln and set up an appointment for the next day.

Friday afternoon, Judy and I met with one of the counselors of the agency, and I was given my introduction to the white cane. In a two-hour session, the counselor instructed me on the basic techniques that I would need to travel independently. It was a simple procedure but profoundly effective. Holding the cane centered in front of me, I would move it in an arc from the outside of one foot to the outside of the other. As the cane cleared an area in front of me, I walked forward. If anything was in the way, the cane would come in contact with it and prevent me from walking into it. I needed no longer to walk tentatively, shuffling my feet and extending my hands to ward off obstacles. I was able to do it alone. Nothing did more to bolster my self-confidence in that first month than the acquisition of the white cane.

The boys seemed to return to their normal activities the following week, and the noise level in the house increased to the usual dull roar.

The pain from the last surgery had subsided when, one afternoon as I was lying on the living room floor, Rusty came in from play. As he stretched out beside me, I grabbed him by the waist and started to tickle him. We wrestled vigorously for a while.

"Uncle?" I asked him as I pinned his shoulders to the floor.

"No, no," he cried, struggling hard to escape my grasp.

"You'll be sorry," I said, pinning him with my left arm and tickling him with my right.

Laughing uncontrollably, he finally gave in.

As we rested on the floor, I gave him a loving squeeze. My face was only a few feet from his, and I lay there facing him. I felt the movement of his arm as he slowly moved his hand back and forth in front of my eyes.

Tears suddenly overwhelmed me and I was filled with a great sadness. I had to turn away from him. I hadn't adjusted to my blindness and neither had he.

Damn it! My blindness might not affect the closeness that I enjoyed with my sons, but it would forever alter the way in which I shared activities with them.

Dr. Knobloch had advised me to have the incision on my eye checked three weeks after I got home, so I called Bill's office to set up an appointment. Since I wanted a chance to talk to Bill, I asked for his last appointment of the day. As I waited for Friday to come, I stayed close to home. Halfheartedly, I attempted to do most of the things that I would have to learn to do myself. After failing to find my shoes for several days in a row, I realized that when I took them off, I would have to put them in a specific place if I wanted to find them the next day. Eating became easier, but I still preferred sandwiches and other foods that I could take in my hands.

I learned a system for identifying my clothes and each day

chose my own wardrobe, asking Judy to check that I had things color coordinated. Two or three times each day, I went for walks with Judy or one of the boys. Other times, I would take my cane and walk alone around the block, trailing the shoreline of the sidewalk. But I did not trust myself to cross the street.

One evening we attended a picnic with some friends. It was a change in the regular routine and it went well. I enjoyed myself but again noticed that my friends chose their conversations carefully. They didn't mention anything about seeing a baseball game or a TV program. They were cheerful and laughter filled the air; yet there was an air of restraint. They were cautious, wanting to respond correctly toward me. They were waiting for me to show them the way, but I could not because I was groping to find the way for myself.

Late Friday afternoon, Judy dropped me at the clinic. I wanted to walk alone to Bill's office.

I settled back in the chair and waited. The conversation in the waiting room, which had stopped when I entered, now began to pick up. The feeling that I had of people watching me was something I would have to get used to.

When the nurse finally informed me that Bill was ready for me, I made my way down the hallway to the room. I walked past the door and bumped up against the back wall. Retracing my steps, I found the opening of the doorway. I went in and sat down by Bill's desk.

"Why hello, Al," Bill said.

"Hello, Bill, how are you doing?"

"I'm fine, but what's more important, how are you? What brings you here today?"

"Well, W. J.," I said, using his initials as I sometimes did, "the docs in Minneapolis wanted someone to check my eye. So here I am."

"All right," he laughed. "Just as long as you remember that I'm an internist and that eyes aren't my specialty."

"Well, Bill, when you're working on me, you don't need to be."

Bill chuckled, and I heard him move to the sink to wash his hands.

"Get up on the table and I'll take a look."

I stood up, taking the cane in my hand, and moved toward the table. As I did so, I swatted him smartly on the ankle.

"Whoops, sorry, Bill," I apologized.

"Damn," he said. "I can see I'm going to have to be awfully careful around you."

I sat on the edge of the table with my legs dangling over the side.

"Are you ready?" Bill asked. I felt his hands push the lid of my right eye back.

"How does it look?" I asked after a minute.

"Puffy and red and sore. But it looks like it's healing nicely. Do you see any light at all?"

"Nope," I replied. "When I go blind, I do it up brown."

He checked my blood pressure and helped me to the scales, where he weighed me. "How's the diabetes doing?"

"All right. I've cut back on my insulin. I haven't been eating as much lately. I don't have too much of an appetite."

For the next five minutes, Bill asked me questions about the diet, insulin dosages, and medications I was taking. Then I heard the squeak of the chair as he pushed it away from his desk, the creak of the springs as he reclined back, and the clump of his shoes as they hit the top of his desk.

He paused and then said, "I haven't talked to you since before the last operation. That's almost a month ago. What's it been like? What have you been going through?"

"Oh, I've been all right."

It was a lie and we both knew it.

"No, that's not true," I admitted. "It's been a bitch, Bill. A real bummer."

I leaned forward in the chair, my elbows on my knees and my hands cupping my chin. Sudden, hot tears filled my eyes as I groped for words to convey what I felt. He sat quietly, and I heard the strike of a match and smelled the cigar.

"You don't have to talk about it, Al. But if you want to, I'll listen."

It was quiet in the room. Down the hall I heard the nurses leaving for the day. I was aware of Bill's calm, unhurried presence. Tears started afresh, but I fought them back. I knew the pent-up sobs—the deep hurt—would have to surface soon if the healing process was to begin. But now was not the time, and I steadied myself.

"Bill," I said, taking a deep breath and letting it out slowly, "I think that what's happened is beginning to sink in a little, but I know that the total adjustment is going to take a long, long time. There seem to be so many things that I have to consider— like what kind of training should I get, and where am I going to get it? What am I going to do after I get through? Then there are the hundreds of adjustments that I am going to have to make in my life. Everyday I seem to be running into something new. Then there are the adjustments that Judy and the kids have to make, that everyone around me is going to have to make."

I continued with my litany of woes, and Bill listened patiently as I tried to exorcise the hurt that was in me.

"I feel as if someone had died. Do you suppose that I'll mourn for my eyesight in the same way I would mourn for a person? I'm close to tears all the time, and I'm so very depressed. How long do you think it'll take before I get over the loss of my eyesight? Months, years? Or will it ever end?"

"It's an old cliché, Al, but how does it work, taking it one day at a time?"

"Not worth a damn. Things seem to be headed nowhere."

"Maybe that's because you operate best when you have things planned, when you have goals set for yourself. Right now you haven't made any long-range plans. When you start to do those things, I'm sure you'll feel better. Give yourself a little time. It'll come."

"I suppose you're right, but I haven't been able to see anything since the last of April. They told me then that I was going to be blind for good, and already I'm tired of it—just sick and tired of it. And another thing, I'm tired of thinking about it. It's always on my mind. The fact that I'm blind fills my every waking minute. I'm tired of that, and I want to do something.

"That's a good sign, Al. If you're tired of thinking about it, maybe you're ready to occupy yourself with other things, to explore the options you have available. I think you have come a long way already."

I mulled over Bill's statement but made no response. I changed the topic, and we talked about the rental properties that we owned. Several small maintenance problems had come up, and we had to decide what to do about them.

The visit with Bill lifted my spirits for the entire weekend. It had been good to talk to someone besides Judy about my feelings. Bringing them out in the open seemed to relieve the tension. That weekend, I began to think of my future and tried to formulate a possible course of action. It was difficult to reach beyond my blindness and forge goals that would give meaning and value to my life. But it was necessary and was the best therapy I could have engaged in.

With lots of family activities and visits to several of our friends, that weekend was enjoyable. My mood was outgoing and cheerful. But by Monday afternoon, I again became depressed.

It was obvious that the key to overcoming my depressions was to keep extremely busy, and although a part of me was searching for activities that could occupy my time, I still was unable to shake the lethargy. I talked about it with Judy; she, like Bill, counseled me to give myself time.

Toward the middle of the week, I walked to the church office and visited with Pastor Meyer.

"Al, you're bound to be upset and depressed about what's happened, and it's going to take you a while to get back on your feet, physically and emotionally. But remember God's promise to you—that He will not allow anything to happen to you that you cannot bear. Right now you're grieving over the loss of your sight. That's natural, but I also believe that you are beginning to look ahead and starting to make plans for your future. Look, you haven't even been blind a month. Let me ask you this. How did you get over here today?"

Not sure of what he meant by that question, I answered, "Why, I walked."

"Exactly. Al, I know that you feel like you're in limbo, that your life right now doesn't have any direction, but you haven't even been home a month. Yet you're able to walk independently from your home to my office."

"Well, Pastor," I replied, "it's only a block and a half."

"Whether it's a block and a half or a mile and a half isn't the point. The point is, you're trying and you'll continue to keep trying. A lot of people wouldn't have done that. You feel you aren't accomplishing anything, but I think you already have. I think you are doing extremely well."

The talk with Pastor Meyer helped, and for the remainder of the week I took renewed interest in learning to be more independent. I also spent an increasing amount of time outside. I walked with Judy and the boys but spent most of the time walking alone, learning how to use the cane. The single most important aspect of walking independently was the sense of wellbeing that it gave me. I liked the feeling of being completely on my own and in control of the situation. I also enjoyed the feeling of accomplishment that came from walking to a specific point and returning home.

But down inside there remained a feeling—a lump in my throat—of being close to tears all the time. On several occasions that pent-up feeling almost broke loose, but I fought it back, knowing even while I did that, sooner or later, it had to come out.

The following week, we made a trip to Lincoln to talk to the people at the Department for the Visually Impaired. The arrangements were made for an instructor to spend half a day each week at my home, helping me with Braille, with typing, and with mobility training.

We discussed the training program the department offered. It was a nine-month program, with the students living in cottages provided by the state. The program was extensive, and it was designed to teach students how to cope with blindness and lead a normal life.

The school in Lincoln, like all others, was not a vocational school. It was for rehabilitation and was not intended to train people for a specific career. Still, the rehabilitation lessons would prove invaluable when applied to the specific job of selling real estate and insurance.

On the way home, Judy and I talked about my going back to work. She encouraged me to consider it. "You've got all of the necessary licenses," she said. "You're good with people, and you know that I'll be happy to drive you and your clients anywhere you need to go. I think it would work."

For the rest of the trip home, I considered the idea, weighing all the pros and cons. The more I thought about it, the better I liked it.

One afternoon Scott and I took a walk. We were about six blocks from home when we heard children laughing. They were across the street ahead of us.

Several days ago, we had encountered the same group of children and now I wondered what Scott would do this time. That first meeting had been uncomfortable. The young children had called out, "Hey, look at that blind man," and, "Mister, what's that stick for?"

They had been displaying curiosity, but instead of talking to them, we had walked past them. I had heard one mother scold her child, "Don't bother that man. He's blind."

Scott had been uneasy then, and his pace had quickened as we left the children. Now on this Fourth of July afternoon, the children were lighting firecrackers.

As we approached the intersection, I gave Scott the opportunity to turn back toward home.

"Scottie, it's really getting hot. If you want to head for home, that's all right with me."

I waited for him to reply, but he didn't say anything. As we reached the curb he paused. I felt with my cane, found the curb, stepped down, and we crossed the street. As we approached, some of the children ran up to talk. Again there were the same questions.

"Hey, mister, are you really blind?" one of them asked.

"Yes, I am," I said.

"Does that mean you can't see anything?"

"That's right."

"You mean you can't even see me?" the child asked, unbelieving.

"Yep, that's right," I said again, this time smiling at him.

Another child asked, "What's 'blind' mean?"

"That means my eyes don't work," I said.

That seemed to satisfy him, and he then told me about the plans for his family's picnic that evening. But my explanation hadn't quite sunk in.

"Watch me, mister," he said. "I'm going to light a firecracker. I'm old enough."

I laughed, for he hadn't caught the inconsistency of his remarks. I talked to the other children, telling them about blindness. Scott was telling them that I was his father and explaining to them, in a shorthand way, the use of my white cane.

Scott and I left them and continued our walk. I had given my nine-year-old son an opportunity to avoid the encounter. He could have turned back a block earlier, but he hadn't. He had led me toward them and had talked to them about me and my blindness. From the tone of his voice, I knew that he had experienced no embarrassment at all. He was adjusting to my blindness, but it still had taken courage for him to do what he had just done. I felt a tug at my heart but didn't trust myself to say anything to him. Instead, I reached over, put my arm around his shoulders, and gave him a hug.

Several days later I took a walk to the church. I checked the time on the Braille watch I had bought when I was in Lincoln. It took a while, but I finally deciphered the time. It was four-thirty and Darlene and Pastor Meyer would still be in the office. I decided to go in for a cup of coffee.

As I walked in the front door, I found the coolness inside the church refreshing after the heat of the afternoon. I climbed the stairs toward the office, but for some reason, I continued ahead instead and opened the doors leading to the nave. I sat down in a pew in front of the pulpit. The sanctuary was quiet and still; the sounds of the traffic outside were barely heard. The quietness, the sense of remoteness, the feeling of being detached from any human contact, made me feel quite alone. I sat there for a long time, thinking about being blind and the fact that it would be with me for the rest of my life. Suddenly I knew, knew that my blindness was a part of me, as much as part of me as any other physical attributes I possessed. I could never run away from it. No longer could I experience the joys that sight could bring. No longer would I be able to see my wife and children, or look into the eyes of a friend. No longer would I be exhilarated by a beautiful sunset or able to see the stars twinkle. No longer would I be able to watch the change of the seasons.

All of those things, and countless more, were forever lost to me. And as I thought about what had been taken from me, I was filled with anger. No, not anger—rage. There was no justice here. Two years ago I had almost died of kidney failure. I had suffered for almost two years and only at the last moment had been saved from death. I had suffered then. I didn't need blindness. This shouldn't have happened to me. I cried out to God that I did not deserve this. A merciful God, a loving God, would not allow this to happen to one of His children.

Angrily, I stood up. I stepped into the aisle, my cane catching on the edge of the pew. Irritated and angered, I took the cane and swung it. The full length of the cane caught the pew along its face. The sound echoed like a rifle shot through the church, and its loudness jolted me.

As I sank back into my seat, the full weight of the burden I would have to carry for the rest of my life came crushing down. I felt alone, helpless and defenseless against all of the trials that I knew would come. The sorrow, the deep sorrow, now burst forth in a torrent of tears. I put my arms on the pew in front of me and rested my head. The pent-up hurts and pains I felt were vented with my tears.

I could not stop the deep aching sobs that wracked me. When they finally subsided, I was spent, emotionless. Gradually a calmness came, and it was then that I was able to pray. In my prayer I asked God to give me strength necessary to face what lay ahead, strength to fight against depression and self-pity, and the strength to achieve all that I would be capable of achieving.

I rested there for some time and then reached for the handle of my cane. I found it lying in a pool of tears.

Setting a Course

❖❖❖❖

July to September 19, 1976

That summer, with the help of the instructor from Lincoln, I learned how to make crossings at intersections and expanded my territory to roughly a twelve-square-block area around my home.

"Now that you're blind," the instructor had told me, "your hearing won't miraculously improve. It's just that you're going to use it more. Your other senses are not more acute than mine, but because you've lost your sight, you will rely on them more."

Before I began walking, by myself, I worried about dogs. But the city has a leash law, and to my pleasant surprise, dogs were no problem. However, I did encounter an unexpected, persistent, and puzzling enemy—water sprinklers. Oscillating sprinklers set in the middle of the sidewalk gave me the most trouble. They operated quietly, and unless the water was falling on the sidewalk, I could not hear them. Several times I got completely soaked, and on one memorable occasion, I straddled one and was soaked from the bottom up. As I gradually depended more and more on my hearing, I learned to avoid them, but on blustery days, when the wind made it impossible for me to hear any sprinklers, I had to grit my teeth and accept the unexpected dousings.

My mood and temperament began to improve slowly. I could now laugh and joke with my friends, and I became more outgoing. Blindness was a challenge that I came to accept. It was going to be a learning experience for myself and all those around me.

My instructor spent one afternoon a week with me, but I found that that was not enough to meet my needs. I contacted Fletcher Shields, the high-school typing instructor, and he agreed to give me lessons at home.

Now that I had started typing and had confidence walking with my cane, I turned my attention to Braille. The instructor brought a book that had the Braille alphabet and simple sentences on one side of the page. On the other side was a printed version of the same material. Someone newly blinded could learn the alphabet, while a sighted person checked his progress. I set out to learn my ABCs, but having a class in Braille once a week did not seem enough. During a conversation with Darlene and Pastor Meyer at the church, I told them that I was learning Braille.

"Do you know Elinor Eggert?" Darlene asked.

"No, I don't believe so. Why?"

"Elinor is a member of Trinity, and in her spare time she prints some of our devotional books in Braille. She sends them to the synodical office in St. Louis when she's finished. If you are looking for someone to help you learn Braille, I'll bet Elinor would be glad to help. Why don't you give her a call?"

I did just that, and later that afternoon Judy and I found ourselves visiting with the Eggerts in their home. They are wonderful people and were eager to help me. Spending several hours three afternoons a week with Elinor would certainly do much to speed the learning process. There was a side benefit as well. The Eggert home was five blocks from mine, in an area not familiar to me. I intended to walk to those lessons, which would force me to use all my newly acquired skills. The trip meant crossing a main thoroughfare without the aid of a stoplight. This would reinforce my ability to use my hearing to judge traffic noises.

Two more decisions had to be made: one had to do with choosing a school for rehabilitative training. The other concerned the pancreas-transplant program that Dr. Sutherland was pioneering at the University of Minnesota Medical Center.

While I was hospitalized in Minneapolis for eye surgery, Dr. Knobloch had told me about the Minneapolis Society for the Blind (MSB). He spoke very highly of the facility, and since I wanted to talk with Dr. Sutherland anyway, I decided to make an appointment for a tour. Several weeks later Judy and I drove to the Twin Cities and arrived at Don and Alice's house after a day-long drive.

The next morning, Judy and I made our way to Dr. Sutherland's office. There, the conversation turned immediately to the transplant program.

"Dave," I asked, "has there been any significant progress made in the program?"

"It's a tremendous success in laboratory animals, but as you know, these animals are all genetically identical, so we don't have to cope with the rejection problems. We haven't done very many in humans, and, of those, we haven't been successful in curing diabetes or even getting the patient to the point where he can reduce or eliminate his insulin intake. We're also short of suitable cadavers, which is a hindrance to the program."

"I'm very interested in it," I told him. "If I decide to participate, would it be helpful if I were to live closer to the university?"

"Once we have a suitable cadaver, it might be helpful if you were within minutes or at least a few hours of the hospital. But I certainly wouldn't recommend that you move to Minneapolis."

"If I like the training program for the blind here, I would be living close by for approximately six months."

"That would have to be your decision, Al. But you have to remember that there's no guarantee that during those six months a cadaver would become available. Also, your antigen types are not the easiest ones to match. When you and Vic had the kidney transplant, you didn't have to worry about that, but now you would. It might take years before one becomes available."

"I know. That's just a chance I would have to take. I'll let you know in a couple of weeks what I have decided to do," I said in parting.

After a hurried lunch we made our way to the rehab center. We sat in the car for a minute while Judy described the building to me: it was an older, two-story structure situated on a corner. The traffic noise was loud, and I thought of how difficult it would be to make a crossing at one of these intersections. Once in the building, we met with the director, Mel Sauterbach. I felt that he was proud of his organization and the work he was doing.

"We are set up mainly to help Minnesota residents," he told us. "It's very seldom that we have someone from out-of-state. Have you considered the program that Nebraska offers?"

At this point I told Mel and the state counselor about my interest in the beta-cell transplant program, explaining that if I decided to enter the program as a volunteer, it might be beneficial for me to be close to the University of Minnesota Medical Center.

"Quite a few of our students share your situation," Mel said. "Diabetes is now the leading cause of new blindness. If you decide to enter the program, I wish you all the luck in the world. Not only could it help you, but it might help thousands of other people. I'll have to check out a few things, but I'll have a definite answer for you by next week.

"Now," he said, standing up, "why don't you let me give you and Judy the grand tour?"

Back home in Nebraska I resumed my study of Braille, mobility training, and typing, all of which were progressing at what the counselor said was an above-average rate. The busier I was, the better my mood was. It was when I took time for a nap or to listen to a talking-book record that I became depressed.

But I was becoming more outgoing, more like my old self. I found that when I laughed at some mistake I made, some unintentional faux pas, the people around me were much more at ease. The value of laughter as a tension-reducer became very clear one evening when I attended a board-of-education meeting at the school. I had walked to the school and entered the conference room. I felt with my cane to find a chair but was having some difficulty determining which way the chair faced when Dale Rohweder, a member of the board and a good friend, said in mock exasperation, "Al, would you please find that confounded chair and sit down? You're making us all nervous."

With exaggerated movements of my cane, I took my sweet time sitting down. I laughed at Dale, and the rest of the group joined in. I felt good and they did also.

* * *

The decision to go ahead with the transplant was easy. On the surface it appeared as though I had nothing to lose. If the transplant failed, I would remain a diabetic. However, if it were successful, I would be cured. Also, I felt that the risks involved were within acceptable bounds. Judy concurred with me. However, when Mel Sauterbach called and said that an opening was available October 4, Judy was not sure that spending six months in Minneapolis was the right thing for me to do.

"You have been blind only four months. Don't you think you're rushing into things a bit?"

In part, I had to agree with her. I wasn't sure how I would handle being away from the family for that extended period of time. Judy was concerned for other reasons, too. She had seen me walk into trees, fall down stairs, and crack my head on half-open doors.

"Look, Judy," I said, "those are the very things I'll be learning not to do." She understood, but when I informed her that I intended to get an apartment and live alone instead of living in a dormitory suggested by MSB, I had a much tougher time convincing her. She had a whole host of reasons to dissuade me.

"It all boils down to this. I don't want to be away from you and the boys for six months and come away having learned only half the lessons I'm going to need for the rest of my life. If I get an apartment and live alone, I'll be able to practice everything that I learn in school. I'm sure that Don and Alice and Gordon and Sandy would help out any time I need them."

That seemed to convince her. Having two brothers close by to keep an eye on me would relieve some of her worries.

One night in July, Ted Wolfram, representative for the Aid Association for Lutherans, and Herb Heider, secretary-treasurer of the local AAL Branch 773, called on us. The message they brought was simple: my friends wanted to help.

Their proposal was for a fund-raising drive that would culminate in an "Al Beckler Day."

Herb explained, "We know that you have been out of work for a while, Al. I'm sure those last surgeries you had in Minneapolis weren't cheap. Some of us want to get together and raise a little money and help you with those expenses."

Then Ted spoke up. "The AAL is a fraternal insurance group for Lutherans. For an approved project like this fund raiser for you, Al, the company will match the money that's raised. The local AAL branch here would like to sponsor the project. We would like you and Judy to take time to think this over and meet with us next week at our committee meeting."

I decided to talk it over with Pastor Meyer. After I expressed some apprehension, he said, "I know how you feel. I guess if I were in your position, I might feel the same way. But what your friends want to do is a real expression of Christian love, and I know you well enough to know that, if the roles were reversed and someone else was in your shoes, you would want to help them. It would be good for you and your family, and it would be good for the congregation. Something like this could really draw everyone together. Think about it real hard, Al. Personally, it is something I would like to see you accept."

The following week Ted Wolfram brought the meeting to order. He didn't waste much time getting to the point.

"Well, Al, what have you and Judy decided?"

"To be truthful, we haven't decided," I answered. "There are a couple of things we should probably talk about. The whole idea of accepting money is one I have trouble with. The other thing that I want you people to know is that I am not destitute. We have several investment properties that we were planning to sell to help meet expenses. Maybe instead of agreeing to an 'Al Beckler Day,' that's what I should do."

"But, those are assets your family should keep," one of the committee members said. "You've been out of work for a while, and it may be some time before you get back."

"Herb, I admit the future is uncertain. I guess I don't know what kind of luck I'll have selling now, but I want to give it a try."

We continued to talk about the future and about what lay in store for me. Later they told me what they had in mind for Al Beckler Day.

There were a lot of contradictory emotions whirling through

my head that moment—feelings of not wanting to accept charity, even in this fashion, and feelings that an Al Beckler Day would be of immense benefit to me and my family. But I liked the honest way the program was presented and the sincerity and warmth of the committee members, so I gave my consent to the fund-raising drive.

Coleman, South Dakota, the spot picked for this year's Beckler reunion, was situated on a flat expanse of prairie having few trees to offer respite from the hot wind and hotter sun. However, Coleman did have a redeeming feature. Nearby at Flandreau, South Dakota, was the homestead of the Ailts family. Two of my brothers and one of my sisters had married two sisters and a brother of that family, and this year's joint reunion promised to be a wild one. Tents, trailers, and motor homes were set up on either side of the entrance lane to the park, close to the restroom facilities and an outdoor shelter. Tennis courts, swimming pool, and a golf course completed the layout. There promised to be activities for everyone.

I was in unfamiliar territory in the campground and still much too new at traveling alone to find my way from one campsite to another. I joined a group sitting in the outdoor shelter and, with beer in hand, entered into the visiting and kibitzing.

Vic sat down beside me and as was our usual custom, we swapped stories about the kidney transplant and inquired about the health of each other's kidney.

"I'll show you how well mine's working," I said to Vic. "See this beer can? I drank it a half-hour ago. Now guess where I have to go?"

We laughed and headed toward the restroom.

Later, the families gathered around the campfire. The singing that had been going strong began to trail off, and now the old stories were being retold: Vic's stint as a trapeze artist in the haymow of the barn when, while hanging upside down, he had laughed so hard he wet his pants and dropped the neighbor boy on his head; Sarah and Priscilla's episode with the toy rubber knife; Gordon's undershorts with his name sewed in the back turning up in the refrigerator of the church basement as members of the Ladies Aid were preparing to serve a church dinner. Everyone knew them by heart, but that didn't matter. We all laughed until our sides ached.

Suddenly I felt a hand on my arm. I knew who it was. I had heard her voice, but we had not spoken.

"Hello, Sis," I said.

"Hello, Al," Sarah replied. Hearing the catch in her voice, I stood there for a moment, not knowing what to do.

"Oh, Al. I feel so bad about what's happened to you."

She kissed my cheek, and I felt the wetness of her tears. She hugged me for a long time and then, patting me on the back, drew away and laughed.

"Hasn't anyone told the story about how you and I ran away after I thought I killed the pig?"

"Not yet," I said. "But give 'em time. Somebody is sure to remember it. And if they don't, I'll remind 'em."

"You would too, big stinker."

I heard someone beside me, and Howard sat down.

"Mind if I join you two?"

"Not at all," I said.

No sooner had he sat down when he hollered loudly, "Say, do you all remember when Sarah hit the pig over the head with a two-by-four and thought she killed it?"

Sarah groaned, "Oh, no. Here we go."

It was very late when I finally made it to bed. I drifted off feeling safe and secure, surrounded by loved ones.

"Breakfast is ready, come and get it," Vic shouted late the next morning.

With the help of several nieces and nephews, he was turning out bacon and eggs, hashbrowns, and toast in copious quantities. Strong coffee helped open eyes that at midmorning were still sleepy from last night's late activities.

Those who were playing in the tennis tournament went to the courts. The first group of golfers teed off, and the more sedentary members of the family settled down in lawn chairs under the outdoor canopy.

I felt a twinge of resentment at my blindness when they headed for the golf course. I had always been able to hold my own with that group, and in previous reunions it had been nip and tuck to see who was going to win.

Judy and I worked on my Braille book for several hours and then gave in to the clamor of the boys wanting to go swimming. I stayed in the pool too long and came out lobster red across my neck and shoulders.

The next day, two things began to claim the attention of everyone. Those who were involved in giving the program that evening gathered and began to practice. I was part of a quartet, and our group drove to Gordon's in-laws to practice our songs with the piano. From their collections, each family contributed twenty slides to be shown that evening. Also drawing everyone's attention was the pig that Bern Ailts was roasting in his homemade portable barbecue pit. My contribution was that of gopher—go-fer a beer, go-fer some ice—and I kept the fellows at the barbecue well supplied.

In other areas of the campground, the various tournament finals were held. After the tennis, golf, and horseshoe champions were crowned, everyone congregated at the swimming pool.

Dinner was a gargantuan feast. The family seemed a bit drowsy as they stretched out in lawn chairs with their belts loosened. But as the program progressed, everyone joined in and the mood again became lively and fun.

When it was dark, a sheet was hung over the side of a motor home and the slides were shown. Oohs and aahs filled the air as people exclaimed over how much the nieces and nephews had grown, or who had lost or gained weight.

"That picture must really be old. Vic's got a full head of hair," someone said.

I felt sad because an event long looked forward to was ending, and in the morning my family would again scatter across the country. We would be leaving early next day, so Judy and I said our goodbyes late that evening.

Once we were back home, August seemed to speed by. I took my walks each day and practiced my typing and Braille. I also found time to swim laps at the YMCA two or three times a week, walk with the boys on their paper route, and help Judy prepare the garden vegetables for freezing.

Since Howard's daughter Tammy was to be married in St. Paul the first week of September and since Judy, Mom, and I were planning to make the trip anyway, it didn't take much coaxing on anyone's part for me to agree to go with Vic and Gret to their home in Marinette, Wisconsin, for a week of fishing.

We were skunked all week long. Rain and gale-force winds combined, and we didn't have a hint of a nibble. With Vic's promise that the fishing would be better next time ringing in my ears, I boarded a plane in Green Bay and flew to Minneapolis, where Don picked me up from the airport.

Judy and Mom arrived at Don's house, and that afternoon we met with a counselor from the Minnesota Department for the Visually Impaired and went apartment hunting. We located a two-bedroom apartment situated on a bus line about thirteen blocks from the MSB. I rented the apartment, rented some furniture, and made arrangements for it to be delivered before my arrival in Minneapolis.

The wedding service for my niece Tammy and Rick Bentz went off without a hitch. This time Gordon provided the musical solo. Tammy, who had been around enough Beckler weddings to know that she wouldn't get away scot-free, seemed to take her "kidnapping" in stride. Not so her husband.

"He really is upset," Sarah told me at five o'clock the next morning, when the couple was finally reunited.

"He shouldn't have been," I said. "Tammy told me she warned him about what usually happens."

With the apartment rented and the arrangements completed for enrollment in the school on October 4, Judy and I left the Twin Cities and traveled leisurely home.

We were driving down South Locust Street the next day when Kevin excitedly shouted, "Mom, Mom, look at that, at that sign. There's Dad's name on it!"

"What does it say?" I asked Judy.

"It says 'Al Beckler Day, September 19th,'" she answered.

That evening I called Ted Wolfram.

"We decided to let the whole community know what we had planned," he said. "That's the reason for the signs that you see around town. There will also be some publicity on the radio and in the newspaper. I hope you don't mind."

I told him no, but I did feel a certain amount of apprehension.

That fall, Judy also started working for the hot-lunch program at Trinity school. With the boys in classes and Judy working at school, I redoubled my efforts to learn Braille and typing. I extended the range of my territory and tried walking in areas barely familiar to me.

I looked toward September 19 with mixed feelings. I had consented to what I thought would be a small group of friends getting together and wishing me well, and, of course, I understood that it was to be a fund-raising event. But things had snowballed and now, instead of just a small group, an appeal had been made to the whole community. I still didn't like the idea of accepting money. I found myself not looking forward to it at all.

Sunday, September 19, was cloudy and cool. The chance of rain had forced the committee to move the program into the school gym. At two o'clock Judy and I left the house.

"Al," Judy said, "the parking lot is just jammed full. There's not room for another car. I'll never be able to find the boys in this crowd."

As we entered the doorway and made our way to the gym, we were greeted by so many people that not all of their names registered.

"The bleachers are full," Judy said. We made our way to some chairs set up on the gym floor.

The program was lively and entertaining. Small musical groups performed, plays were given, pie-eating contests were held, a German band played, and the Trinity choir sang. Between acts, someone announced how much money had been collected, and as the amount grew larger applause would break out.

Toward the end of the program, Wayne Gilmore, a representative for AAL and emcee for the afternoon gave the crowd a brief sketch of the last three years of my life.

"After the kidney transplant, Al didn't give up. He went back to work, and now, after blindness, he's not giving up either. The man is tough. What he wants is a chance, and all of us here can help give him that chance."

There was more applause.

Scheduled last was the singing of the benediction, which was to be performed jointly by the Trinity choir and the Grand Island City Singers. I felt a tug on my arm as someone urged me to stand up.

"Al, come to the stage. We want you to sing this with us."

For a moment I wanted to refuse, but suddenly, the meaning of what it was all about came over me. The people gathered here were my friends. They were supporting me with help and encouragement when I needed it. The day was a generous out-pouring of love. Suddenly I felt very, very good. I took the arm and walked to the stage.

I joined the combined choirs and sang the beautiful words of the benediction.

"The Lord Bless You and Keep You" had special meaning for me as I thought of the separation from family and friends that lay ahead in the next six months.

Several hours later, Darlene and her husband, Al Knoepfel, close friends and neighbors, joined us at home. We talked about the day's events. The phone rang and Judy answered it. While she was gone, Darlene asked me to guess how many people had been there.

"I wouldn't have any idea," I replied.

"At the last count, between twelve and thirteen hundred."

"What?" I exclaimed.

"That's right," she said.

I sat for a moment in disbelief, and then Judy came back in the room.

"Al, come quick. It's Barney Turnbull. He wants to talk with you."

Something in the tone of Judy's voice made me hurry to the phone. Barney was my mom's next-door neighbor. I picked up the phone and said, "Barney, this is Al. What's the matter?"

"Your mom's fallen. I think she's broken her leg. You better come over right away."

Late that evening as we left the hospital, I reflected on the day's events. Mom had broken her leg above the knee and would need surgery to repair it. Her bones were very brittle, and it would not be an easy operation. She was in a great deal of pain; the ambulance ride to the hospital had been difficult. She seemed settled now, and I would call the rest of the family and inform them what had happened.

I felt weary and tired after the tremendous high of that afternoon and the emotional low of Mom's accident that evening.

School

◊┼◊┼◊

September 20 to December 31, 1976

M y first Sunday night in Minnesota I felt very lonely. The noise on Hennepin Avenue outside my apartment was loud, even for a Sunday evening, and I knew it would take some getting used to. The unpacking that had taken most of the weekend was over; my family, who had helped me move in, had gone to their homes.

I fixed myself a drink, guessing at the amount of whiskey I was pouring, tasted it, and diluted it with more water. I moved cautiously from the kitchen to the living room and found the couch. I sat down, sipping slowly on the drink, and recalled the past two hectic weeks.

Sarah had come to Grand Island, and five days after Mom's fall, we found ourselves in the hospital, anxiously waiting the outcome of the surgery on her broken leg. She came through it fine, but it would be some time before she would be able to get about, and then she would probably have to use a walker.

Much of my time was devoted to selecting the items that I would need for my stay in Minneapolis. I tried to be selective, but my "necessities" completely filled Sarah's car, leaving only enough room for us in the front seat. Judy and I worked many hours labeling my clothes and other items with Braille tags so I would recognize them. Also included were two sets of gauges, calibrated to the correct dosage of insulin, which fit over the end of the syringe.

On the day of my departure, I said goodbye to the boys before they left for school and then helped Sarah load the car. Shortly before noon we stopped by the north side of Trinity school. Seeing us through the window of the school kitchen, Judy came out and sat in the car with us. She was calm and resolute, but there was a catch in her voice as she said, "It seems like such a long time."

We drove to the Twin Cities and my brother Don and my nephew Reed and his wife Cindy helped me move into the apartment.

Across the living room against the opposite wall were the TV and stereo. I went to the stereo and tuned in a station that was playing instrumental music. But the music didn't capture my attention, and my thoughts wandered to Grand Island, to Judy and the boys. I had been gone only three days, and already I missed them deeply. The more I thought about them, the more melancholy I became, and the beginnings of depression set in.

"That's enough of that," I said to myself. "Get busy and do something, or you're going to get in a lousy mood."

I walked to the front door of the apartment and got my cane. I wasn't going to venture outside, but I did want to learn how to get from the front door of the building to my apartment.

I went into the hallway outside my door and downstairs to the front door. I familiarized myself with the entryway, the location of the steps, and the entrance to the hall that led to my apartment. I retraced my route five times, until I felt comfortable with it. Then I set about exploring my apartment. I walked through every room until I was familiar with everything in it. I went through all the kitchen cupboards, feeling each pot, pan, and utensil until I memorized their location. I tried to review the order in which I had placed the canned goods, chuckling because I knew that I didn't remember what some of them contained, which meant that some of the meals would be surprises.

MSB had promised me a ride, and promptly at seven the next morning there was indeed a knock at the door.

"Hi, are you Al Beckler?" a quiet, low voice inquired.

"Yes, I am."

"My name is Doug. I'm from the Minneapolis Society for the Blind. I'm the mobility instructor, and I'm here to give you a ride. Are you ready to go?"

Doug took me to a large room filled with other students and informed me that he would be back later.

I was seated only a short while when a member of the group introduced himself. He was an older gentleman and had half completed his training. After gaining the attention of the others, he introduced me to them.

"This is Al Beckler. He's starting his schooling this morning. He comes to us all the way from Nebraska."

"A Cornhusker," a male voice said, in obvious reference to our football team.

I grinned, not at all ashamed of the mastery that the Big Eight Conference had shown over the Big Ten.

"Now, now, let's not hold that against him," the older gentleman said.

They introduced themselves, each offering a brief history of his family and his situation, and I responded in kind.

I was genuinely surprised to learn that of the fifteen people in the room, only two others were completely blind like myself. The rest had varying degrees of sight, ranging from legal blindness to the capacity to perceive light only.

A bell rang and the group dispersed to individual classes. Doug arrived and we began a tour of the facilities; special emphasis was placed on those areas that would become references for me. The secretary's area, the louvered divider at the end of one hallway, and a small inclined ramp all took on special significance as I tried to make sense of what seemed to be a maze of corridors and hallways.

"Here's an area that you will find without any trouble. See if you can tell me what it is."

The smell of food told me where we were.

"Doug, I don't know about you, but if they serve coffee in this cafeteria, I'm ready. How about it?"

He agreed amiably and as we progressed down the cafeteria

line, he pointed out various items—trays, silverware, a cooler where sandwiches were stored on different shelves, and a soda dispenser. As we arrived at the cash register, he introduced me to Tillie.

Tillie, who was legally blind, said, "We're glad to have you here, Al. If you have any trouble finding what you need, just sing out, and I'll be happy to help you."

I was to learn later that Tillie made the best German potato salad in town. And when she served it, I was her best customer.

The balance of the day was spent visiting the different classrooms and meeting the instructors.

Braille was taught by Sandy. She was in her twenties and was congenitally blind. Born premature, Sandy had been blinded when an early incubator had allowed too much oxygen into her system. Braille was one of my priorities; a minimum of two hours a day would be spent in Sandy's classroom.

John, in his mid-fifties, taught the abacus, the Chinese method of arithmetic calculations. He was totally blind, having lost his sight in an accident in World War II.

Peggy was sighted and in charge of personal management, which involved everything from cooking, to sewing buttons on a shirt, to writing checks. She possessed an infectious laugh and a sincere desire to help people. A staff of three other persons assisted her.

Nelda, also sighted—she was a native of Jamaica and owner of one of the most distinctive British accents I have ever heard— was in charge of typing. At first meeting, I felt that she would brook no nonsense. But despite her stern demeanor, toward the end of our meeting a rather racuous laugh on her part led me to believe that she was not so strict as she had first seemed.

As Doug was leading me to the counselor's office he said, "The first couple of weeks I'll be working with you to help you get acquainted with the building and to help you find your way to your classes. After that, we'll start working in a residential area, then move up to a semi-commerical area, and finally, you'll be walking independently in downtown Minneapolis. We want you to become familiar with using the buses. Minneapolis has one of the finest bus systems in the country, and you'll be able to go anywhere you want."

"But don't worry," he added as he ushered me into the counselor's office, "we'll take it at your speed."

Dave, the counselor, had a very limited amount of vision. As he talked about the things he enjoyed doing, he said exactly what I wanted to hear. He was actively involved in a wide gamut of activities ranging from boating to bicycling. In was obvious that he did not let his severely restricted vision limit him in any way, and this was exactly the way I wanted things.

"Al, what do you see as being most essential to you at this time?"

"I want to graduate with all the skills I will need to lead a full life, socially and vocationally. I want to take everything you have to offer, but the priorities are Braille and mobility. Mobility inasmuch as I want to be able to go anywhere on my own. And I think Braille will be important to me for recreational reading and also in business."

"What kind of business are you involved in?"

"I have my real-estate and insurance licenses, and when I'm finished here I want to get back into selling."

Dave and I planned a course of study, placing heavy emphasis on my priorities.

I shared the day's experiences with Judy that evening, and it was with a feeling of eagerness and anticipation for school to begin that I went to bed.

Several weeks later in Braille class, I sat hunched over my desk.

"Sandy," I complained, "up here in Minnesota, you make these Braille dots a lot smaller than the ones we have back home."

My right forefinger seemed numb, and the six-dotted Braille cells that I could distinguish early in the hour had become a series of rough lumps on the paper.

"Oh, listen to this," Sandy said. "You outstate students are all the same. All you do is bitch, bitch."

I chuckled and again bent over my lesson, trying to decipher the few remaining words in the paragraph. When I finished I checked my watch, and, noting that there were only five minutes left, I closed the book and sat back in my chair.

"Giving up already?" Sandy asked with a lilt in her voice.

"Look," I said, "my fingers feel numb and I can't read at all. By the time I finally figure out the last letters of the words, I've forgotten the first letters. I'm ready for a cup of coffee."

As I reached to put my book in the desk drawer, my hand came in contact with what felt like a deck of cards.

"What's this?" I asked.

"It's a deck of cards, of course," Sandy responded.

"Does Mel know you have those in here?" I whispered to her kiddingly.

"Yes, yes. It's all on the up-and-up. Do you like to play cards?"

"Yes," I said, reflecting. "I used to play cards once in a while, poker mostly."

"For money?" Sandy asked with a conspiratorial air.

"Well, I didn't play for matches."

"Mmmmm, anything else?"

"Once in a while I played pinochle and sometimes cribbage."

"I love to play cribbage," Sandy said. "In fact, there's a group playing every noon hour."

"Let me feel one of those cards."

My finger felt the two Braille cells in the upper left-hand corner.

"If you like," she said, "we can spend some time using the cards in class. It might help you to recognize the numbers and letters more quickly. Of course, if you really want to learn them, you're welcome to join us during the noon hour for some cribbage."

"Hey, that sounds like fun. And I'll bet that if I really want to learn them soon, there'd be nothing like a penny a point and a quarter a game to help the process along. Huh, Sandy?"

"I suppose I could be talked into that," she shot back.

"Somehow, I get the feeling I've been set up," I told her as I walked to the door.

The next morning I was standing in front of the stove in the personal-management class. Peggy's instructions were easy to follow.

"Find the handle of the frying pan with your gloved hand, Al. Be careful you don't burn yourself. It's hot."

The padded glove was on my right hand, but for some reason I reached for the handle with my left and instead of touching the handle, I touched the pan. Wincing from the burn, I completed the procedure as she had directed. This time using the gloved hand, I carried the pan to the sink. Peggy inspected my hand.

"Better sit down and I'll see if I can find some salve and Band-Aids."

As I waited for Peggy, I started thinking that cooking in the personal-management class was something I would enjoy. I had just finished cooking some concoction Peggy called "three-bean burger bake" and had been preparing to clean the pan when the accident happened.

"Do you serve coffee with your first aid?" I shouted in the direction Peggy had gone.

"What do you think I am, a nurse?" Peggy chuckled, standing not two feet from me.

"Whoops, sorry, I didn't hear you come back."

With my hand tended to and coffee before me, I settled back in the chair.

"What foods are you fixing for yourself at home now-a-days?" Peggy asked.

"Well," I said slowly and expansively, "I'm eating pretty good, really. I always have vegetables, potatoes, and some type of meat. Sometimes I even have soup and dessert."

"Really. Sounds like you're eating better than I am. Are you having any trouble preparing the food?"

"Oh, no. I bought myself several compartmentalized metal baking pans. All I have to do is make sure that the different foods are in their separate areas, and then I just pop it in the oven and bake it. It's really pretty handy."

"Compartmentalized baking pans?" Peggy said aloud, almost to herself. "Were did you get hold of something like that?"

"In a store."

"Well, that's obvious, but what are they called?"

"I think they're called TV dinners."

"Jeeees!" Peggy cried, and the laughter exploded. "Did I fall for that."

She poured herself some coffee and sat down across from me at the table.

"Seriously, Al, are you having any problems getting along at the apartment?"

Peggy had inspected the apartment three weeks before, paying particular attention to the kitchen, but at that time she had not made any comments.

"I seem to be getting along fine, at least as far as I'm concerned."

Then remembering the day of her visit, I added, "You know, when you made your visit, you really didn't have too much to say about the way I had things set up. Am I doing something wrong?"

"Wrong? No, no," she laughed. "You had things so damned organized, it almost made me sick. I've been here almost ten years, and you're the first student I've worked with who's gotten himself an apartment, moved in, and set up housekeeping before he started school. And you've only been blind four months."

"I knew school was necessary, and I couldn't see any sense in putting it off."

"But all the same, you're attempting an awful lot in a short period of time. Are you sure you've adjusted to it yet?"

"It would be nice if I had, but I don't think so. Maybe some people adjust quickly and others never do. I do know that I feel good about what I'm doing right now, and it really helps me to keep busy."

"Speaking of keeping busy, I'll show you what I have in mind for next month," she said.

She proceeded to outline the activities designed to help students face all kinds of everyday situations and equip them to live at home totally independent of outside help. Subjects ranged from cooking a five-course dinner and sewing on buttons to doing the laundry and setting the timer on the Braille alarm clock. As each area was covered, I gained more and more confidence in my own abilities.

The mobility lessons with Doug were also progressing at a steady rate. We were working in a residential area southeast of school. The area covered was a grid ten blocks square, bounded on four sides by busy thoroughfares.

At intersections, when I missed the sidewalk on the other side of the street, his advice was, "Project a straight line and walk a little faster." When confused by coming upon gravel at the end of the sidewalk, he counseled, "Remember which way the alleys run in this area, and you'll learn to expect them."

When I failed to find a house number he had assigned and instead ended up on the wrong side of the street, he said, "Remember, even numbers are on the north and west sides of the streets; odd numbers on the east and south. And remember also, the number of the house on the corner of the block ends in four, the next one ends in eight, the next one in twelve, and so on. Just count the sidewalks that lead to the houses and you won't have any trouble finding the correct address."

I tried to incorporate all of his advice into the walks I took, but the weekend before Judy and the boys were to arrive for a four-day visit, I found myself lost four blocks from my apartment. I walked to the corner, meanwhile listening intently for the traffic noise from Hennepin Avenue, but heard nothing. I retraced my steps and walked to the other end of the block, hoping to encounter an alley that would tell me which direction I was heading, but I found none.

I stood on the corner waiting for someone to come by, but no one did. All of the people whom I had greeted before had mysteriously disappeared. I was lost and, for a moment, I was filled with panic.

I turned around and started down the sidewalk, feeling for the sidewalk that would lead to a house. I then heard the sound of someone raking leaves. I walked toward the sound, and my cane came in contact with a heavy, wrought-iron fence. I heard a noise and waited, half expecting someone to greet me, but no sound came. I turned to the sound of leaves being raked. I grasped the top of the fence, cleared my throat, and said, "Excuse me, could—"

That was as far as I got. A large dog emitted a loud, angry growl a split-second before I heard him thud into the fence. The dog continued to bark viciously, clearly oblivious to his master's commands.

"Max, be quiet. Get down, Max. Max, come here!"

I was startled by the dog, and, in stepping back from the fence, I dropped my cane. As the animal's wild barking subsided, I dropped to one knee and, feeling the ground, finally found it. I stood up to hear the voice of an elderly man say consolingly to me, "Now sonny, you don't have to worry. Max isn't going to hurt you any. If you want to, you can pet him."

"No thanks," I replied, "I think I know him well enough."

The old man chuckled and then asked, "Say, what's that cane for? Are you blind?"

"Yes I am."

"Oh," he said, his chuckle now turning to laughter.

"That explains it."

"Explains what?" I asked.

"Why you started talking to Max."

"Well, I don't know about that," I said, "but I'm lost. I heard someone raking leaves and came over here to ask directions."

The old man's laughter grew louder.

"That noise ya heard wasn't somebody rakin' the leaves, it was Max finishin' up after he done his duty. And I guess he didn't like bein' interrupted in the middle of his chores." He laughed and wheezed some more.

The scene must have been ludicrous; the dog, in the yard squatting, straining, and covering it with leaves; me, standing at the fence asking him directions; and the dog, interrupted, clawing at me through the fence.

Politely I managed a laugh and asked for directions to my apartment.

I thanked him, oriented myself, and started to walk. On the next block, the embarrassment that I felt passed, and I began to chuckle, then laugh out loud. But as I walked further and thought about it more, I became angry. I'm no different than anyone else, I thought. I don't like to look like a fool.

Thursday of the next week was a red-letter day. Judy and the boys would be arriving late in the evening for a long weekend. The housecleaning that I had been putting off for at least a week could no longer be denied.

All day long the thought of the dirty apartment plagued me, and at three o'clock I could stand it no longer. I called a cab and went home early, rolled up my sleeves, and dug in. Soap suds flew as I scrubbed down the kitchen and bathrooms. In the bedroom that served as the weight-lifting room, the vacuum rolled dumbbells and barbells across the floor until I felt satisfied that the floor was clean. In my bedroom, the carpet presented no real challenge to me or the vacuum until I got to the other side of the bed. A sudden screeching coming from the power-driven brush told me that it had encountered something. I dislodged the sock that had found its way into the hose leading to the stomach of the monster, and then I found its mate by feeling on the floor under the bed. I didn't know what color they were, nor did I remember taking them off on that side of the bed, but I tied them together and put them in the laundry bag.

The few dirty dishes in the sink didn't stand a chance; five minutes later they were reposing in the cupboard, clean and, I hoped, sparkling. I rearranged the cupboards, cleaned the oven, and wiped down the counter and stove top, and I even took a halfhearted swipe at the inside of the refrigerator.

Ten o'clock that evening found me in the parking lot, emptying three bags of garbage. I knew that I might be able to explain dirty dishes in the sink or socks on the floor, but three bags of garbage would be too much for Judy to accept.

After a shower, I sat down in the living room to relax and turned on some music. My anxiety that they would arrive before I finished housecleaning now gave way to apprehension that something might have happened to them on their way to Minneapolis.

Enough time elapsed for me to work myself into a lather before

I heard the knock on the door. I opened it to a stampede of three boys. Three hugs and greetings of "How you doin', Dad?" and my sons were investigating the apartment.

"Gee," Rusty said in utter amazement. "Look, Dad's got two bathrooms right next to each other."

"Hey, you guys," I yelled after them, "where's your Mom?" As I reached to the side of the door for my cane, Judy stepped into my open arms. "Hi, honey," she said.

"They're still sawing logs," Judy said the next morning as she surveyed the boys in the living room; one was on the couch and two were on the floor in sleeping bags.

"I didn't think they'd ever get to sleep last night. Want some more coffee, hon?"

I nodded. The large breakfast Judy had prepared was delicious and now, with a third cup of coffee and my family around me, I sat there feeling fat, dumb, and happy.

"What's on the schedule for today?" Judy asked.

"I thought we'd spend most of the day at the school. I've arranged for Doug to give you and the boys a tour, and you're also welcome to attend classes with me."

"That sounds like fun."

The tour that Doug gave Judy and the boys later that morning took an unexpected twist. As we entered the building, Doug met us, and, after introductions, he handed Judy a blindfold. "I want you to wear this. I'll be your guide, and you'll get acquainted with the building the same way Al did."

An hour later Judy met me as I entered Sandy's room for Braille.

"Well, how'd it go?" I asked her.

Judy didn't respond in words. She only took my hand and squeezed it tightly, and I knew she had come to understand better what it was like for me.

I introduced Judy to Sandy and the other members of the class.

As I was reading the Braille text I heard Judy ask Sandy, "How's Al doing?"

Clicking her lighter and inhaling on the cigarette, Sandy said, "I really hate to say this, but he's doing exceptionally well."

And then to me she added, "Now don't go getting a swelled head."

Sandy showed Judy the various reading materials that I was using and explained Grade II Braile, which I was just beginning to delve into.

"Grade II Braile is like shorthand. Certain letters standing alone in a sentence can represent whole words. The letter B, for example, represents the word *but;* C represents *can;* K represents *knowledge,* and there are other abbreviations or simplifications as well. Once you've memorized all the rules, Grade II Braille is much faster to read. The other good thing about it is that it's much more condensed."

Then Sandy urged, "Show her the crowning achievement so far."

"The what?" I asked.

And then, chuckling softly, she said, "Just a minute. I'll get the deck. Once in a while Al uses the cards in class, but we play cribbage almost every lunch hour."

And as she dealt the hand for cribbage, I said in a stage whisper to Judy, "Watch her close. I think she cheats."

Sandy, not to be outdone, said, "Anyone who plays with you doesn't need to cheat."

"I suppose we're going to play Minnesota rules again," I added.

"Minnesota rules? What are those?" Judy asked.

"Minnesota rules means Sandy wins."

And, of course, she did.

I had played a lot of cribbage but had never run up against a player as good as Sandy.

"Judy, I hate to tell you this," I said, "but I owe Sandy over five hundred dollars."

"How much did you say?" Judy exploded.

Sandy hastily broke in, laughing. "No, no, he doesn't owe me five hundred dollars. It's only five dollars and twenty-five cents."

"That sounds better, but five dollars and twenty-five cents still adds up to an awful lot of cribbage."

"Braille is really tough to learn," I said.

"But he's getting better," Sandy said. "He used to owe me nine dollars."

After church on Sunday, I treated the family to brunch at one of the fine restaurants in the Twin Cities. We spent the balance of the day with Don and Alice, and all too soon the long, very enjoyable weekend drew to a close.

When I went home to Grand Island for Thanksgiving, I was greeted by a new member of the family. Early in November Judy had told me that she had found a small male Schnauzer at the Humane Society. For her and the boys it had been love at first sight.

The return home after being away almost two months was a very happy one. I spent the time with my family and friends. Thanksgiving dinner was hosted by Judy's sister Sharon and her husband, Jim Livingston, with all of Judy's family in attendance.

The flight back to MSB on Sunday was uneventful. Monday morning found me in Doug's car. I was to receive a lesson in buses and was feeling a bit nervous as Doug said, "Buses are going to take a little getting used to."

The December wind was bitterly cold as we left the car and made our way to the huge garage that held the buses of the Minneapolis Transit System. When we reached the vehicle that Doug had selected, I followed his instructions and, with my cane, made an examination of the outside of the bus, trying to gauge its length, width, and the locations of the tires and doors. Then we entered the bus, and Doug pointed out the steps and handrail and told me how to locate the coin slot.

I proceeded down the aisle trying again to estimate the length of the bus along its interior and to acquaint myself with the placement of the other seats. I also found the rear exit.

When we finished our investigation, I stood at the front of the bus with my foot resting on the bumper. Here, immobile and in the quiet vastness of the huge garage, the monster seemed benign, almost benevolent.

It was a different story the next day as I stood at the bus stop with the cold wind whistling through me and the traffic noise loud in my ears.

"Just take your time, and we'll see how it goes. Remember, I'm here in case you need me," Doug said reassuringly.

As the bus pulled to a stop, I completely forgot Doug's first instruction and headed toward the noise of the motor, walking away from the open front door. I walked into and through a group of people exiting from the rear before Doug caught up with me and told me what had happened.

"Remember, the motor is always in the back of the bus. It's a natural tendency to head toward it, but you have to stay where you are and listen for the sound of the door opening. Always head toward that sound."

We retraced our steps and entered the bus. As I fumbled through my pockets to locate the change, I dropped my cane, and it slid down the steps out onto the street. Doug retrieved it and the two of us sat down.

The rest of that lesson wasn't any better. I seemed to do everything wrong, and it was a relief that I was finally able to hang up my coat in the closet at school and head to Tillie's for a badly needed cup of coffee.

Subsequent lessons with Doug improved my skills, and by the end of the week I managed my first solo trip, remembering this time even to ask the driver to tell me when we had reached my stop. Although it was scary at first, working with the buses was a necessary experience and a valuable lesson.

Now freed from relying on someone from the school to pick me up or deliver me home, I regained one more aspect of being independent. I felt damned good about it.

Mobility instructions had progressed from a residential area to a semi-commerical area. The difference between the two was profound. In the latter not only was the traffic denser and the noise louder, but the speed of traffic had increased dramatically. I felt as if I were going to be sucked into the street when a large truck or bus sped by. However, the increase in pedestrian traffic proved to be helpful. At the stoplights of busy intersections, generally there was a crowd of people waiting to cross. Listening for and following the sound of their footsteps made these crossings easier. The only drawback was that I received quite a few offers of assistance during the two hours spent on mobility training. At these times, Doug or I would politely refuse, much, I'm sure, to the amazement of most of the people. Finally I began explaining that I was newly blinded and a student, and needed to practice on my own.

One of the areas that I wanted to visit was the University of Minnesota and its hospitals. When I broached the idea, Doug readily agreed. Aware of the possibility of a transplant and my need to familiarize myself with the hospital, he said, "It will be a good experience all the way around. You'll have to change buses twice to get there and the campus will give you good training in walking with large groups of people around you."

After successfully making the round trip on the bus twice and dealing a little less successfully with pedestrian traffic, I called Dave Sutherland and made an appointment to see him in the Clinical Research Center (CRC).

"Al, how are you doing? You're looking really well," Dave said to me as we seated ourselves in the nurses' lounge.

"I'm still waiting for that call from you telling me you have a pancreas."

"I wish I did. We did try a transplant earlier this fall, but it didn't seem to be successful."

"Why not?"

"Probably the same old problem. Rejection."

"How good a match was it?"

Dave paused, "I'm sure that it was a two-antigen match. If we had been transplanting a kidney, we probably wouldn't have had any problems, but the islet cells seem to behave differently. They seem to be more susceptible to rejection, " he replied. "But one of these years we will achieve a breakthrough and find better immunosuppressant drugs," Dave added optimistically.

After testing my speed at reading Braille, Sandy, who was never free with compliments, said, "Thirty-two words per minute! That's pretty good even though I know that 'if you were back in Nebraska' you'd probably be reading around sixty."

The memorization process for Grade II Braille had been drilled into me. To reinforce it, I started working on the brailler, the machine used for printing Braille. It has six keys, one for each of the Braille cells, as well as a spacer, return carriage, and two adjustable knobs for inserting the heavy craft paper.

Checking what I had just written, Sandy would stand in front of me, place her finger on the page, and pronounce it fit or unfit. To me and the rest of the class, that was no mean accomplishment, for she had to read it upside down and backwards.

I became involved in the Christmas season and sent Christmas cards to some friends. I also attended the Guthrie Center and listened to *A Christmas Carol,* and at Orchestra Hall, to a performance of *The Messiah.*

I decided to have a Christmas party and invite some friends from school. I asked Peggy if I could use class time to prepare some of the food that I wanted to serve. She agreed, and I started putting together the refreshments I would serve later in the week.

I set the date for my party on a Saturday evening. Toward the end of the week I cleaned the apartment and set up a small Christmas tree I had purchased. To make sure that all the lights on the tree were on, I held each one until I felt its heat. Then I searched through the records that I had brought with me, looking for the Christmas music. Since I hadn't labeled them in Braille, I had to listen briefly to each one, a process which took a full hour.

I had invited three guests, all of them totally blind like myself. I placed the hors d'oeuvres and sandwiches that Peggy and I had prepared on one end of the dinette table, the bowls of chips and dip in the center, and a tray of olives and garnishments on the other end. And I set up the bar on the counter between the stove and the sink. I put the beer and liquor in the refrigerator and set the glasses, napkins, and straws on the counter.

Right on time a knock at the door announced the arrival of all three guests. After ushering them into the living room, I offered drinks. The orders came back—two beers and a bourbon sour.

The beers were no problem, especially since the guests wanted them served in the cans. Then I poured the bourbon sour and made a whisky and water for myself. As I put the bourbon back in the refrigerator and shut the door, I heard a thud, but I paid no attention to it.

I put on some Christmas music and joined my guests in conversation. As we chatted it seemed remarkable to me that our conversation wasn't very different from a conversation I might have held a year before, when I still had sight. When I asked, "Did any of you fellas watch the game on TV today?" one of the guests replied, "I missed the first part, and I only got to see the last half."

Of course, we had only heard the game, but in our vocabulary *see* was deeply ingrained. While I was home over Thanksgiving vacation, I had told some friends that I'd see them around Christmas time, and one of them later asked me why I had said "see."

"I guess it's from thirty-three years of habit," I said. I had considered eliminating the word from my vocabulary, but that night I decided that I wouldn't. People would understand that "See you later" is just a phrase, not something to be taken literally.

The conversation flowed easily, and as I listened I realized that subconsciously, I had invited only blind guests because I was afraid that otherwise the conversation would lag and that we would not find common interests. It was a mistake that I would not repeat.

When I opened the refrigerator to get two more beers, I noticed a strong odor of bourbon but didn't pay any attention to it.

"Got anything to eat over here, Al?"

"Listen, you guys, you're in for a real treat. The food's on the table, and most of it I made myself."

The loud chorus of groans and shouts made me amend this statement quickly. "Well, Peggy helped a little bit."

When everyone had filled his plate, I asked Tom, "How about another drink?"

"I thought you'd never ask. I've been dry for ten minutes."

I took his glass and put it on the counter. I reached in the refrigerator to get the bottle of bourbon but couldn't find it. Then,

reaching lower, I found it on its side, laying in—of all things—
a dish of butter. It was tilted precisely so that all the bourbon
had drained out. No wonder the smell was so strong.

I felt the bottom of the refrigerator. The bourbon seemed to
be collected in one corner. It was saved from draining out the
open door by the ridge that ran along the bottom. I felt in the
corner; about an inch of bourbon was trapped. But how to get
it out? I took Tom's glass and put it next to the ridge, but that
didn't work.

One of the guests, noting the unusual amount of time that I
was taking, asked, "Having some trouble, Al?"

"No, no," I lied. "I just want to get some ice cubes to freshen
up this drink."

Suddenly, it became important to me that I mix this drink
and that no one know I had spilled a full bottle of bourbon. I
decided to try soaking it up with a dishcloth and squeezing it
into the glass. I went to get a handkerchief from the drawers in
the bedroom.

"A man could get sober waiting for you to fix a drink," Tom
said.

"Be there in a second, Tom," I replied.

I put the glass in the sink, dipped the cloth in the bourbon,
let it soak, and then squeezed it out over the glass. I repeated
this three times, guessing at the amount. I added the ice cubes
and the mix and gave Tom his drink.

"I think I'll switch to beer this time," I said.

Later, during a cribbage game, when Tom asked for another
drink, I asked, "Sure you don't want to try a beer this time,
Tom?"

"Might as well, that's what everyone else is drinkin'."

Around midnight with the food and beer gone, and with all
of us in a jovial Christmas mood, I bid my three guests goodnight.
Reluctantly, I started to clean up the mess that awaited me in
the kitchen. As I started to stack the dirty dishes in the sink, my
hand came in contact with the cloth I had used to soak up the
bourbon. I turned on the hot water and, as I unfolded the cloth,
felt an elastic band.

"Good night," I shuddered. "I've used a pair of my shorts to mix Tom's drink! Well, at least the shorts were clean."

And with that thought, sudden waves of laughter engulfed me. The more I thought about it, the harder I laughed. I sat on the couch and, holding my sides, reached for the phone to call Tom. As I dialed his number, I realized he wouldn't be home yet—and anyway he might not think it was as funny as I had.

I flew home the next week for the Christmas and New Year's break. I was loaded with Christmas presents that I had bought while on training with Doug.

"Gosh, Al, you look like you've put on a couple of pounds. Those pants look a little tight around the waist," Judy mused. From the amount of food she had prepared for the holidays, it was obvious that Judy was prepared to send a starving, underweight husband back to Minneapolis in good shape.

The Christmas Eve service was beautiful as always, and as I listened, I couldn't help reflecting over the past years.

Nineteen seventy-three had been a low point in my life as I had faced what I thought was the inevitability of death. The tide had turned dramatically, and in 1974 I had attended this service full of joy about the success of the kidney transplant and the prospect of a full life. Last year had found me with the cold, raw fear that blindness was looming ahead. And now, this year, I was blind, not yet fully adjusted, but optimistic about the future even though I knew a tremendous amount of work lay ahead. My life these past four years seemed to resemble a roller-coaster ride. Then I shivered inwardly. If this year was a peak, would next year be a valley? My prayer to God during that Christmas Eve service was that He would stop the roller coaster on its wild, mad dash.

The holiday was spent in many enjoyable ways. There were the long walks Judy and I took in the evenings with the bite of the cold, north wind on our faces and the sound of snow crunching under our feet; the time spent alone with each of the children, renewing our relationships; time spent with friends, laughing and renewing friendships; time spent alone late at night in front of the fireplace, dreaming, planning, setting goals for the rest of my life, with the low strains of Christmas music issuing softly from the stereo.

All too soon, it was time to go back, this time to complete the last and the longest session away from home. March had never seemed so far away.

Bad Times

✿❀✿❀✿

January 1977

"**A**l," Dave said as we sat in his counselor's office early in January, "you've come a long way in a short period of time, and I think we can find time to add several new courses. One would be an introduction to a talking calculator, and I don't think that would take too long. But the other one would be a mini-course introducing you to an optacon."

"A what?" I asked.

"Optacon. That stands for Optical to Tactile Conversion. The optacon is designed to enable a blind person to read print. The right hand holds a small portable lens that sees each individual letter of a word. It transmits it back into a computer that's about the size of a Polaroid camera. On the front and to the right is a grooved space that accommodates your left forefinger. This grooved space is a grid of 144 vibrating needles. As you move the lens across the print from left to right, it picks up the letter and transmits it to the grid. The letter will also move across the grid from left to right, and you will be able to distinguish it by feeling which needles are vibrating. The letter W is probably the easiest."

"How fast can a person read with it?" I asked.

"That depends. Fifteen to twenty words a minute is about average, I would say."

"That's not very fast," I said. "In fact, that's a lot slower than I can read Braille."

"Well, it does have one other application," Dave said. "It can be mounted on a typewriter."

And immediately I saw the value. Whenever I was interrupted while typing, I would have to ask someone to read the last sentence or two in order to pick up my thoughts. With this device it would be possible to back-space the typewriter, read a sentence or two, and pick up exactly where I had left off.

We concluded our conversation with Dave assuring me that he would also schedule extra time for mobility training and Braille, the two areas I felt were the most important to me.

Doug and I had begun working in commercial areas shortly after my return from Christmas vacation. The corner of Lake and Hennepin, only three blocks north of my apartment, was a major intersection with six lanes of traffic on each street. Doug now began to put more distance between us as my skill at crossings increased.

"If I'm too close," he explained, "people will know I'm your instructor and will act differently toward you. I want you to walk in a crowd and get used to the idea of people offering assistance and giving directions that sometimes may not be helpful at all."

Crossing Hennepin Avenue went smoothly enough, and I stepped up on the curb, walked five or six steps forward, and turned left in order to cross Lake Street in the direction of a small key shop that was my destination. I waited through one complete traffic-light sequence, trying to orient myself to the flow of traffic on Hennipen, which paralleled my left side. I distinguished the sound of a bus on my left; it had stopped, I assumed, for a red light. When the bus started across the intersection, I started crossing Lake Street and almost immediately found myself in trouble. I had made it approximately one-fourth of the way across when I heard a car passing behind me from left to right, and then I heard the loud blast of a car horn almost on top of me. I continued to move forward in an attempt to get away from the traffic that was crossing behind me, but as I did so I was caught in the flow of traffic coming from my right. By now I had gone too far to try to retreat to the center.

"Where in the hell is Doug?" I thought as I tried with mounting panic to complete the crossing against the flow of traffic. Cars bore down on me with screeching horns and squealing of brakes. One of the drivers tried to shout hurried instructions, but his voice was lost in the roar of the traffic. Finally, after endless seconds, my cane came in contact with the curb on the opposite side and I stepped up to safety just as I heard the roar of a large truck behind me.

As soon as the traffic light changed, Doug made the crossing and stood beside me.

"Why don't we head back?" he said, shaken. "You look like you've had enough for this morning."

Without saying a word, I took his arm.

Over a steaming hot cup of coffee in the lunchroom, Doug told me what had happened.

"You made the crossing of Hennepin with no trouble at all. But before you went across Lake Street, you waited for a whole sequence of traffic lights. I saw you start across as soon as the bus pulled away. What happened was that the bus was not waiting for a red light to turn to green but for loading passengers. His light was green, but when he pulled out, it turned yellow. You'd only gone about ten feet into the street when the light turned red against you."

We both sipped our coffee for a minute, pondering what a close call it had been.

"Where were you, Doug?" I asked somewhat angrily.

"I was down the block from you," he responded. "I was watching you all the time. I guess I didn't think you'd cross when you did. By the time I got to the corner and started yelling at you, the traffic was so loud you evidently couldn't hear me."

The experience had badly shaken me, and it would be some time before my confidence returned to normal. For the next several weeks, I was tentative and overly cautious during mobility sessions. Instead of walking assertively and purposefully, I found myself holding back and accepting more help than was necessary.

One cold, blustery morning the whole thing came to a head. Walking slowly, I had negotiated eight blocks in the busy downtown area. The crossings at the intersections had been rough, but without mishap. Now I was at the corner, waiting for the light to change for the second time. When it did, I started across the street, trying to project a straight line to the corner and also trying to keep parallel with the traffic noise on my left. Half way through the crossing, I realized that I had veered too close to the traffic flow on my left, so I over-corrected and came in contact with the front of a car on my right that was waiting to cross the intersection.

I was taking too much time to make the crossing, and when I became aware that there was no traffic in the intersection, I knew that the light was about to change. I hurried, walking too fast and not using proper cane technique. I came in contact with the curb, and, without clearing the area in front of me with my cane, I stepped up. I was moving too fast, and my head cracked sharply into a metal pole set close to the curb. The blow jolted me so hard that I dropped to my knees, stunned. For a few seconds I stayed in that position. Then I put my hand at the base of the pole and shifted to one knee in an attempt to get up. I found that I couldn't. Then I became aware of people standing around me, none of whom offered any assistance. When I heard shuffling feet, I knew they were moving away from me. Shortly, I heard the sound of a bus pulling up, and the people who were standing close by boarded it. Not one of them had spoken, much less offered assistance.

"My God," I thought in anguish. "And I have a lifetime of this to look forward to."

When Doug and I arrived back at the school, the nurse examined me.

"It looks as if you may have hit your eye," she said softly.

And the rest of the morning was spent at the eye clinic at University Hospital.

That afternoon, we had one of the group-encounter sessions that were, in my estimation, scheduled much too infrequently. I arrived in a terrible mood. My anger boiled out in loud, hot words, heavily laden with invectives, as I told the others what had happened.

"Why didn't anyone offer any help?" I demanded of them.

For a long while no one spoke, then an older lady who was partially sighted said meekly, as if offering a plausible explanation, "Al, maybe they thought you were drunk."

"Drunk," I shouted, "they saw me walking across the street using a white cane. What do you mean, drunk?"

And then another voice spoke. It belonged to a young woman who was rapidly losing the last vestige of sight that she had remaining. Her words were laced with an icy venom.

"What the hell's the matter with all of you?" she exploded. "Al's out there trying to cross that damned frozen street, and when he finally makes it across, he damn near kills himself on that pole, and not one of those jerks out there would do a damn thing to help him. And you've got the guts to sit here and tell him they thought he was drunk?"

She continued to speak, her voice quivering with rage. Finally the gnawing fear, the feelings of helplessness and uncertainty deep within her, came to the surface.

"You should hear what those damn doctors told me was happening to my eyes. Some day that's going to be me out there on the street corner, and I'm going to need some help, and all everybody is going to think is 'Leave her alone, get out of her way, she's drunk!'"

Sobbing openly, she stood up so quickly that the chair crashed into the wall behind her.

"I've got to get out of here. Where's my cane?"

And then, when no one responded, in a voice heavy with impotent rage she said, "Can't you see I don't know where the son of a bitchin' thing is? Somebody give it to me."

The door shook behind her as she left, and the sounds of her harsh sobs were audible as she retreated down the hallway.

The people in the room sat in subdued silence until finally the counselor announced, in a voice barely above a whisper, "That'll be all for today. It's a little early for your next class, but maybe you can all have a cup of coffee."

As I remained in my chair, she asked, "Are you coming, Al?"

"No," I said slowly, "not for a while. Tell Sandy I'll be late for Braille."

I sat rooted to the chair. What had I done to deserve this, I thought? What sins of my forefathers were being visited on me? As I considered my blindness and all that it held in store for me, I knew that I was not being punished for something I had done. Blindness was something that God had allowed to come into my life—for what purpose I did not know—and all that I had to cling to was His promise that He would send me nothing more than I was able to bear. But to accept that promise seemed to require more faith and strength than I possessed.

I thought back to that sunny morning when Duane and I were working on the house on Sixteenth Street. Then, I had seen God as someone close, personal, a being possessed even of a humorous side. Now He seemed remote, distant, and aloof. My prayer for faith and strength was not couched in words, but sprang from a deep need within me. At last I stood up and reached for my cane wearily. I had to go on and I knew it, and I also knew that when enough time had passed, I would feel better.

But now another matter needed tending to. Another person was hurting and I wanted to help. I heard the sound of my cane beat an unsteady tattoo on the walls of the hallways as I went to look for her.

Graduation

❖✝❖✝❖

January and February 1977

By January I was studying the optacon with Peggy. I dutifully brought the machine home with me every evening, setting it up on the dinette table. But something else often claimed my attention. The talking books or cassette tapes, which at first had seemed much too slow for me, now became a source of enjoyment. I ordered books by several of my favorite authors, and also included on my literary menu a book on quantum mechanics that Bill Landis had suggested.

At school, my studies were progressing nicely. I was now typing at the rate of forty to fifty words a minute, and Sandy was genuinely pleased when she told me at the conclusion of the last speed test, "You've really worked hard at Braille, and it shows. You're reading at a rate of fifty-six words a minute. I've never had anyone do any better."

Now, Sandy had to make good on the wager we'd made—if I exceeded fifty words a minute, she would bake a batch of cookies, but if I were under fifty words a minute, it would cost me lunch. True to her word, Sandy arrived with the cookies the next day.

"Here, try one of these. I made a double batch."

When I picked up one of the cookies, I felt that it was huge.

"You know, Sandy," I said, "on windy days I'll put a cookie in my coat pockets, and they'll serve as ballast to keep me from blowin' away."

"Ah, knock it off," Sandy retorted. "I started these dumb things at midnight, and I wasn't going to spoon out thirty-six little cookies to each pan, so I made four to a pan. If you don't like 'em, you don't have to eat 'em. Nobody's forcin' you to," she said laughing.

Mobility sessions with Doug were going better. By now I had gained most of the confidence that I had lost, and we wound up what was left of the mobility training working in the downtown area, so I could become acclimated to walking in shopping malls.

"So the big day is just around the corner," Peggy said one morning in late February.

"That's right, Peg. Pretty soon I'm going to make like a big bird and fly south."

"Hah. Before you stretch your wings, fella, you've got one last thing to do before I'll give you a passing grade in personal management."

"Now look, Peggy," I said, pretending to bristle at what I thought was coming, "I will under no circumstances clean out the men's john again."

"No, nothing like that," she laughed. "All you have to do is prepare and serve dinner for four. You can serve anything you want, except I get to choose the meat."

"That sounds okay with me," I said, "as long as the meat is chicken."

This was in reference to the fact that chicken could be picked up with the hands and eaten.

"Nope, no such luck. Pork chops is what you're going to fix. I'm going to see how good you are with a knife and fork. If you can cut up a pork chop, I'll know you will be able to handle anything."

The morning of the day I was to serve luncheon, I cornered Rick, a fellow student.

"Now look, Rick, here's what I want you to do. At precisely 12:15 call Peggy at the personal-management class. I don't care what you talk to her about, but just keep her on the phone for a few minutes."

"What's going on?" he asked.

"Never mind," I said, wanting to keep what I had in mind a secret. "I'll tell you later."

About eleven-thirty that morning Peggy walked into the kitchen.

"Boy, it sure smells good in here, and I'm starved. What's for lunch?"

"Mashed potatoes and gravy, peas and carrots, those abominable pork chops you insisted on, a fruit salad, and for dessert, chocolate brownies." And slinging a towel over my left forearm and assuming the pose of a waiter I concluded, "And to drink, madam, we offer coffee, tea, or milk."

"Don't get smart with me, bub," Peggy laughed, "or I'll hide your cane."

She recited the list of food that I was preparing.

"What about a pusher?" she asked (the pusher is a piece of bread or a roll used to push items of food onto the fork).

"Oh, I forgot to tell you," I said, "The pusher is in the oven."

"Good, good, good," Peggy said, walking around the kitchen, lifting lids on different pots and sniffing approvingly. And then when she had reached the corner of the kitchen where the table was set, she said, "Who's coming to dinner?"

"There's you and I, and I invited Sam and Sandy."

"That's quite a foursome," she said. "What do we do after we eat? Play cribbage?"

"Peggy," I cried, "what an excellent idea. I only wish I had thought of that."

"You're not very subtle, Al. The cards and cribbage board are on the counter top."

Twelve o'clock arrived and so did Sam and Sandy. Everyone sat down at the table, and at 12:05 we began the fruit salad. A few minutes later Sandy asked, "What's next? I'm hungry."

"For cryin' out loud, Sandy, don't you know that good conversation goes with good food?"

I changed the subject, stalling for a few more minutes of time. When I could hold out no longer, I relented and began serving.

I was the last one to fill my plate, and just before the last serving bowl was handed to me, the phone rang.

"Excuse me," Peggy said, "I'll be back in a minute."

Quickly, I ladled the gravy over my potatoes and made sure that Peggy was still on the telephone down the hall. Then I picked up the pork chop with my fingers and neatly and cleanly ate the meat from the bone. But the telephone conversation was much too short, for just as I was replacing the bone on that plate, Peggy walked into the room and took her seat. With the exception of the pork-chop bone, everything on my plate was as untouched as a vestal virgin.

Obviously, something had to be done.

"Peggy," I said, "would you check to see if the coffee is ready?"

"Wait a minute, Al," she said. "You forgot that I'm a guest here. Do it yourself."

After I had poured coffee, I took my place at the table. I had to do something with that damn pork-chop bone before Peggy took a look at my plate. I pushed it to one side, hoping that it would end up somewhere close to the peas and carrots, but no such luck. I had pushed it smack in the middle of the mashed potatoes and gravy.

Now the offending bone was hidden, but its absence from my plate would be conspicuous. Quickly I placed the large glass of tea in front of my plate so that Peggy, sitting across the table from me, might not notice. I switched the roll from my left hand to my right and held it so that it would, I hoped, hide a portion of the plate from her. I picked up my fork with my left hand and made a valiant attempt to herd some willing carrots and unwilling peas across the plate to the roll.

Blind, left-handed eating was not my forte. My fork completely missed the roll, scattering the peas on the table. Holding back choked laughter, I rounded them up with my little finger as inconspicuously as possible, depositing them under the rim of my plate, all the while carrying on a conversation with Sam. Suavely, my left hand guided the fork toward my mouth. Its tines struck me somewhere between the nose and the upper lip, and peas and carrots rained past my open mouth.

I returned the fork to my plate, certain that the jig was up, but still no word came from Peggy. She and Sandy seemed engrossed in their conversation.

I decided that a frontal attack on the potatoes was in order. But my left hand, unaccustomed to holding a fork, made only a stabbing attempt. This time, as my fork made its way toward my mouth, the pork-chop bone was impaled on the end of it.

Dryly, from across the table, Peggy asked, "Having a little trouble, Al?"

I couldn't contain myself any longer and I started laughing hard. I was caught and knew it.

"Thought you were going to pull a fast one, didn't you?" Peggy said, laughing.

And then with all pretenses gone, Peggy and I sat there and literally howled, and between chokes and loud peals of laughter, we explained to Sam and Sandy what had happened.

"You should have seen the look on your face," Peggy told me later as she and I were cleaning up the kitchen, "when you had that bone on the end of your fork."

"Oh well," I chuckled, "it was fun trying."

"Personal-management class will never be the same without you," she said.

Friday of the last week I made my rounds of the different classes, saying goodbyes to the instructors. After lunch Sandy and I had our final cribbage game.

"You know, Sandy, I don't know how many games we've played in the past five months, but after all of them I don't owe you very much."

And I counted out $1.25 and pushed it across the table.

Judy was waiting at the apartment, loading the car, and visiting with Don and Alice and Gordon and Sandy.

"How do you feel?" Judy asked me as I pulled the apartment door shut behind me for the last time on Monday morning.

I didn't answer her then. I regretted the time that I had spent away from the family, but I did not regret making the decision to attend Minneapolis Society for the Blind, even though a transplant had not been possible. And I did not regret my decision to live alone. It had forced me to become self-reliant and had reinforced the lessons that I had been taught. I was coming home from Minneapolis confident and secure that I was capable of handling almost any situation that came my way.

"You know, I just can't wait to get home," I said eagerly to Judy as I lit my first cigar of the day and cracked open the window of the car.

We reached Bern and Sarah's early in the afternoon and were promptly snowed in for four days.

Readjustment

❖❖❖❖❖

March to May 1977

For the first few weeks after I returned home, I eased slowly into the familiar routines. Judy was still working at the school, and her day started at seven in the morning. After rising early and fixing breakfast, she would leave for work and I would make the rounds of the boys' rooms. Scott and Rusty needed only one call, but Kevin, already a late sleeper, would require a second stop, this time accompanied by a vigorous shaking.

The boys needed to be off at eight-fifteen, and as that time approached the house beat to an ever-increasing tempo. Shouts of "I can't find my shirt, Where are my books? Dad, will you help me with my math?" all came at once. When the frenzied whirlwind of activity died down as the boys left the house, I'd pour myself a cup of coffee and sink down at the kitchen table.

Judy didn't return home until two-thirty in the afternoon. I filled my time alone reading, walking, and visiting with the neighbors. Before the boys came home we would shop, run errands and, on several occasions, stop at Da-Ly Realty, where I caught up on what was happening in the real-estate and insurance markets.

With Judy driving and acting as guide, I showed several investment properties to former clients. I didn't make a sale, but getting back into the business world filled me with a great deal of satisfaction. I had been keenly aware of how my clients might react to me now that I was blind, so I had done my homework thoroughly. I was able to field all questions, and after a brief period of uneasiness on the part of the clients, our dealings were very relaxed.

I also became more active in managing the rental properties we owned with Bill Landis and helped Duane and Bonnie with the ones we owned with them. Bill Landis had purchased some rental property while I was in Minneapolis, and it had been an astute move. When Bill offered me the opportunity to buy a half-interest in the property, I jumped at the chance. He wasn't interested in the day-to-day management of the property, so these homes also became my responsibility.

As my days became busier with work, I felt better and better. The only real disappointment in the last three months was the absence of a call from Dave Sutherland telling me that he had a pancreas ready for transplant. But I didn't give up hope, and I continued to keep in close contact with his office.

Memorial Day weekend found us back in Canby for the wedding of Sarah's daughter, Phlayne, to Larry Anderson. I had been asked to sing.

On Saturday morning I rehearsed my solo at the church. Sandy, my sister-in-law, the organist for the wedding, walked with me to the motel where some of the members of the family were staying.

Howard exhaled slowly in protest against the morning heat.

"Yeepers," he said, "it's really hot. I hate to think about what it's going to be like this afternoon. The church better be air-conditioned, or everyone in the wedding party is going to faint."

"It's hot," Don agreed, "but it's still not as hot as the day when Priscilla got married."

"You ought to know," Vic joined in, laughing. "You really had a problem with it then."

Don, who had been one of the groomsmen when our sister Priscilla was married, growled, "Ah, up yours."

But Vic continued, "Did any of you guys ever hear the recording of that wedding? You can hear Dad as he's 'preaching' and then all of a sudden you hear the sound of Don's heels dragging across the carpet of the altar as they carried him out."

We all laughed, remembering the incident.

Then Alice called from the door of the motel room and said, "Why don't you come in where it's cool?"

A while later when Don and Alice left the room, I stretched out on the bed. The coolness of the motel room was a welcome change from the heat and humidity outside, and I fell asleep.

Later Don and Alice and Judy arrived simultaneously.

"You'd better get up, you lazy bum," Alice said to me as I continued to lie on the bed. "You've only got forty-five minutes until church time."

"How much?" I said, sitting up abruptly.

"Forty-five minutes."

"That's what I thought you said." Then rubbing my stomach, I added, "Boy, these butterflies are coming in earnest now."

I joined Judy and the boys in the motor home. On the way to the church, Judy asked, "Nervous?"

"Who? Mmme?" I replied, and we both laughed.

Don had been right. The church, even in spite of its air-conditioning, was hot. But I was sweating for another reason, too. It had been a long time since I had sung a solo.

"How'd it go?" I asked Judy as we headed for the basement where the reception was being held.

"It was fine, except we couldn't hear you. The PA system must not have been working."

"Not working?" I said. "It was this morning at rehearsal."

Feeling a little upset, I joined Judy in the reception line. We left the church shortly after four in the afternoon to go to the wedding dance.

"This place is jam-packed," Judy shouted to me above the roar of the music and the tumult of countless couples on the dance floor. The music, which had varied from Western to 'forties and 'fifties numbers, suddenly took on a hard-rock sound.

"Want to dance, Becky?" I asked Vic's oldest daughter.

"Well, uh, sure, uh, I guess so," she said dubiously.

I took her elbow and she walked apprehensively to the dance floor.

"You sure you want to try this, Uncle Al?" she said hesitantly.

"Sure," I said.

And as I moved into the rhythm of the dance that she thought would be completely foreign to me, she said, with total surprise sounding in her voice, "Why, you do know how to dance."

Later, out of breath, she asked, "Where'd you learn to dance like that?"

"Come on Becky," I chided her as we left the dance floor, "I'm not that old."

We had taken only a few steps when someone said, "And just where do you think you're going?"

"Sarah! I haven't talked to you all day. How's the mother of the bride?"

"I'm just fine," she said, giving me a kiss on the cheek. "Say, you two were really cuttin' up the rug out there."

Then as the music changed to a slower beat she added, "Come on, Al. Let's dance." We headed for the dance floor.

"I don't think we've ever danced together before, have we, Al?"

"Nope. Lucky you," I said.

"Say," she said, suddenly realizing that she had a blind partner, "how do we do this?"

"You just let me lead," I said, "but don't let me run into other people." And then we were off.

The wild din of the ballroom made conversation difficult, but the mood was infectious. The last number was a fast one, and we flew around the dance floor, careening off other couples, shouting hurried apologies, and laughing continually. We were both ready to collapse when, mercifully, the music ended.

"Whew," Sarah said, "that's work."

After we had both caught our breath, she urged, "Come on. I want to introduce you to some of my friends."

We crossed the floor, but not without being bumped every step of the way. At various times Sarah would shout out the names of couples standing in front of us, and I would extend my hand and greet them.

"This is my brother Al," Sarah said.

After a long pause, a woman's hand took mine and a very feminine voice said, "I'm pleased to meet you."

I don't remember whether I shook her husband's hand or not, because Sarah was walking away very fast, bent double with laughter.

When she finally slowed down and straightened up, I asked her, "What the heck's the matter?"

"You," she said laughing, "put your hand out right in her boobs."

"Did I really?"

Sarah was convulsed with laughter.

"You should have seen her face!"

"How'd she look?"

"Very, very surprised," Sarah giggled.

And now, a safe distance from the surprised but not I hoped, offended woman, I laughed too, and we stood in the center of the dance floor, hugging each other and howling.

Much later that evening I found myself seated comfortably on the curb, beer in hand, listening to the roar of my niece and new nephew's car as it disappeared down the street. By now, the centrifugal force had pinned the rocks I had placed in the hubcap to the inside rim. Oh, what a beautiful sound they had made when the car had started to pull away!

The next morning we said our goodbyes to the family. Another niece, Jeanette, was to be married in August in Minneapolis, and most of us would be there for that wedding. Jeanette and her fiance, Jerry Kallstrom, had been in attendance at this wedding. After witnessing the shenanigans at the wedding, Jerry looked white as a sheet. "Jeanette will be lucky if he sticks around," someone said.

We loaded up the motor home and Judy, with Kevin acting as co-pilot, headed us for north central Nebraska to Niobrara State Park.

We set up camp and that afternoon made our way to the Niobrara River.

"Now come on, Dad, you promised you wouldn't move. You're gonna wreck it if you do," Kevin complained again for perhaps the twentieth time.

The hot sun was beginning to do a number on my exposed head. The rest of me was completely covered with sand. The boys had found me lying on a sand bar in the middle of the narrowed river. Although at this point the river was not very wide or deep, the current was strong and the sandbar had offered a welcome respite. While I was lying there to catch a little sun, the boys buried me in sand, and now Kevin was attempting to build a sand castle on my back. With only my shoulders and head exposed, I felt as if I were attending a clambake—as the clam.

"Scott," I said, "find the matches and light my cigar."

I didn't dare move my arms under the sand lest I jeopardize the building project on my back.

The strike of the match sounded a little too close to my nose, but Scott said reassuringly, "OK, Dad, now puff."

With one cheek on the sand and my cigar pointing skyward from the corner of my mouth, I asked, "Hey, fellas, where's your Mom?"

Judy's voice came from nearby. "I'm right over here."

"Watch out for the sharks."

"Sure, fresh-water sharks," she teased me, and I heard her hand slap the water.

The cold water in my face caused me to erupt from the sand-prison, to the wails of dismay from the three boys.

"Boy, Dad, you really wrecked it this time," Kevin said dejectedly.

"If you think that's bad, take a look at this," I said removing a very soaked, very ruined cigar.

Later that evening, with the boys and Sam busily investigating all the wonders of the playground, Judy and I rented a small self-propelled boat. Seated side by side we pedaled away, accompanied by the sound of the paddles dipping into the water behind us.

"Thinking about something?" Judy asked, panting with exertion.

"Sorry, my mind's a million miles away."

"So are your legs."

Turning a watchful eye on the boys, Judy asked, "What's on your mind?"

"You know," I said expansively, voicing something that had been on my mind ever since my return from Minneapolis, "some day I think I would like to open my own real-estate and insurance agency."

Now that it was out in the open I sat back, applied myself to the task of doing at least my share of the pedaling, and waited for Judy's reaction. It wasn't long in coming.

"That's a great idea," she said. "I think you'd really enjoy it."

Seeking a Cure

✧✦✧✦✧

July 1977

During July, I began making plans to meet the goal I had now set for myself—owning and operating a real-estate and insurance agency.

Since Nebraska state law stipulates that agency owners must possess a broker's license, my first order of business was to qualify to take the examination for a broker's license. To do that, I had to complete two years of full-time activity in real estate and go through sixty hours of classroom study. I was close to meeting the first criterion and, in order to fulfull the latter requirement, decided to take two correspondence courses later that fall. Then next winter I would be ready to take the examination in Lincoln for my broker's license.

In the meantime I decided to move my real-estate sales license and work under Dick Cavenee's license. Dick wasn't actively involved in listing and selling property, most of his activity in real estate being geared toward appraisals. He had his office in his home. But although it felt good to be getting back to work and planning for the future, something else was occupying my mind.

Earlier that month, I had had a telephone conversation with Dave Sutherland, during which he had proposed an islet-cell transplant so revolutionary that I'd been able to think of little else.

"The one thing that seems to prevent success in this type of transplant is a rejection factor," he had said. "And there's a real scarcity of human cadavers from which we can harvest a pancreas. In your case, we just haven't been able to find a suitable match. But you're one of the really special people in our program. Your brother Vic was a four-antigen match, and because of the closeness of the tissue types, the kidney he gave you should last you for years. But what's unique about you is that your sister Sarah is also an identical match. Theoretically, if we could transplant some of the islet cells from either one of them, the chances of success would be extremely high."

I was incredulous.

"You mean," I had asked Dave, "that someone can donate a portion of his pancreas?"

"Al, I want you to understand, no one has ever donated a portion of his pancreas for a transplant. However, it's been well established—through years of followup study—that a person who has a portion of his pancreas removed, say, because of an accident, continues to lead a normal life and is not diabetic at all. In fact, years later, glucose-tolerance tests remain in a normal curve."

Dave had gone on to outline in detail both the procedure that would be performed on me and the operation that either Vic or Sarah would undergo.

"Don't misunderstand me, Al, the removal of a portion of the pancreas is major surgery, and there is always a risk involved in any surgery."

He had also explained that, because this procedure had never been attempted, should I and Vic or Sarah agree to it, permission would have to be obtained from the seventeen-member Human Resources Committee at the University of Minnesota.

"Think it over, Al," he had concluded, "and if you have any more questions, don't hesitate to give me a call."

Now, weeks later, the question foremost in my mind was whether or not I should approach Vic or Sarah and ask them to consider being a donor.

"I'd like to see you get a cure for diabetes," Judy told me, "but

I know how bad you'd feel if something went wrong. It's a real tough decision and I wish that I could help you more. Whatever you decide to do, I'll understand."

For the moment, what I decided to do was discuss it with Bill Landis, hoping he'd be able to shed some light on the subject.

At five forty-five the next afternoon I was sitting in one of the office rooms at the clinic, waiting. I had long since been to the laboratory and had had blood drawn, and was working on my fourth cup of coffee when Bill entered the room.

"All right, all right," he said as he watched me make an exaggerated motion of checking the time on my watch, "I'm not that late today. When was your appointment?"

"At four-fifteen," I said caustically.

"Oh," he said, somewhat abashed, "I must have been busier today than I thought."

"Well," Bill said, "let's see what we've got here." He picked up the laboratory slip and looked over the results.

"Good, good, all the readings are right where they should be," he said. "The lab results look great."

Then he offered me a cigar, lit his own and mine, leaned back in his chair, and plopped his feet on the desk.

I told Bill about my conversation with Dave Sutherland and outlined Dave's proposal in detail.

"How do you feel about it?" he asked.

"Well, strictly from my point of view, I have everything to gain and nothing to lose. If the transplant is successful, I've gotten a cure for diabetes. If it isn't successful, I'm no worse off than I was before. I'm still diabetic."

"That's assuming, of course, that you tolerate the surgery well."

"For me the surgical risks appear to be minimal. They would make a three-or-four-inch incision midline right under my breastbone and transplant the islet cells by means of a sophisticated syringe into the portal vein. Traveling through that vein, the cells become lodged in the liver."

"You'll also be taking a load of immunosuppressants after the surgery. Have you considered that?"

"Yes. I don't particularly like it, but I don't see any real risk there."

"What's bothering you, then?"

"The question is whether or not I should—or even have the right—to ask Vic and Sarah," I admitted.

"You've got your diabetes under control. What do you hope to gain from this transplant?"

"The main reason is to protect the kidney Vic gave me. But there's another reason, too.

"I'm in really good health right now, and I don't have any of the other problems you might expect in a person who's been a diabetic for over twenty years. If this transplant can help protect the kidney Vic gave me, it can also protect my other organs—my heart, nervous system and vascular system. I know I've had the small blood-vessel disease. It's claimed my kidneys and my eyes, but damn it, Bill, if I can cure diabetes now, maybe I can prevent some of these other problems from occurring."

"That's a good point, Al. It's true that some doctors hold to the view that a diabetic will run into problems regardless of his control over the disease. They think there's some kind of a biological time clock that triggers complications.

"But the preponderance of evidence seems to indicate that the culprit really is elevated blood sugars. For example, I just read about a study in which pregnant diabetic women, those who really are prone to serious complications during their pregnancies, do much, much better and have a safer, easier time during their pregnancies when they exhibit tight control of their diabetes. I think it's perfectly reasonable to assume that if the transplant is successful, and you're able to control your blood sugars and keep them in a normal range, that it may be possible to forestall any future complications."

"All right then," Bill went on. "Let's come back to what's really bothering you—Vic and Sarah."

Bill's chair squeaked as he turned to face me.

I paused for several moments, searching for the words to convey my thoughts.

"When I needed the kidney transplant, the whole family volunteered to donate. They knew that if I didn't receive a kidney, I was going to die. But this time I'm not facing death. And if I decide to go ahead, it isn't the whole family who's going to be asked. It's narrowed down to two, Vic and Sarah. And to top it off, this type of transplant has never been done before. Sure, it looks good on paper, but nobody's going to give me an ironclad guarantee it will work.

"You know I've been waiting over a year and a half for a suitable cadaver, and nothing has come along. Now I'm presented with this opportunity. I just wish I knew which way to jump."

"One thing you may not have considered is the benefit that this transplant could have for others, particularly hundreds of thousands of other juvenile-onset diabetics. Diabetes is now the number-one cause of new blindness and the primary cause of countless numbers of heart attacks and strokes. Someone has to be at the forefront; someone has to be a pioneer."

"Well, I don't know what I'm going to do yet. I have a niece getting married in Minneapolis in the middle of August, and Vic and Sarah will both be there. Dave said that before any decision could be made about their suitability, both would have to have a glucose-tolerance test."

Then, pacing across the room, I added, "Maybe the thing to do is to present it to them. I feel secure enough in my relationship with both of them so that if they said no, it wouldn't cause any rift between us. All I can do is ask. It would be up to them to make the decision."

I spent the first two weeks of August in Minneapolis, attending a refresher course on the optacon. Peggy taught the course, and for two hours in the morning I worked with her. Then I spent several more hours in the afternoon in individual study. My lunch hours were spent in lively conversation with Sandy, dueling over hotly contested cribbage games.

I finally decided, after endless soul-searching, to call Vic and Sarah, tell them as much as I knew about the program, and leave the decision to them. When I spoke to them, both seemed eager to help. Both would be in Minneapolis for Jeanette's wedding.

Dave scheduled them into the Clinical Research Center on an outpatient basis to have the glucose-tolerance tests run the following Saturday morning. His office had sent out the 300-gram carbohydrate diet that both Vic and Sarah were required to follow for four days prior to the test.

When I told Sarah about the diet, she groaned and said that she would never be able to eat that much. Now sitting alone in the motel room on Wednesday night, I wondered again whether or not I had done the right thing, but somehow the die seemed to be cast. Although I had told them all about the program, I had not explained my reasons for wanting to attempt it. I was eager to talk to them and yet, at the same time, somehow reluctant.

Dave wanted me to meet and talk to Dr. John Narjarian, who headed the entire transplant program, and after I finished the optacon refresher course and bid farewell to Peggy and Sandy, I made my way to his office in the Mayo Hospital building on the university campus. Dr. Najarian had come to the University of Minnesota from San Francisco in 1967. The chief of staff at the hospital and professor of surgery, he had placed his considerable reputation squarely behind the program and was one of the pioneers in transplanting kidneys into diabetics.

The receptionist ushered me into Dr. Najarian's office and gave me a cup of coffee. Some minutes later, he entered the room.

Introducing himself he said, "You must be Al Beckler. I'm Dr. Najarian."

His voice was deep and rumbling, and the moment I heard it I knew that I was going to like this man. His day must have been very hectic, but his voice remained calm, purposeful, and completely unhurried as we exchanged pleasantries. His large, broad hand gripped mine firmly, and I had an immediate impression of strength. The hand belonged to a large man and its proportions amazed me. An absurd thought flitted through my mind: Good night, if this man operates on me, the incision will be gigantic.

We talked at length about the proposed transplant.

"What's the surgery like for removal of a portion of a pancreas?" I asked.

He moved around the desk to stand in front of me.

"The incision would be here," he said, leaning down and tracing an imaginary line under the left side of my rib cage.

"It's deep abdominal surgery, comparable to the removal of a kidney. It is major surgery. You've had your kidneys removed, so you know what I'm talking about."

"We'd use approximately 50 percent of the gland and then seal the capsule. By that I mean we'd stitch the incision on the remaining portion. This type of surgery has been done thousands of times, mostly on people who have been in accidents or another type of trauma, but it's never been done for the purpose we propose."

After he had returned to his chair, I asked him the other burning question on my mind.

"Doctor, in your estimation, what are the odds of success in this transplant?"

"Everything seems to point to rejection as the stumbling block preventing success. With you, rejection should be minimized, and I'd say the chances of success would be in the 70-80 percent range."

Later, at Tammy's, I groaned, slipped off my shoes, and rested my feet on the coffee table.

"Man, this day's been going on forever," I said to myself, "and it's not going to end soon."

The apartment of my niece Tammy and her husband, Rick, was filled with noisy people. Jeanette and Jerry's wedding was over, and the inevitable had already occurred. Jerry had been spirited away to some unknown destination, and Jeanette had been "kidnapped" and was being "held" at Sarah's motel room.

"Come on, Al," Tammy said urgently, "everybody's heading for the motel."

I gulped down the third drink I had been nursing along, and we headed for her car.

"You did a good job singing tonight, Al," Tammy said as she opened the car door.

"At least if they threw something, they didn't hit me," I said, chuckling, and I entered the car occupied by Tammy and three other attractive nieces.

We left the car in the parking lot, and the five of us entered the lobby of the large motel, singing loudly and laughing.

"All right, gals," I said, bringing the group to a halt. "Who knows where Sarah's room is?"

No one did, so we walked to the front desk. There I stood, an attractive niece on either side, both of my arms encircling shapely waists. I asked the clerk for Sarah's room number.

The rustle of the ledger was drowned out by the sudden noise of laughter and loud music as the door of the bar opened behind us and someone stepped out. After a few seconds the clerk gave us the room number.

I asked joshingly, "Is that the bridal suite?"

I pivoted on my heels as my two nieces turned me toward the direction of the elevator. We had taken a few swaying steps when a voice came from the direction of the now closed barroom door.

"Shay, buddy," a drunken voice said, filled with complete incredulity and a tinge of envy. "I don't know how you do it." Then, his voice almost a whisper, the man concluded in awe, "Bridal suite? You must be quite a man."

The laughter and noise coming from Sarah's room would have enabled us to find it without the aid of the number. Inside, the party was gathering a head of steam.

"Uncle Al," Jeanette's voice rose above the noise, "come over here and sit by me."

Jeanette, still dressed in her wedding gown, was seated on the bed. I sat down beside her, swung my feet up, and leaned back against the headboard.

The conversation was centering around Jeanette's plight.

"This is nothing," Sarah assured her. "Why, when I got married, your uncles hid my suitcase in a corn field and filled our car with two loose bales of straw."

Jeanette's sister, Donnell, a bride of more recent vintage than

Sarah, said of her wedding night, "When Jules and I finally got away and got to the motel, I tried to put on my nightgown, but I couldn't because Grandma Beckler had sewed the bottom shut."

As the evening progressed others joined the throng in the small room, and the noise level resembled that of a convention center.

A loud, angry knocking erupted from the door, closely followed by the sound of a strident voice demanding admittance.

Bolting upright I said with bravado, "I'll handle this," and promptly fell off the bed, spilling my drink.

Once outside in the hallway, I had to grin amiably through a torrent of abuse and invectives. During a short lull in the tirade I tried a witticism, but somewhere between the time my mind went in gear and my mouth went in motion, something happened, and what came out was garbled and completely unintelligible. Its humor was lost to everyone but me. I found it hilarious. After the spasms of laughter were spent, I stood, slack-jawed, bleary-eyed, one hand supporting a wall that seemed to be moving. Then it really did move as our complainant, after a loud "har-rumph," slammed his door.

Late the next afternoon all of us gathered at Don's house.

"Al," Vic said, "let's go for a walk."

We walked down Don's driveway, heading for a park a short distance from his house. At the end of the driveway Sarah joined us, and arm-in-arm the three of us entered the park's cool interior. We paused and talked at the bottom of the hill.

I told them all I knew of the beta-cell transplant program.

"I guess the only thing I haven't told both of you," I concluded, "are the reasons why I want to try it."

Linking arms again we strolled slowly down a winding path.

"There are two reasons," I said. "The first is to protect the kidney you gave me, Vic. But that's not the only reason. If the diabetes is cured it won't only protect the kidney. It'll protect the rest of me, too. That's really important to me. I'd like to get in some trouble-free years without worrying about a lot of other complications."

"I can understand that," Sarah said, squeezing my arm.

"I can too," Vic added. "You've got to think about Judy, and those boys of yours need to be raised."

"Look," I told them as we reached Don's driveway, "I want you to take your time with this. Get a second opinion about the surgery from your doctors at home. Then when you decide, you can give me a call."

"Now listen," I said, taking one of their hands in each of mine, "whatever you decide, it's okay with me."

Vic shook my hand and then, unexpectedly, he was giving me a hug.

"I'll let you know," he said quietly.

Sarah held me and squeezed tight. She started to say something, but her voice choked. Laying her head on my shoulder she shook her head to indicate that she couldn't speak.

It was an emotional time for the three of us. Vic handled it best, Sarah better, and I rather poorly. There were tears in my eyes as I left them and walked to the house.

I sidestepped a group of people in the kitchen and went to the bathroom. After closing the door, I doused my face with cold water and leaned against the counter top.

I thought of what I had just asked Vic and Sarah to undergo. The reasons I had given them, why I had wanted to try it, now seemed somehow inadequate, somehow puny.

"Why the heck did I ask them?" I accused myself bitterly as the tears started anew.

The door opened and Alice stepped in. Without saying a word she stood beside me and put her arm around my shoulder. Don, too, came into the bathroom and closed the door behind him. The tears streamed down my face.

"Here, buddy, you can use this," he said as he handed me a cold, wet washcloth.

I stood there with Don on one side and Alice on the other. I was upset and confused, and I wished desperately that I had not asked Vic and Sarah. I was feeling utterly dejected.

The front door opened and shut, and I heard a commotion of people in the foyer.

"Where's Al?" Sarah was asking, her voice rising with urgency. "Where's he at?"

Don opened the bathroom door and called, "He's in here, Sarah."

Sarah rushed in past Don, and I held her close until the sobs that shook her shoulders subsided.

"Ah, Sarah," I told her, "I shouldn't have asked."

"No, don't say that. You've gone through so much, and I feel so bad about it all. I'm so proud of you. I want to help you if I can."

I pushed her shoulders gently back until her face was close to mine.

"Look, don't decide now. I want you to talk it over with Bern. Tell him all about it, and then the two of you make up your minds, just like Vic and Gret will do."

The tears were still wet on our cheeks, but we were calmer now.

Don growled, "It's damn crowded in this bathroom with the four of us in here. I'm gettin' out."

Sarah dabbed her eyes with a Kleenex and said, "I have to go, Al. Bern's waiting for me in the car. We're driving back to Canby tonight, but I couldn't leave until I told you."

She kissed me and walked out, turning down the hallway, and I stood leaning against the counter top.

"Al," Sarah's soft voice spoke from the doorway, "I've always loved you, even when you were little and I had to take care of you."

"I know, Sarah," I said, turning toward her. "I've always known."

Bitter Failure

✿✦✿✦✿

August to December 1977

The next week Dave Sutherland called me at home to inform me of the results of Vic and Sarah's glucose-tolerance tests.

"Both of them are in a completely normal range," he told me, "but the numbers on Sarah's are slightly better. Our choice would be Sarah."

Early the following week, Vic and Sarah called, and both told me that they would participate in the program if chosen.

"Well," Sarah said, upon learning of the results of the tests, "looks like it's you and me."

Toward the end of August, the last call finally came through from Dave—the Human Resources Committee at the university had approved the transplant, and surgery was scheduled for September 27. In the meantime, although I found it difficult to think about anything else, I involved myself wholeheartedly in the usual round of fall activities. School started, and with it another football season. Some evenings would find me and the boys on the church lawn. Scott and Rusty would alternate at center and would hike the ball to me while Kevin, with a whistle in his mouth so I could throw the ball toward the sound, would go out for a pass.

In the middle of September, Duane and Bonnie and Judy and I spent a long weekend at Estes Park, Colorado. To our surprise, the unit we were staying in was for sale. It didn't take us long to make up our minds.

"It would be a good investement," Duane said. "Not only can it be rented out, but it would provide a place for our families to enjoy."

Shortly after my return from the mountains, Sarah and I checked into the Clinical Research Center. She was scheduled to undergo exhaustive physical tests to determine the general state of her health, and was also slated for another glucose-tolerance test.

"We use the results of this test as a benchmark," Dave told us. "Then shortly after the transplant we will rerun the test and compare it to this one. There shouldn't be any difference."

A glucose-tolerance test, which measures the body's ability to handle sugar, was also run on me. It involves drinking a large dose of glucose, after which blood samples are drawn at regular intervals over a five-hour period to determine blood-sugar levels.

On Sunday, the resident entered my room.

"Mr. Beckler," he said, "we want to start the ALG treatment and I'm going to put in a line."

The ALG treatment, anti-lymphocyte globulen, was one I was familiar with. It was intended to keep my body from rejecting the cells that would be transplanted from Sarah's body.

Later in my room, the resident, now joined by two others, explained the procedure further. "The line I'm going to put in is a central-venous-pressure line, CVP for short. The ALG is so concentrated that it would burn a vein if we administered it through a normal IV-line. The CVP-line will end up in a large vein above the heart, and the blood flow will disperse the ALG before it has a chance to harm the surrounding tissue. I'll give you a little novocaine here," he said, tapping the crook of my left elbow. "We'll thread it up your arm, and it'll end up about here," he added, his finger indicating a spot on my upper chest above my heart.

It wasn't an easy procedure, and I wasn't at all comforted to hear the resident warn his colleagues, "Be careful now. We don't want to puncture his lung."

But it went smoothly, and after the x-rays confirmed the position of the CVP-line above my heart, I touched the tubing where it exited from the dressing on my arm.

"Good Lord," I said to Judy, who had entered the room, "that feels about the size of clothesline wire."

After dinner the nurse started the ALG treatment. Several hours later I was in the midst of a severe reaction to it, which continued until dawn the next morning. I experienced sweats and chills alternately. The vomiting emptied my stomach early in the evening, and the dry heaves that continued all night long left my muscles sore and stiff.

"You've had a tough night, Mr. Beckler," the nurse said sympathetically. "But along with the ALG tonight we'll give you some medicine that should prevent another reaction."

My dosage of Imuran, the immunosuppressant drug, would remain the same, but prednisone, a member of the same family of steroids, had been substituted for Medrol. Although its dosage would taper down over the next two months, its initial dose was very high. Taken in pill form and therefore quite painless, its effects were still profound: increase in appetite, weight gain, a retention of fluids, and a puffy appearance. Through all this my insulin dosage would be monitored very closely and adjusted to handle the amount of calories that I took in.

Although the ALG treatment that evening went much better, it was late when I finally fell into a fitful sleep.

Most of Tuesday remains a blur to me. I do remember the early morning routine: the pre-surgery hypo, hurried goodbyes to Judy and the family, a brief conversation in the surgical suite with Dave and Dr. Najarian, who would be doing the surgery on Sarah, and my quick prayer before losing consciousness.

My next recollection of that day is late evening and my niece Tammy, who was taking a break from her nursing duties on the obstetrics floor, leaning over me and saying, "Uncle Al, how are you doing?"

"It hurts," I said, still groggy from the effects of the anesthetic and a shot taken for pain.

"It's bound to, silly."

"It's not the incision," I said. "It's my shoulder."

The incision was only a dull ache, but the CVP-line had made my shoulder feel as if it were on fire, particularly on top of the ball-and-socket joint, where nurses had placed a heating pad that had warm water circulating through it. Tammy, noticing that it had slipped off my left shoulder, moved around to that side of the bed and readjusted it.

"I've been to see Sarah and she's doing just fine. She said to tell you hello."

"Good," I muttered, more awake now. "Is she having much pain?"

"She didn't seem to be."

We talked briefly and then Tammy said, "Look, I've got to run. You take care, Uncle Al. I'll be back to see you tomorrow."

As she leaned over to plant a kiss on my forehead, I experienced a warm, wet feeling along my whole left side.

"Uh, Tammy, you better check this," I said, indicating the hot-water pad that was now sending a small stream coursing down the left side of my body.

Tammy took in the situation and muttered something not at all ladylike under her breath.

"Your nurses are going to kill me," she wailed.

"What happened?"

"I just disconnected your heating pad."

"Well turn it off. I'm about to float away."

Tammy left the room and returned shortly, and I heard the bed linen plop on the chair beside the bed. A nurse stuck her head in the room.

"Are you sure you don't want any help?"

"No, it's my fault. I'll take care of it."

Tammy proceeded to change the entire bed with me in it. With her help, I rolled on my side and held on to the bed rail while she rolled up the soiled sheets from the part of the bed I wasn't occupying and tucked them under me. She replaced these with clean sheets and tucked their loose ends under me also.

"Okay now, all you have to do is roll back over that hump," she said, and, as she held the catheter tubing, the IV-line, and the CVP-line, I slowly did as she commanded.

By now the incision was really beginning to hurt, and my left shoulder was throbbing angrily. But I couldn't help laughing at my panting, frenzied niece.

"Tammy," I said, chuckling as everything was once again in place, myself included, "have I ever told you that sometimes you can be a real pain in the butt?"

"Oh, goodnight," she laughed. "I'll see you tomorrow."

The next day I insisted on seeing Sarah. With the nurse guiding the IV-pole and Judy pushing me in a wheelchair, we made the trip to Sarah's room.

"Well, look who's here," I heard her say as my wheelchair bumped into her bed.

I leaned forward and found her hand.

"How you doin', Sis?"

"I'm fine," she responded, her fingers tightening around mine.

I sat there holding her hand, struggling for something to say to her. Nothing came; then the pressure of her fingers increased around mine, and I knew that I didn't have to say anything. I leaned forward and kissed her hand and rested my cheek on it.

Judy and I visited with Sarah and Bern and their children until the nurse came back into the room and said, "Mr. Beckler, we'll have to take you back now."

In the hallway I asked Bern earnestly, "How's she doing, really?"

"She's doing fine. The doctors say she's doing fine. Don't worry about her."

The next morning Judy bustled about my room, arranging my toiletries in the drawer of the stand by my bed and placing my tape player on top of it.

"I wish we knew how long you'd be up here," she murmured.

"That's hard to tell. Dave said that the cells could begin to function at any time within the next six weeks. We'll just have to wait and see."

"You've been gone so much this last year."

"I know. But if we can get through this, maybe that will be all for a while," I told her.

The following day Dr. Najarian visited me.

"Dave taking care of you all right?" he joked, taking my hand.

"This isn't the Waldorf," I said, marveling at the size of his hands, "but Dave's doing the best he can."

And then I chided him, "Doctor, no wonder my incision's so long. It had to be in order for you to get those meathooks in me."

He laughed.

"Your incision's hardly four inches long, and these meat-hooks—as you refer to them—are only large in comparison to those small mitts of yours."

"How's Sarah doing?" I asked, as our laughter subsided.

"I'm really pleased, Al. She's undergone major surgery and she's bouncing right back. In fact, she's doing very, very well indeed."

"Did everything go all right during her surgery?" I asked.

"Yes. We removed approximately 60 percent of her pancreas."

"I didn't think you'd take that much."

"That's where the seam was in her pancreas, and that's where we cut it. But don't worry about it. The pancreas is like the kidneys. It has tremendous reserve built in."

"How are Sarah's blood sugars doing?"

"They're exactly where they should be, right in a normal range, and that's where we expect them to remain," he reassured me.

Then in reference to my blood sugars he said, "I see that yours haven't changed, but it's still awfully early."

On October 11, two weeks to the day after the transplant, I completed the last ALG treatment and was transferred from Station 22 to the Clinical Research Center. I was delighted because it meant I could spend some time with Sarah before she was released.

It was a beautiful, early autumn day, and we walked east of the campus, heading toward the Mississippi River. We descended several hundred steps to reach the river level, found a park bench, and sat down.

Sarah, who was scheduled to leave for home the next day, asked, "What was your fasting blood sugar this morning?"

"Two hundred eighty-five," I said.

"Shoot. What did you say normal range is again?"

"Seventy to 110. But don't forget, Sarah, it's bound to be high right now with all the prednisone I'm taking. Prednisone is an antagonist to insulin, and my blood sugars will be high as long as I'm on a high dose of prednisone. As for you, I talked to Dave this morning. He said the glucose-tolerance test they ran on you yesterday didn't show any change from the one they ran on you before the surgery. Sarah," I said, giving her a hug, "I'm really glad."

"Me too," she said. "Now all we're waiting for is for you to have one as good as mine."

"Yes," I said excitedly. "Won't that be great? When that happens you and I are going to uncork a bottle of champagne."

We sat in the bright sunlight, feet outstretched, soaking up the warmth and talking. The sound of the river gently lapping at its banks provided a counterpoint to our conversation.

"We've got to get back," Sarah said, checking her watch. "Let's see how good a shape you're in."

When we had completed ascending the steps and stood, panting, on the sidewalk, I said, "I can't believe that you had major surgery a little over two weeks ago."

Sarah left the following afternoon. I missed her presence, and I needed something to occupy my time while I waited for the beta cells to begin to function. I approached Dave.

"Is there a gym or swimming pool around here that I could use during the day? I'm going nuts just sitting around this room."

Dave checked the incision.

"It looks fine," he said. "How would you like to go to physical therapy and work out with some weights and maybe spend some time on the exercise bicycle?"

"That'd be great," I exclaimed.

I was scheduled for physical therapy twice a day, once in the morning and again in the afternoon, and now the daily pattern for the next month was set. I had blood drawn before breakfast and again at two o'clock in the afternoon to monitor my blood-sugar levels, I exercised in physical therapy in the morning and afternoon, and I spent the evenings visiting with other patients or listening to tapes that Judy sent. Occasionally, I obtained a pass and spent an evening out either with Don and Alice or with Gordon and Sandy. It wasn't the most exciting routine, but I managed to keep busy while I waited, with mounting excitement, for some sign that the transplant had been successful. And I didn't have long to wait.

Several weeks later, I experienced a very severe insulin reaction. These occur when there isn't enough sugar in the body for the insulin to work on, either because there's not enough food available or else because sugar has been burned up after strenuous exercise. Any insulin that is injected burns up the little sugar that remains, causing an insulin reaction. The person becomes weak and faint, perspires heavily, and if a reaction isn't checked, can even become unconscious.

The reaction I was experiencing now was very severe, and the antidote was, as usual, to take in some carbohydrates immediately, which I did by means of sugared orange juice.

I had just returned to my room after physical therapy when the reaction struck, and now the lunch tray sat on the table in front of me. As I ate, I thought about the reaction that had just taken place and the others that had preceded it over the last three or four days. I was excited. My daily insulin dosage and calorie intake had been watched closely for the past five weeks, and even with the high dose of prednisone, I exhibited very good control, but now something else was happening. Something else was driving my blood sugars low. The amount of food I ate every day, the amount of insulin I took every morning and evening, and the amount of exercise that I performed twice a day were all constant. Nothing had changed, so clearly, something else was at work. The simple fact was that I was taking too much insulin. And the reason, I hoped and prayed, was that Sarah's beta cells were beginning to function and produce insulin.

As I finished my lunch, Heidi, the nurse, reentered the room with the results of the blood sugar she had drawn while I had been in the midst of the reaction.

"Guess what your blood sugar was? It was 39," she said excitedly.

"Thirty-nine," I whistled, "no wonder I felt so punk." I was exhilarated.

Dave entered my room late in the afternoon with the chart in his hands.

"Thirty-nine," he exclaimed. "You certainly were hypoglycemic around noon, weren't you?"

"Yes," I said. "I've been having quite a few reactions for the last three or four days."

"I know. I've been watching your chart. It's possible that Sarah's cells are beginning to function."

He tried to keep his voice matter-of-fact, but I caught a note of excitement.

"We won't know for sure, though, until we get some results back from the C-peptide tests."

The tests he was referring to measured the C-peptide level in the urine. C-peptides are a waste product of insulin that is manufactured in the body, and they are not present in the urine when insulin is artificially injected.

"While we're waiting for the results of the C-peptide tests," Dave continued, "you'll be the one to provide the clue as to whether or not those cells are working. If we drop your insulin intake and your blood sugars remain constant, the only reasonable cause for the difference would be the transplanted cells. This is the first week in November. That would place us just about six weeks post-transplant. So the timing is right."

During the next week, that's exactly what happened. I continued to have insulin reactions, and when my insulin was decreased, my blood sugars, although not completely normal, stayed in a very acceptable range. Never in my whole life as a diabetic had my blood sugars been this consistently good on such a low dose of insulin.

I felt certain that the cells were beginning to function, and when Sarah called I shared the news with her. After I talked to Sarah, Judy called.

"I'm sure they're working," I said to her, trying to be calm but not succeeding. "I've been a diabetic too long not to know when something different is happening."

"It's just what we've been praying for," she cried happily.

The nursing staff of the Clinical Research Center also seemed to be caught up in what was happening. My blood-sugar readings were common knowledge, and enthusiasm abounded. All of the other patients in the eleven-bed wing were also aware of what was taking place and shared in the excitement. All, that is, except one—an elderly woman who occupied the room several doors from mine. She was very mobile and very vocal, especially in her opposition to transplants.

"Young man," she accosted me in a thin, reedy voice, "I hear you're the one who's had that transplant."

"Yes, ma'am, I am," I said in high spirits.

Then she demanded, "How do you feel now that you're running around with a part of your sister's body in you?"

I didn't quite know what to make of that question, but I wasn't going to let her ruin my high.

"You know," I said to her, grinning a little too wickedly, "I do feel a little different."

"How's that?"

"I don't quite know how to explain it. It's just that every time her husband walks by, I get this sudden urge to nibble on his neck just below the ear."

As I approached the middle of November, I was in a state of euphoria. My blood-sugar level remained consistently good even in the face of what was now a moderate level of prednisone, and my insulin dose was revised downward almost daily.

"If things keep going this well," I thought to myself happily, "I'll be home for Thanksgiving."

It was several days later that I began to notice an aching in my joints and muscles, particularly in the small of my back.

"I must be getting old," I said to the orderly as we walked to my room following a physical therapy session. "I ache all over."

I reported how I felt to Dave that evening.

"I must have overdone it lifting weights, because I sure am sore."

Dave examined me thoroughly.

"We'll watch it real close," he said to me.

Then to the nurse he added, "Get his temperature every hour."

That evening my temperature rose to 101.9° and I suffered the effects of the fever. All through that night I fretted and worried. Something was wrong. I had caught the concern in Dave's voice.

I was reassured the next morning when my temperature returned to normal, but that feeling was short-lived, for later in the morning it rose again. For the next two days this pattern continued.

On the third evening, Dave was noncommittal when I pressed him for an explanation. He had ordered some tests the day before, and now he said, "We should know the results in the morning."

It was almost noon the next day before Dave came into my room. It was November 13.

"Al, I'm afraid your problem is cytomegalovirus," he told me. "CMV strikes some people who have had transplants and are still on high doses of immunosuppressant drugs. If it's not treated properly, it can affect the bone marrow and even cause death. But don't worry. We've caught yours in the very early stages and it shouldn't present any problems."

"How do we treat it?" I asked.

Slowly and with compassion evident in his voice, he said, "We're going to have to withdraw you from the dosage of immunosuppressant drugs we've been giving you since the beta-cell transplant. We'll have to cut back to the minimum level that is sufficient to protect your kidney."

"What?" I cried out in dismay. "But what about the beta cells?"

"Right now our first concern has to be getting rid of the CMV. If we let it go, we could be placing your life in jeopardy, and we can't do that. There's an outside chance that the beta cells may survive even though you're on a low level of immunosuppressants. We'll just have to wait and see."

"Isn't there any other way we can treat the CMV?" I implored him. "Isn't there anything else we can do?"

"No, Al. I wish there was, but there isn't," Dave said quietly. "We've got to cut back the immunosuppressants, and we've got to do it now."

I was numb. I felt as though the bottom had fallen out. My thoughts flew to Sarah and of the surgery she had undergone in order to give me this chance. Would all of her pain and suffering be for nothing?

The withdrawal of the high dosage of the immunosuppressant drugs had its desired effect, and by the following week all evidence of CMV was gone. During that week my blood sugar levels began to rise, and with that rise my daily insulin dosage was increased. That week also brought the now heartbreaking results of the C-peptide test—the beta cells had indeed functioned.

What followed were long, excruciating days that offered no glimmer of hope for the survival of the cells. My blood sugars were at diabetic levels, and my insulin needs were that of pre-transplant days.

I exercised doubly hard in physical therapy to try to burn up excess sugar. In the evenings, I walked the four flights of steps at the rear of the Clinical Research Center ten times in a vain, futile attempt to do anything possible to help the beta cells along. I railed inwardly at what had happened, and I was sick at heart for having asked Sarah to donate a portion of her pancreas.

"There's one other thing we can try," Dave told me after Thanksgiving. "It's possible that with all the insulin you're taking, the beta cells recognize it in the bloodstream and consequently don't manufacture any insulin of their own. If we stress them, that is, if we remove you completely from insulin, it's possible that they would again begin to function."

And so for the last ten days of my stay, I was not given any insulin. I manifested the symptoms of an uncontrolled diabetic: excessive thirst, excessive urination, and extreme hunger coupled with a rapid weight loss.

When December 4 arrived, the day I was to fly home, Bern and Sarah came to take me to the airport. And when I put on my pants, Bern had to use a large safety pin to gather over two inches in the waistline.

I said goodbye to Dave and the nursing staff and left the hospital that I had entered with such high hopes two-and-a-half months ago.

Vic was also in the Twin Cities for the weekend and he, Don, Bern, Sarah, and I drove to the airport.

"Al, we tried," Sarah said to me as we lagged behind the others on the way to the boarding area for my flight.

"Sarah, I'm sorry," I blurted out, holding her arm and standing quite still. "I wish to God I'd never asked you."

"Oh, Al, don't say that," Sarah said close to tears. "I don't regret doing it. I wanted to do it. It didn't work out. But, Al, it's not your fault."

Sarah, whom I love so dearly, had been a part of my life even before my first memories were formed. She had always been there, and now as I stood facing her, people rushing by on both sides, the clamor and noise of the airport surrounding us, I tried to tell her my feelings, but no words came. I had asked her to give of herself and she had responded in love, and it was with that shared love that we had attempted the transplant. Now it was over, and it had been a failure. She had given everything that had been asked of her, endured all, and through it had remained positive, cheerful, and loving. But a sense of failure gripped me hard, and now I felt almost as if I had used her, exploited her for no good purpose at all.

"Sarah," I said to her finally, still groping for words, "Vic told me when he gave me the kidney that he felt it was going to work. That's how I felt this transplant would be."

"I know. I felt exactly the same way."

I began again, still struggling to express myself. "I tried to do everything I could to make this transplant work. When the CMV hit, I felt as if my body had betrayed me, and after that, there wasn't anything I could do."

"Don't think about it like that," she said urgently. "You couldn't help what happened. Neither could I, and neither could anybody. It just happened."

But I was not to be comforted. The transplant had failed. I was bitterly disappointed, dejected, sick at heart, and I needed time to heal. I wanted desperately to be home.

The three weeks I spent at home before Christmas were quiet. But as Christmas Day neared, my prayers were answered, and my deep depression lifted. As I sat in the Christmas Eve service, the smell of the evergreen tree and roping pungent in the air, I thought of the past year, its great hopes and small triumphs, the one huge, bitter disappointment, the wild, crazy roller-coaster ride I was still on, vacillating between peaks and valleys. For the moment, I felt very sad.

New Ventures

✧✦✧✦✧

January 1978 to November 17, 1979

A s the late winter months of 1978 went by and early spring
approached, the ache of deep disappointment over the failure of the transplant receded. I was busy during that period taking
and completing two real-estate correspondence courses I needed
in order to qualify for my real-estate broker's examination. With
Pastor Meyer serving as proctor for the tests, I completed both
courses in just over two months.

I had the results forwarded to the Nebraska Real Estate Commission, and, since I had now met both requirements, I took the
examination. The Real Estate Commission provided a reader,
and she and I and my talking calculator were tucked away in a
corner of Pershing Auditorium for the four-and-a-half-hour exam.
Three weeks later I was informed that I had passed the examination.

Dick Cavenee and I were also becoming more and more active
in the Grand Island real-estate market. We had properties for
sale, and, between the showings and open houses and managing
of my rental properties, I was very busy. We also had the
opportunity of purchasing a very nice, brick five-plex, and I
approached Ray Block, VP of the Overland National Bank, for
my half of the sizable down payment.

As the spring days lengthened, however, I began to get restless,
and an idea that I had been formulating in my mind for over a
year demanded attention.

"Dick," I said one night at his house after dinner, "would you be interested in forming a partnership with me, building an office, and really getting into real estate with both feet?"

Dick, some fourteen years my senior, was already successful in several other business ventures. His common-sense approach, not only to business but to all aspects of life, was one I envied. Dick and his wife Colleen are an attractive, fun-loving couple. Their home on Kuesters Lake exudes warmth and friendship.

It became obvious that he had given this matter some previous thought when he replied. "I think it's a good idea. Let's give it a try," he said.

The partnership was formed that simply, and it was a good one. I was to be responsible for hiring the office help and sales people. There was a lot of work in the offing. The new business had to be put together, and the next months would be busy and challenging.

The highlight for the month of May was Kevin's confirmation and graduation.

"Our boys are growing up," I thought to myself as I helped Kevin into the coat of his new suit prior to the confirmation service. I couldn't help remembering my own confirmation, twenty-two years before, when my father, hands on my shoulder, emotion in his voice and tears in his eyes, had performed the rite of confirmation for me just as he had for all his children.

"I'm sorry, Alfred," he had said, embarrassed by his show of emotion. He went on, "The last one was harder than the first."

Several weeks later we were again in the church, this time for the graduation service. I felt a great deal of pride as the principal, Bill Chandler, called out "Kevin William Beckler," and I, as chairman of the Board of Education, offered my oldest son his eighth-grade diploma.

"Congratulations, son," I said to him warmly.

"Thanks, Dad," he replied, in a voice that had not decided whether it was going to be soprano or bass.

Construction was the keynote for the summer. Dick and I had decided to build an office rather than lease an existing one, and we planned to use an open lot in a commercial subdivision Dick had developed. Building was to begin in late summer, with a completion date of approximately November 1. Until that time we would operate the business from an office in my home.

I was now ready to focus on another construction project. In the spring Duane and I had purchased two lots located five blocks from the house that we had remodeled during the summer of 1975. We had hired a contractor to build a house on each lot. He had completed the construction with the exception of the shingling, siding, and painting on the exterior, and the insulation, cupboards, staining, and painting on the interior. Now a few weeks into the summer, both houses awaited us.

"Doggone it, Al, now you be careful," Duane said to me as I climbed the ladder leading to the roof.

As I cleared the ladder and stepped up onto the roof, I heard Bonnie say, "Whew, he made it!"

My boys and Christi, Adriene, and Aaron, Bonnie and Duane's children, let out war whoops and clamored to be given permission to join me on my perch.

"Nope," I shouted down to them, "only roofers allowed up here."

I had taken several investigatory steps when I heard Judy's no-nonsense voice say, "Stay put until Duane gets up there."

Duane soon joined me on the roof. The lumberyard had distributed the compact squares of shingles across its expanse.

"OK, Duane, I'm ready when you are," I told him.

"All right," he said dubiously, "but you be sure to use your cane to feel for the edge of the roof."

"Don't worry. I'll be careful."

I broke open the first square of shingles and tossed them gently toward the sound of Duane's hammer, which was pounding vigorously on the roof. We crossed the roof in this fashion, he doing the nailing and I keeping him supplied with shingles. By mid-afternoon, having taken only a short lunch break, we had made quite a bit of progress on one side of the roof. The sun was blistering hot and its heat was reflected off the white surface of the asphalt shingles.

"We're going to have to call it a day," Duane told me. "We're going to ruin these shingles if we walk on them any more."

I stood up, groaning. The muscles in my back and shoulders and arms were rebelling at their unaccustomed workout. Sweat poured off my face and into my beard, but I felt great. I stood on the apex of the roof and caught a cooling breeze as it whistled through the trees by the side of the house. I was happy. I felt healthy and strong. Summer days beckoned to me, busy and filled with work, and at their end lay the promise of a new venture, the opening of the business.

I turned slightly and balanced on the ridge of the roof.

"Duane," I shouted to my friend, "I feel like I'm on top of the world."

The four of us and our kids made steady progress on the two houses. When the siding, which I held while Duane nailed, was up, Bonnie and Judy applied the first coat of paint. While I wouldn't be of much help to Duane with the rest of the house, especially when it came time for the really close work such as hanging the doors, trimming them out, and setting the cupboards, there was one thing left that I could do on my own—hang the insulation. And if our days were filled with hard work, our evenings were devoted to enjoying the usual summer complement of picnics, barbecues, and an occasional weekend at Johnson's Lake.

Then one evening, I got the chance to expand my activities. Dolly, Scott's piano teacher and a member of the City Singers, called with some exciting news.

"Guess who's going to be the guest conductor at their fall concert?" I asked Judy as I hung up the phone.

"I don't have any idea. Who?"

"Norman Luboff," I said.

Judy caught the excitement in my voice. I had a number of his albums.

"What did Dolly want?" Judy asked.

"She asked me to audition."

"Well, you're going to, aren't you?" Judy asked.

"I don't know," I said, reaching for my shoes. "I asked her to stop by and bring the music for the concert. She'll be here in a few minutes."

Judy went to the kitchen to make coffee. A little later, Dolly arrived. She showed me the proposed program for the concert. It ran the gamut from the music of the seventeenth- and eighteenth-century classical composers to popular songs of the 'sixties and 'seventies.

Judy, joined us, listening as Dolly completed the list of songs. She laughed, "Al will love to sing that one."

"Which one?" we both asked.

"That one called 'Hasty Nymphs.'"

Dolly nearly lost herself laughing.

"It's not 'Hasty Nymphs,'" she said at last. "It's a piece by Handel called 'Haste Thee Nymphs.'"

Judy laughed.

"It really doesn't make any difference. Al will be for anything that has to do with nymphs."

I agreed to audition for the concert.

Several nights later, with the audition successfully behind me, a new thought occurred to me. "I hope Luboff knows how to direct a blind singer," I said, chuckling.

August brought with it its usual quota of Nebraska heat. When I was not able to be of help to Duane, I spent my time learning the music for the Luboff concert. And as August drew to a close, construction of the real-estate office was in full swing.

I also turned my attention to staffing the office. In addition to Dick and myself, three other persons would join us as realtors. Early in the summer I had approached Duane about obtaining his real-estate sales license.

"I'll give it a try," he agreed.

Norm Grobe, a veteran salesman whom I had worked with at Da-Ly Realty, approached me when he heard that we were opening an office.

"I've been wanting to make a change to a smaller office," he said. "It looks real good to me."

Maurine Mercer, a friend of long standing and another member of City Singers, brought additional real-estate sales experience to the staff. She is charming, gracious, and witty, and our relationship had always been characterized by lively banter.

"I don't know if I can stand it, having to take orders from you," she said to me one evening after a City Singers rehearsal.

"I suppose from now on, you'll want to be called Mr. Beckler."

"No," I replied laughing. "I prefer something a little more formal like 'Your Majesty.'"

Linda Lavelle was hired as secretary-receptionist. Now there was one other position left to fill—a part-time assistant for me. Although I planned to make many calls independently, I wanted the assistance of a sighted person for those occasions when my blindness might be an embarrassment for me or a possible irritant to my clients. I wanted someone with whom I could be comfortable and who could be comfortable with me and my blindness.

I interviewed several applicants, but found none suitable. And there the matter rested until one evening in late August at the board of education/faculty dinner.

"I hear you're opening a real-estate office," Karen, my partner in the foursome, said as she dealt the cards for pitch.

"Yes, I'm going to give it a try."

We finished playing out the hand and lost. During the lull as the two winning players advanced to another table, I asked, "Are you still working at the car dealership?"

"Today was my last day," she responded. "I'm going to take it easy for a while."

Karen and her husband, Wayne Gross, are the same age as Judy and myself. Their oldest son, Brian, and our son Kevin had been friends ever since kindergarten, and their daughter Sheri and our son Scott were in the same grade at Trinity. Wayne and I both served on the board of education, and the four of us had known one other for a long time.

I thought briefly of the position I wanted to fill, and, knowing that I would be comfortable working with Karen, asked her, "How would you like to go to work for me?"

Before she could answer I quickly explained the duties of the job I was offering her.

"I don't know anything about real-estate closings or insurance. You'd have to help me with that," she said. I detected a note of interest in her voice.

"Don't worry about it," I said. "I'll give you all the help you need."

"Well," she hedged a bit, "I was going to take some time off before I started another job."

"That's all right. I'm not going to open the office until November."

She was silent for a moment, and I was about to offer her some time to think it over when her answer came back.

"All right. I'll take it."

"Good. We'll get together in a couple of weeks and go over the forms you'll be working with."

October was drawing to a close in a whirlwind of activity. With the business slated to open in a few short weeks, I felt that I might not be able to get away for some time.

"Why don't we spend a long weekend in the condominium in Estes Park?" I told Judy. "The aspens should be turning by now and the mountains will really be pretty."

Judy agreed enthusiastically.

"Duane and Bonnie have been wanting to go. Why don't we see if they can join us?"

And by the time all the arrangements had been completed, two other couples were coming along—Bob and Marie Meyers and Oscar and Rose Ann Bredthauer. To accommodate all of us, we rented another condominium below ours.

The weather was perfect and the walk around Bear Lake, high in the Rocky Mountain National Park, couldn't have been more enjoyable.

The mystery of who put hand lotion on the toilet seats and hid the toilet paper remains unsolved to this day.

Monday, November 6, found us moving into the office even though the carpet had not arrived and some minor touch-up work needed to be done to doors and woodwork. Linda and Karen spent most of that week unpacking, organizing files, and getting accustomed to office routine.

I grinned to myself almost everytime I heard one of the girls answer the phone, "Good morning. Beckler-Cavenee Realty, Beckler Insurance." It was a dream, a goal I had set for myself, and now it was coming true. Before me lay a lot of hard work, and I couldn't wait to get at it.

In addition to the long days spent at the office during the first week, there were long evenings spent in rehearsal with City Singers. Norman Luboff had arrived in town early in the week, and from Monday through Friday we spent three and sometimes four hours each evening rehearsing for Saturday's concert. Mr. Luboff made two announcements late in the week.

"I think it would be best if you had your music in front of you at the concert," he said, concerned about our performance of one particular song.

Jokingly, I lodged a vigorous protest.

"I memorized the whole concert," I bemoaned.

My suggestion that if I had had to do it, everyone should have to do it, was soundly defeated in a chorus of good-natured boos and hisses.

Then as he was announcing his selection of soloists, he said, "Al Beckler will be singing 'Amazing Grace.'"

Saturday started out as a crisp, fall day, but by late afternoon an ice storm had gripped the city. Nevertheless there was a near-capacity throng in the 1,500-seat auditorium of the senior high school that evening as Mr. Luboff took his place in front of the singers.

Later in the concert it was a very nervous first tenor who sang this verse of the well-known hymn:

> Through many dangers, toils and snares
> I have already come,
> 'Tis grace hath led me safe this far,
> And grace will lead me home.

One morning early in the following week, Karen and I made our first joint excursion. As we stepped out of the office door and I took her arm, we were both apprehensive.

"What do I do?" she asked, preparing to head for her car.

"We won't have any problems. I'll keep my hand on your arm." And, gesturing with the cane in my right hand, I added, "I'll use this, too. Later on I'll give you some tips that will help me."

"All right," she said, and began to walk purposefully toward her car, which was parked along the sidewalk that ran parallel to the building.

Karen, five-foot two, petite and attractive, wasted no time getting where she wanted to go. This fact had only begun to register in my mind when I came in contact with the bumper of a car that protruded over the edge of the curb. I banged my shins, recovered, adjusted my gait to hers, and tried to coordinate my cane to ward off any further metal intrusions on my ankles. But I failed and came in contact with a second car. I bounced off that one, readjusted myself, took three more steps, and sailed off into space at the end of the curb. Brushing off my knees where I had landed on them, I took her arm again.

"Whoops," she said softly, laughing nervously.

"Don't worry about it," I said, limping exaggeratedly to the car. "We'll get the hang of this yet."

And we did.

Several weeks later, I complimented Karen on how well she was doing as a sighted guide, and how comfortable I felt walking with her.

"Gosh," she laughed merrily, "there wasn't anything I could do but improve!"

The first month was hectic but nonetheless very enjoyable. Duane, who had by now obtained his sales license, held an open house at the second home that he and I owned together. Not only did he make an immediate sale on this home, he had also listed the buyer's home.

"Right out of the gate and you land one," I laughed. "Well, good for you!"

I was exhilarated at what was happening. I couldn't wait to get up in the morning and get to the office.

But despite my preoccupation with business, there was something else on my mind. During the summer, I had had a long conversation with Dave Sutherland, during which he proposed another transplant. Now, as Christmas approached, I took the time to examine his suggestion thoroughly and make a decision.

"We'll try a different approach," Dave had told me. "Instead of taking a portion of the pancreas, harvesting and transplanting the beta cells, we are now transplanting a segment of the gland itself, just like we would a kidney, and placing it into the abdominal cavity. The pancreas has two functions. One is the endocrine function, which involves the ability to manufacture insulin and distribute it into the blood stream. The endocrine function shouldn't be impaired in any way as a result of the procedure, since the pancreas will be connected to an artery in a vein. The second is the exocrine function, which involves the manufacture of enzymes that flow from the gland through the pancreatic duct into the duodenum of the small intestine. Once these enzymes are in the intestinal tract, they react on the food to digest it. But when we transplant the pancreas into the abdominal cavity, we won't be able to hook the pancreatic duct up to an intestine. So what we do is to sever the duct where it exits from the pancreas, and let the digestive enzymes flow freely into the abdominal cavity. These enzymes are then absorbed through the peritoneum, which is the lining of the abdominal cavity, and are finally excreted by the kidneys in the urine."

I had listened to Dave's explanation. I knew that in my pancreas, as in every diabetic's pancreas, the endocrine function was impaired. But the exocrine function continued normally.

"The digestive enzymes act on protein, don't they?" I asked Dave.

"Yes they do," he replied. "The gut is nothing but protein."

"Won't those enzymes start eating away at the intestinal tract and other internal organs?" I queried.

"No. In laboratory animals and with a few humans on whom we've tried this procedure, that doesn't seem to happen. But there is one complication that you should be aware of. The abdominal cavity can't absorb the enzymes as fast as they are produced, and a condition called ascites can develop. When that happens you become bloated with fluid, and it can be very painful."

Dave, as always, had been completely honest in his appraisal of the procedure.

"It's a new wrinkle, very experimental, and because of that we will only use cadavers as donors. It also involves deep abdominal surgery. Those surgical risks, to you, would be much greater than those you faced in the transplant with Sarah."

After our talk, I mulled it over in my mind for several weeks. What bothered me most was the thought of those digestive enzymes that would be excreted from the transplanted pancreas and then float around in my abdominal cavity, and the probability of ascites developing. What I needed was a crash course on the pancreas, and I called Mary Boehle, a friend of mine who headed the laboratory at the St. Francis Hospital.

Mary was an excellent teacher, but I still wasn't able to reach any decision. My next step was to discuss it with Bill Landis.

"What time did you say Dr. Landis is going to pick you up?" Linda asked me from her desk as I paced to and fro in front of her.

"He said he'd be here around twelve."

"It's twelve-thirty now. He must have been held up at one of the hospitals."

"When Bill says twelve," I laughed, "that means anywhere from twelve to one-thirty."

Eventually, Bill picked me up and we headed for the restaurant. Bill's attitude when acting as a sighted guide was more or less every man for himself, and I still vividly remember when once in this same restaurant my right elbow had come in contact with a lady's head, jarring something loose: her hat, I had hoped, and not a hairpiece.

We ordered our lunch and I launched into the subject of a segmental pancreas transplant, describing my conversation with Dave Sutherland and my interest in the transplant. Bill assimilated this information while the waitress served our food.

"What kind of success have they had?" Bill asked when she had left.

"There are a couple that they're cautiously optimistic about. In those two cases, the patients are insulin independent with normal blood sugars."

"How many have they done so far?"

"Nine."

"What about the other patients?"

"That's where it gets kind of hairy. Five of them have rejected, and two have died. One died from a peritoneal infection and the other from a pulmonary embolism."

Bill was silent for a moment, considering. Then he said, "So what you've got is this; two have been successful, five failed, and two have died. The mortality rate is about 25 percent. That's very high."*

"I know it," I said. "I know it."

Bill was concerned.

"Do you really understand the risk you're taking, entering a program where the mortality rate is 25 percent? Statistics are funny things. Sometimes we listen to them and sometimes we don't. Look at it this way. You and Judy can get into the car and drive to Omaha, and you do so, knowing that there is a statistical chance that you might be killed in an accident. But those odds are very small. You'd never get into that car if you knew that the odds of your being killed were one in four?"

"That's true. I wouldn't even consider it."

"Then why," he asked me quietly, "would you want to consider this transplant?"

I shifted in my chair and pushed the food from me. I wasn't hungry. Bill's question was crucial, and I considered it as I lit a cigar.

---

*Author's note: Today, the mortality rate for this procedure is much lower. Of the fifty-seven transplants done to date, the mortality rate is under 10 percent. But at the time I considered this procedure, the 25 percent mortality rate was of concern to me.

"All right. I'll see if I can explain why."

And I ticked off the same list of reasons that I had given Bill a year and a half earlier—protecting the kidney Vic had given me, protecting myself from further diabetic complications, and increasing my chances for a longer life.

"I'm not going to argue with any of those reasons. In you, diabetes has claimed your eyesight and your kidneys. But that's all it's done. It's not at all an absolute certainty that it will claim more. Right now, you're in really good shape. You watch your diet, you exercise, and you've got your diabetes under control."

"That's right," I broke in. "But all I've achieved is a good defensive posture, and with it I can go sailing along for years, maybe without any problems. But the chances are that, sooner or later, some complications are going to show up and then all I will be able to do is treat the symptoms, the complications, while the real cause, the diabetes, is left untouched. I don't like to play that kind of waiting game. Why not try and do something to get at the root of the problem?"

We were both silent for a moment after my outburst.

"You've already had a kidney transplant, and you were one of the pioneers with the beta-cell transplant. Let's assume for the moment that you go through a third transplant. Does it have to be right now? Why not let somebody else be first? You've paid your dues. Don't you feel that you have time to wait for them to improve the technique?"

"I can't plan when to have this transplant as I could with Sarah's. My tissue types are hard to match. I waited over two years for a cadaver to become available for the beta-cell transplant, and I never did get one. The same thing could happen again. Also, since they aren't able to keep a pancreas viable for any length of time after it has been taken from a cadaver, the pancreas will have to come from a cadaver in the Twin Cities area. That means it could take even longer."

Bill finished his lunch and ordered more tea.

"It's not an easy decision, is it?"

Bill was stating a fact, not asking a question.

"No," I said, sighing deeply. "It sure isn't. The other two

transplants were different. With the kidney transplant there were risks involved, but I had to accept them because there was no other choice. With Sarah, even though it was an elective surgery, the risks to me were minimal. But now, with this third transplant, it's an elective procedure and the risks are really high. Not only would I be placing myself in jeopardy, but if something went wrong, I could jeopardize my family's future. Sometimes I think I'm selfish even to consider it, but damn it, Bill, I want a cure for diabetes. I guess in here," I said as I tapped my heart, "I think it's worthwhile. It's not selfish. A cure wouldn't only help me but would provide help for millions of other diabetics. I've tried once and it failed, but I guess I don't believe that's sufficient reason not to try again. Does that make any sense?" I asked urgently, my hand on his forearm.

Bill didn't answer, and we were both quiet as he drove back to the office.

"Al," he said as he parked the car by the front door, "I'm awfully close to the situation, and sometimes it's hard for me to separate my feelings. As your doctor you know I'll do anything I can to be of help if and when the time arises. But as your friend, I wish you'd wait a while. You always seem to be faced with tough decisions, and this one isn't any easier. I just want you to know that whatever you decide, I'll be supportive of you decision."

For the next several days I couldn't think of anything but the transplant, and one evening Judy asked if I'd made any decisions.

"I'd like to try it," I replied slowly. "How do you feel about it?"

She was silent for a moment, and I waited for an answer.

"I don't like to have them cutting you," she said. "I don't like seeing you lying in a hospital bed, I don't like seeing you in pain, but I know what you're trying to accomplish and I want that for you, too. I know that if you don't try, you'll always wonder whether or not you should have. It seems so risky though, and I just don't want anything bad to happen."

"Neither do I, but I have a lot of faith in Sutherland and Najarian. I wouldn't let anyone else do it."

Judy's voice, filled with emotion, was a little calmer.

"All right, I'm with you on it. Tomorrow we'll have to tell the boys. I hope this time you won't be gone as long as you were for the last transplant. The boys really need you now, and it's not easy for them when you're gone."

"I've thought about that a lot," I told her. "I've had to spend too much time in hospitals, and then I was in Minneapolis for six months, and now with this third transplant ahead of me, I'll be gone even more. I want the boys to know where I've been and what I've been doing. Maybe I'll write a book," I said jokingly.

The next day when I told the boys, Rusty and Scott—one was in the fifth, the other in the sixth grade—understood in general what I wanted to accomplish.

"You won't have to take any more shots then, will you, Dad?"

"No, Scott, not if it's successful."

"Will they put it down here?" Rusty asked, touching my lower stomach area.

When I had told him they would, he asked, "Will you have another big scar?"

Again I told him that I would.

"You sure have lots of 'em," he said speculatively.

Scott evidently knew what Rusty had on his mind because later he told me, "It's a good thing Rusty isn't in kindergarten, or he'd take you along for 'show and tell.'"

Kevin, a ninth grader, took in everything I told him.

"When do you think you'll have the operation?"

"I don't know. It could come today, or it might not come for two years. I just don't know. We'll have to wait and see."

As with any decision of major importance in one's life, the hardest part is determining which path to follow. Now, with the decision made, I turned my attention back to the office, but I could never hear a phone ringing without wondering if it would be Dave calling to tell me he had a pancreas for me.

Between the holidays Dick and I threw an impromptu party at the office for the staff and their spouses. I stood, leaning on the divider behind Linda's desk, enjoying the laughter and talk. Duane joined me.

"Al," he said, taking a sip of his champagne, "I think the office has gotten off to a really good start."

I agreed with him wholeheartedly. However, there was one other aspect of the business that I wanted to develop and that was the insurance agency. The real-estate agency was a natural source of leads for the insurance department. Every time we sold a home, I made certain that the purchasers received a bid from us on their homeowners' insurance, and once we had successfully placed that business, it was a natural extension to talk to them about auto, health, and life insurance. Now an opportunity presented itself to expand the insurance department.

"Karen," I said one late-winter morning, "I've been thinking about the insurance department."

Karen, who had just refilled our coffee cups, sat in a chair by my desk. The bulk of our mail concerned insurance, and I handled those items with her.

"Oh," she said, "what do you have in mind?"

"Doubling its size."

"That won't take long. At the rate we're going, we'll be twice as big at the end of the year."

Karen, who had begun working full-time in December, now had her insurance licenses and was able to handle quotes and claims that came into the agency.

"No, that's not what I had in mind. There are two other small agencies in town that are for sale, and I'm going to buy them and combine them with ours."

"Oh," Karen said slowly, and I could hear the cogs whirring in her mind as she considered what lay ahead.

"Here's what it'll do for us. First of all, I think that the price is right on both of them. Secondly, besides increasing the book of business we now have, we will pick up the insurance companies the other agencies represent, and that's important. We need more companies in the agency."

"Yes, I can see that. Right now, I'm only able to quote from several companies, and sometimes those quotes aren't competitive. The more companies I have access to, the better chance I'll have to give a quote that's acceptable to a customer."

"Now you've got it. That's the point."

"Wow," Karen said enthusiastically. "I'm really going to be busy. When do you take over the other two agencies?"

"March 1."

The addition of the other agencies would dramatically alter Karen's work load, so I decided to hire someone to take over the trust accounts and real-estate closings. And I was especially pleased to be able to get Elaine Wilson for the job. Elaine, like myself, held a broker's license and was experienced in that field. She also had a way of describing individuals and situations that made them come alive. Her wry observation after fielding a call from an irate tenant that "she was as sour as an old prune sucking on a lemon" gave me a clear picture of the individual on the other end of the phone.

I was also pleased that my sons were interested in the office and what I was doing. Kevin and Karen's son Brian spent several hours one evening a week cleaning the office, a job which later they passed on to Scott and Karen's daughter Sheri.

"I don't think they're spending all of their time cleaning," Karen told me one morning. "There's a footprint of a tennis shoe right in the middle of this table."

When I asked Kevin about it he 'fessed up to the footprint.

"Brian was after me with the vacuum cleaner," he said, laughing, "and I tried to jump the table but I didn't quite make it."

By now Scott knew that the name of the game in real estate was having the listing. Rusty seemed particularly interested in how I spent my time at the office, and he asked questions as he and I strolled home after a visit to the grocery store. He didn't ask about my sales activities, but his curiosity was piqued when I told him that I dictated letters.

"What'd you call that again?" he asked.

I reviewed the process of dictation for him once more and explained shorthand. He assimilated all this information, and for perhaps a half a block was completely silent.

Finally he asked, "Is your secretary any good at taking dictation?"

When I told him that she was, he dismissed the subject from his mind with an observation that left me doubled with laughter.

"And boy, Dad, I'll betcha that you're a real good dictator."

The summer months found me again knee-deep in construction projects. Bill and I had a four-plex built next to the duplexes we owned. Dick and I purchased some properties that we turned around and listed for resale with the agency. Some of them needed minor fix-up, and I supervised those activities.

One problem that I always faced when considering new construction was getting a sense of the floor plans. I tried having someone take my finger and trace on the blueprints the outline of the house and the individual rooms, but that wasn't the ideal approach. Then Karen suggested that someone glue toothpicks along the lines of the drawings on the blueprints. By first feeling the toothpicks placed along the drawing of the outside wall I ascertained the dimension and shape of the house, and then, by starting at the front door and literally letting my fingers do the walking, I toured the interior and located the various rooms.

When fall arrived, I heeded the adage that all work and no play makes Jack a dull boy and gave myself up to the annual autumnal rites of the football season.

"Dad," Rusty said to me between bites of the food he was bolting down one mid-October Sunday noon, "guess who's playin' in the first half of the double-header game?"

There was only one reason why Rusty, whose eating habits were slow and picky at best, would rush to finish a meal.

"Dallas," he shouted, answering his own question as he flew by my chair and down the stairs to the family room.

As I lay ensconced on the couch, and Scott and Kevin were sprawled out on the floor in front of me facing the TV, waiting for the game to begin, Rusty asked me the question that had been on his mind all morning.

"Dad, who you gonna be for today?"

The answer to that question would indicate to us all where

Rusty would watch the game. Kevin and Scott, who had nothing against the Dallas team, invariably chose the other team simply to annoy Rusty. If I were for Dallas and lent my vocal support to the cause, it would be two to two. If, for more practical considerations, I wished the outcome of the game to swing away from Dallas, it would be three to one, with Rusty the sole champion of Tom Landry and his Cowboys. In which case, Rusty couldn't watch the game with us. When Dallas was winning, we couldn't stand him, and when Dallas was losing, he couldn't stand us. Today my choice was the opposition, and Rusty settled glumly in his chair awaiting the eviction notice that would come from the three of us if Dallas should happen to forge ahead and he, deliriously happy, would lose his head, raise the roof with his enthusiasm, and rub salt into our wounds—or if, heaven forbid, the opposite should occur and he, being unable to withstand the taunts from his brothers, would have to leave.

Today, things weren't going Dallas's way. Rusty suffered silently the slings and arrows from his two brothers stretched out on the floor. Finally Rusty had had all he could take.

"Now don't get so upset," I shouted after his rigid back as he stomped up the steps.

I followed his progress across the house by listening to the thunder of his footsteps above me, and heard them come to a halt by the TV in the den.

"Oh, oh," Scott said, referring to a dramatic change in the game that led to a Dallas score. "He'll be back now!"

And sure enough, seconds later I heard his footsteps running across the house. "Did you guys see THAT?"

The second half of the doubleheader found Rusty joining me in the family room. His devotion to the Dallas team was total and complete. A loss was a catastrophe. A win was bliss untold, and if that win should be a come-from-behind win, euphoria reigned.

I stood in absolute awe of such football frenzy. I don't know where he came by it.

And now with the second game in progress, Scott and Kevin

deserted the family room, for, of all things, some fresh air. Rusty and I sadly considered such heresy on their parts for a moment, then shook our heads and riveted our attention to the game.

My team was doing poorly all day long. Heavily favored, they found themselves behind in the closing minutes of the final quarter. Rusty, forgiving me for my abdication to the opposition in the previous game, bore me no ill will. He placed himself in support of the team that I wanted so desperately to win. But it seemed to no avail. Now I even considered the ultimate sacrifice—the highest and best thing that I could do to ensure my team's victory.

"Yes, Lord, yes. You see to it that they win, and I'll give up cigars."

Then it happened—the reversal I had been seeking. With seconds remaining, my team found itself parked in front of the enemy's end zone and the field-goal team came on the field.

I was living proof that miracles do happen, and now another was about to be wrought on the football field. I sat back on the couch exhausted, waiting only to savor the victory that I was certain would come.

"Well, Rusty, it looks like the best team's going to win after all."

Rusty's roar of "Oh, no" and the roar of the crowd coming from the TV were simultaneous, and I knew disaster had struck. Victory had been snatched away, and in its place was bitter, bitter defeat.

"What happened?" I shouted.

"He missed it," Rusty cried. "He just plain missed it."

"Phooee," I yelled and, with my back rigid, I stomped up the stairs, grabbed a cigar, and thundered out the front door.

Kevin was coming in as I was going out.

"Hi, Dad," he said, stepping back to let me pass.

"Hello, Kevin," I growled at him.

"Where you goin'?"

"For a walk," I said shortly.

Kevin passed me and went into the house. I stood and applied a match to the cigar, sucking on it to get it started. Behind me

I heard him say to his mother, "Dad's team lost again, huh?"

As I stood there, I understood Rusty's football addiction. It was a case of like father, like son.

The first part of November brought a last-minute party at the office.

"You opened the doors a year ago," Maureen said. "How do you think we've done?"

"I'm really pleased," I said to her.

"If you ask me, it looks like it's been awfully hard on you," she kidded me. "You're really getting thin on top," and she mussed up the sparse hair on my head.

But Maureen's kidding aside, I was pleased with the business. My fears that my blindness would inhibit me as a real-estate broker, insurance agent, or an employer had proved groundless. Nor did people seem to feel awkward and constrained around me. A few embarrassing incidents had occurred with clients, but I felt that the people of the community accepted me as a businessman.

Earlier in the fall, because other business interests were claiming more and more of his time, Dick had offered me a chance to purchase his half of the partnership, and I had taken it. I was especially pleased with the insurance department. The acquisition of the two agencies had provided a base from which to expand, and our growth had been steady and solid. I was extremely pleased with my first year in business, and my mind was filled with plans and goals for my second year.

I bid goodby to Karen, who had given me a ride home from work. "See you Monday morning."

It was one o'clock P.M., Saturday, November 17, 1979.

The Call From Dave

✧✦✧✦✧

November 17, 1979

"Al, hurry, there's a telephone call for you. It's Dr. Suth-erland."

Judy's voice was urgent.

I stood for a moment, frozen. I knew what the call meant.

"Hello, Dave," I said, taking the phone from Judy's hands.

"Hello, Al. We've got a pancreas for you. Do you still want to try the transplant?"

"Yes. How good is the tissue match?"

"It's a good one. It's two-antigen for sure and possibly three. How soon can you get here?"

"I think there's a flight that leaves in about a half-hour. It's direct to the Twin Cities. I could be there late this afternoon."

"That'll work out. The donor is a child, killed in an accident. He was placed on a respirator earlier, and the encephalograph showed no brainwave activity. After the child was pronounced dead, the parents decided to donate the organs. The respirator will keep the organs viable until they're needed, but we'd like to do the transplant just as soon as possible. Have you had lunch yet?"

"No."

"Don't eat anything solid. We'll want your stomach to be empty when you get here. If you need to cover the insulin you took this morning, drink some orange juice or soda. Do you have any other questions?"

"No, I don't think so."

"All right then."

I replaced the phone. "So this is how it happens," I said to myself.

"Is it the transplant?" Judy asked, standing beside me.

"Yes," I said.

We both stood still as if rooted to the floor, neither of us speaking. I was considering for a brief moment what lay ahead.

"Well," I said, drawing a deep breath, "we've known it would come sometime."

I called the airline. A flight was scheduled to leave in twenty minutes, but when I explained the situation to them, they agreed to hold the flight until I got there.

"We've got to hurry," I told Judy, and we were both galvanized into action.

Judy raced upstairs and I sat at the desk and reached for the telephone.

I cancelled several personal engagements, and as I dialed Elaine's number to tell her that I would be gone from the office, I was almost angry for an instant at this intrusion into the plans I had for the office. "Of all the times for it to take place, it's just when I'm the busiest," I thought to myself.

I finished my telephone calls and joined Judy upstairs.

"There won't be time for you to get the boys settled somewhere and join me on this flight. When we get to the airport, we'll try to book you on a flight tomorrow."

"Okay. I'm finished packing here. See if you can find the boys and tell them goodbye."

I found the boys outside, and, while Judy backed the car out of the garage, I told them about the impending transplant.

"Will you be gone long?" Rusty wanted to know.

"I hope not."

"Good luck, Dad. We'll be praying for you," Scott told me.

And as Kevin hugged me goodbye, I again noticed how tall my oldest son was getting.

Judy and I entered the airport on the run and checked in at the ticket counter.

"Your flight's ready to leave," the agent said as she came around the counter. "I'll help you get boarded."

Before I took her arm, I gave Judy a hurried embrace.

"I'll call you after I talk to Dave. And see if you can get a flight tomorrow." We headed for the small twin-engine turboprop plane that waited for me, one engine already running.

It wasn't until the small plane reached its cruising altitude that I took stock of what had happened in less than an hour. Before Dave had called, the thought of a transplant was the furthest thing from my mind. This morning I had been occupied at the office, completely immersed in work, and when I had left, I had been looking forward to spending a weekend at home with my family. Dave's call had changed all that, and I knew that things wouldn't be the same for some time to come. The roar of the engines completely filled the small cabin, and I experienced a minute of fear and apprehension. Was I really doing the right thing?

The pilot had radioed ahead, and there was a cab waiting for me at the far end of the terminal building where I deplaned.

"Where to?" the driver asked.

"The University of Minnesota Medical Center," I said. "And hurry."

The driver did everything but hurry and succeeded only in getting us lost. An hour later we finally reached the university campus, but now we were trapped by the throng of football fans emerging from the stadium. I was in a fury as I left the cab at the hospital entrance, and with sharp, terse words happily rid myself of the driver. I'm sure that he was as happy to be rid of me.

In my room on Station 22 I had a chance to cool off as I unpacked and stretched out on the bed to wait for Dave.

"Hello, Al," he said a half-hour later as he entered the room. I rose from the bed and we shook hands warmly.

"You're looking good," Dave said as he took a chair in the corner. "How have you been feeling?"

"No complaints at all."

"Good."

Dave then asked me more specific questions about the state of my health.

"Give me a list of medications you're on now," he concluded.

"The same old thing. One hundred seventy-five milligrams of Imuran and 4 milligrams of Medrol. That plus insulin, of course."

"That's all?" he remarked, surprised. "Most of our other patients take quite a bit more medication than you do. It always surprises me when I remember that you're on so few."

He tossed the chart on the bed.

"What time is surgery scheduled?" I asked him.

"Probably not till later this evening. The donor is here in the hospital, but we want to get you ready first," Dave explained.

"Once we've run all the tests and concluded all the pre-operative preparations on you, we'll take you to the surgical floor. Your operation will begin first, and once we have you open and ready to receive the pancreas, we'll harvest it from the donor. The donor will be in an adjoining surgical suite.

"There are some things that I want to go over with you before surgery," he continued. "The problem of ascites occurs in most pancreas transplants that we have done. We're going to try something different with you to see if we can alleviate that problem. Since the pancreas kicks out digestive enzymes when it becomes aware of food in the stomach and intestinal tract, we're going to withhold food from you for seventeen days. By doing that, it's possible that the portion of the pancreas that controls the exocrine function may atrophy and that the digestive enzymes won't be produced. Eventually, the pancreas will realize that the exocrine function isn't needed and will stop producing digestive enzymes. But we want to see if we can alleviate this problem immediately after the transplant. We're also going to try to keep the pancreas from producing those enzymes by treating it with radiation therapy."

"With what?" I asked Dave quickly.

"Radiation therapy," he said, catching the note of alarm in my voice. "But don't worry. The level of radiation that you'll be exposed to is well below accepted minimal safety standards, and it will be localized in the pancreas. Radiation seems to inhibit the ability of the pancreas to manufacture digestive enzymes."

"If I'm not going to eat for seventeen days, can I get everything I need through an IV?"

"No. We'll feed you through a process called hyperalimentation. When you're in surgery, I'll insert a Hickman catheter in your right shoulder. One end of the tube will be inserted into a large vein, and I'll thread the other end under the skin and bring it out right about here," he said, indicating a spot approximately two inches above my right nipple.

"The hyperalimentation, which is highly concentrated proteins and nutrients, is too thick to go through a regular IV-line, so it will be given to you through the Hickman catheter."

"Will the hyperalimentation be all that I need for those seventeen days I'm off food?"

"Yes. It will provide all the vitamins and nutrients that your body will require. There are quite a few calories in it, which will raise your blood-sugar level. And since we don't want to stress the new pancreas too much, you will also be hooked up to an insulin-infusion machine that will be programmed to give you three units of insulin every hour around the clock. Even with that much insulin, your blood sugars will be high as long as you're on hyperalimentation. But don't be alarmed by it. We will expect those blood sugars to be high."

"Will I have the anti-lymphocyte globulen treatment again?"

"Yes. We'll give you a fourteen-day course on that treatment also."

"Are you going to put the CVP-line in my arm again?" I groaned, remembering the difficulty I had had with it during the previous transplant.

"No. While we're in surgery I'll insert it under your collarbone. We'll also insert the naso-gastro tube through your nose into your stomach, and, of course, you'll also have a catheter in your bladder. We'll put those in while you're in surgery, too."

I considered all of those tubes while Dave gave instructions for my pre-op care to a nurse who had just entered the room.

"Any questions, Al?" he said to me when he had finished.

"What about the incision? Where will you be going in?"

"I'll go in midline. You'll have an incision approximately two inches above your navel down to your pubic bone. This is going to be major abdominal surgery, Al. After that type of surgery, your intestinal tract is going to stop working for about five days." Then, turning to the nurse who stood at the foot of the bed, he added, "Be sure enemas are given till clear."

After he left, I called Judy.

"Surgery is scheduled for later tonight, probably around ten or ten-thirty. Could you get a flight tomorrow?"

"No. There aren't any flights on Sunday, but I've got one early Monday morning."

"That's all right. I'm not going to be awake much tomorrow anyway."

"How do you feel about the surgery?"

"Oh, I'm nervous about it, but I think it's the right thing to do."

We talked a while longer, and then I visited briefly with each of the boys. When Judy was again on the line, she said, "We'll all be praying for you, and I'll see you on Monday morning."

I called Don next and told him about the transplant.

"Alice and I will be up to see you as soon as we can get away from here."

The two nurses on the floor who were in charge of preparing me for surgery were as coincidence would have it, called Don and Alice. Don, the male nurse, told me as he prepared to shave me for surgery, "You're going to get the full treatment."

"What do you mean by that?" I asked dubiously.

"Nipples to knees. I'm going to shave you from your nipples to your knees."

When that task had been completed, he brought in a metal basin filled with Betadine and a packet of small sponges. He gave me a pair of rubber gloves and said, "Scrub the shaved area for half an hour. The Betadine will kill most of the germs that are on the skin."

I completed that chore and slipped on a clean hospital gown only minutes before Don and Alice arrived.

"How you doin', buddy?" Don said, gripping my hand hard.

I explained the transplant to them, and we talked about it. Then a nurse informed me, "Mr. Beckler, Dr. Sutherland called from surgery. They're almost ready for you. I'm going to give you a shot to make you drowsy."

Shortly afterward the surgical orderly appeared in the room, and I clambered aboard the cart. Don and Alice each bent over the cart to give me a reassuring hug.

"Call Judy for me when surgery is over, will you, Don?"

"Don't worry. I'll call her," he said, and the cart moved toward the elevators.

On the surgical floor the cart was parked outside the door to the operating room, and I had a few minutes to myself. Periodically through the day I had offered prayers asking God's help through the upcoming surgery, and now once again I prayed deeply and earnestly. When I had finished I berated myself for the lack of prayer in my life. It seemed as though I only presented myself to God when I was in trouble, while the prayers of praise and worship were few and far between. I vowed to try to do better.

I was drowsy and didn't feel the movement of the cart through the doorway or its approach to the operating table. A slight bump as the cart was positioned parallel to it brought me awake. Somewhat later, after I was on the table with surgical drapes placed over me, I felt someone start an IV in my arm. Dave stood by my shoulder.

"Are you getting along all right?" he asked me.

"Yes."

My tongue was thick and my lips were dry, and I licked at them to moisten them.

"What time is it?" I asked thickly.

"It's ten-thirty," someone said.

I tried to relax, but I could only lay rigid. I was tense with apprehension. I wished to be unconscious, to have the surgery over, but even as I wished that, I was afraid. I lay on the operating table waiting for the anesthetist to ask me if I was ready, but he did not, and I was unaware of the swift, deep slide into unconsciousness.

The Pancreas Transplant

◊(◊(◊

November 18 to December 16, 1979

O f the day following the transplant, I have very little memory. I do recall Dave speaking to me in a loud voice early that morning, saying, "The surgery is over and you're doing fine. The pancreas is in. We've brought you back to your room to recover. The nurses will be staying with you."

I tried to make a feeble movement with my head to indicate that I understood.

"It's six-thirty," he said, with his hand on my shoulder. "You've really made me work. I'm going to get some rest. Just take it easy. Everything's fine."

Later in the day I became aware of Don standing by my bed, saying something to me. I tried to talk to him but I couldn't. The plastic air passageway was in my mouth and partly down my throat. It was irritating, and I made movements with my left hand to try to remove it. Someone restrained my arm, and I rolled my head violently from side to side, trying to dislodge it from my mouth. The rest of my body seemed completely paralyzed from the effects of the anesthetic. I panicked momentarily, and a nurse held my head and told me to take slow, deep breaths. As I did so, I slipped under again.

Judy arrived early the next morning, and the first recollection that I have of her being in the room is not the greeting we exchanged but the feeling of a cold washcloth on my forehead and her asking, "Does that help your headache?"

I was having a lot of pain, not incisional pain but pain from deep down inside. It spread throughout my abdominal cavity steadily, intently, like thousands of angry, burning pinpricks. There wasn't any one position that was really comfortable, although raising the bed to a full sitting position seemed to be the most acceptable. The daily trips on the cart to radiation therapy completely wore me out, and when I returned to bed, I lay there exhausted. There wasn't anything I could do for the pain except call for more hypos.

Dave stopped in the room two or three times a day, and Dr. Najarian also checked my progress. It was only after Dave assured Judy that I wasn't in any danger that Judy reluctantly left on Wednesday to rejoin the boys.

As the week lengthened and the pain persisted, few things penetrated the fog that I was in. But two things did register. One was Dave's concern about the severe pain, and the other was his cautious optimism about the way the pancreas was functioning.

"Your blood sugars are high because of the hyperalimentation," he told me, "but they're not way out of sight. They're just where we expected they would be."

On Saturday the pain was still with me, but perhaps it had begun to subside, or perhaps I was better able to accommodate it; anyway, I tried to lengthen the time between shots.

Late that afternoon Dave took out the catheter that was in my bladder.

"We're collecting all your urine for C-peptide tests," he told me. "From now on when you urinate, be sure to use the urinal. You're awfully weak, so call for assistance when you want to get up."

I should have heeded his admonition. During the night I had to urinate and so I rang for the nurse, but they were busy at the other end of the hall. Impatiently, I worked the controls of my bed, bringing it to a full sitting position. I swung my feet over the side of the bed and planted them on the floor. I felt along the railing until I located the urinal hooked over it by its handle. I waited some minutes for a nurse to enter the room, but none did. I decided to stand on my own and gingerly I moved even closer to the edge of the bed. With one hand on the railing and the other hand on the bed, I pushed off and stood up. The sudden pain in my right shoulder and chest was excruciating and I fell back. The nurses, hearing my loud cry, came running.

"What's the matter, Al?" one of them asked urgently.

"I don't know," I said between clenched teeth. "It's my shoulder."

I rubbed tentatively at my shoulder and chest.

"Don't do that," one of the nurses said. "Take your hand away and we'll have a look."

"Be careful," one of the other nurses said. "There's a spot of blood on his gown."

One of the nurses was reaching behind my head to untie my gown as the resident on duty entered the room.

"What happened?" he inquired.

"I was going to use the urinal, and when I stood up I got this terrific pain in my shoulder."

Slowly the resident removed my gown, but the procedure was hampered by the tubes leading to the IV in my arm. When my right shoulder and chest were exposed, he immediately exclaimed, "Where's the Hickman?"

There was a pause, and then a nurse said, "Here it is, doctor, on the floor."

"On the floor? How the hell did it get there?"

"I don't know. It's still connected to the hyperalimentation tubing."

The resident turned his attention back to me. "I'll have to put a stitch in here to close it up. How's the pain?"

"It's not so bad. It stings right through here," I said, tracing a line from the incision in the shoulder to just above the spot he was preparing to stitch.

"That doesn't surprise me a bit. That's where the Hickman was. When you stood up, you must have had one of your feet on the hyperalimentation tubing, and when you straightened up, you pulled it out of your shoulder. Ouch!" he whistled slowly.

"That makes me hurt just to think about it. Those little dacron flaps on the catheter were probably pretty well anchored in your skin."

"Won't you have to do something about the vein in my shoulder?" I asked apprehensively.

"No, we don't have to worry about that. The vein will take care of itself and seal off, but what I am worried about is how we are going to feed you for the next ten days. I'm not going to bother Dr. Sutherland tonight, but I'll talk to him about it in the morning."

When the stitch was in place and a small dressing placed over it, I was given a new robe. The skin on my shoulder and chest still smarted, but it was nothing compared to the stubborn, sharp initial jolt when the catheter had been displaced. I apologized to the resident and the nurses for the trouble I had caused, and feeling very upset at myself for what had happened, I promised faithfully to wait until someone was in the room to assist me before I stood up again.

"I don't think it would be wise to put in another Hickman right now," Dave told me the next day, "so we'll use the CVP-line for the hyperalimentation. But we also need that line for the ALG treatments and also for your other medications. There's only so much we can put through one line, so we'll have to start IVs in your arms to give you fluids."

But that presented other problems. Blood sugars were drawn four times a day, and the veins in my hands and arms had been used so often that many of them had collapsed. It became increasingly difficult for the interns to find a suitable vein from which to draw blood, and with the added requirement of finding a vein suitable for an IV-line, the procedure became a nightmare for me as well as the staff. My arms and hands felt like two gigantic pincushions. Because of the fistula that had been put in my left wrist for the kidney transplant, many of the veins in my left forearm were not suitable for an IV-line. And when an IV was started there, it lasted only a short while before it infiltrated into the skin and surrounding tissue, causing my arm to swell. Hot packs were then applied to reduce the swelling and the pain.

Unlike the nurses at the Clinical Research Center, who were allowed to draw blood and start IVs, those at Station 22, because the hospital was a teaching institution, were not, and only doctors performed these procedures.

One intern and I didn't hit it off well at all. He was new in his tour of duty on the transplant floor and relatively new to his internship. On one occasion, I had suffered through five hours with one of his IV-needles stuck, of all places, below the first joint of my right thumb. I gritted my teeth every time he came into the room, but I was patient with him; he had to learn his profession and this was part of it, and it wasn't his fault that my veins were in such rough shape. But he had an exasperating habit of sitting by the side of the bed, applying a tourniquet to my forearm and—for perhaps five minutes—studying it as he searched for an appropriate vein. He could only complete this inspection by an unnecessary ritual that involved moving his chair, standing up, walking around it, and sitting down again, all the while talking to himself in a low mumble. If, at the first stab, he was unsuccessful in finding a vein, he would immediately withdraw the needle, walk out of the room, and the whole process would have to be repeated again. My repeated requests to "just get in there and try it" fell on deaf ears. Late one night during the second week after the transplant, I was not in a very good mood when I rang the nurse and told her a new IV would have to be started in my right arm. I knew "he" was the intern on duty. Forty-five minutes after he had made his first attempt, there was still no IV-line going, and he and I were addressing each other sharply, both of our tempers frayed.

"All right, Mr. Beckler, this isn't any fun for me, either. Just where do you suggest I start this thing?" he said, icily.

"I'm so sore I don't care where you stick the damn thing," I barked back at him.

"Oh, really. Well let me get to it."

And the laughter that erupted from both of us broke the tension. We both knew that the part of my anatomy in which he wanted to stick the needle wasn't my forearm.

The abdominal pain that had been with me since the transplant persisted. On Thursday of the second week I returned to my room from radiation therapy in a wheelchair. As I moved to the bed and sat down, I knew something was wrong. The pain that had been a steady ache now increased dramatically, and the upper part of my stomach all along the width of the rib cage turned into one huge mushroom of extremely severe pain. It felt as though there was a hot wire inside me being twisted to constrict my stomach. I could only breathe in rapid, shallow pants. I tried to lie down but couldn't. I sat up, pushing my shoulders back, but that did nothing to relieve the pain. The pain was becoming unbearable, and I cried out. I made an attempt to stand, failed, and passed out, falling into someone's arms. Seconds later, lying on the bed, I came to and heard the sound of running footsteps in the hallway coming toward the room.

"What happened?" Phil, the senior surgical resident said, bursting in the room.

"He just came back from radiation therapy," one of the nurses said. "We were helping him get into bed when he got this attack."

Phil turned to me.

"Al, can you hear me? What's wrong?"

I was drenched with sweat.

"It hurts all through here, bad." I moved my hand to indicate where the pain was.

"Here?" Phil asked, pressing gently on my stomach below the ribs.

Even that small pressure was too much, and I cried out again.

Phil finished his examination and said, "Al, we've got to get you to x-ray."

Then to the nurse he added, "Call x-ray and tell them that he's coming down, and we want to get him in stat. And give him 50 mg of Demerol. Hurry!"

Demerol is a narcotic used to help the pain. I knew that my usual dosage was 100 mg.

"Phil, 50 mg isn't going to touch this," I groaned.

"I'm not going to give you more until we see what's going on. I'll see you in x-ray."

As he left the room he told one of the nurses, "Page Dr. Sutherland to Station 22."

The trip to x-ray and the time spent there were agonizing. When the technicians brought the table on which I was lying to a full upright position, I passed out again.

The x-rays were inconclusive. I was returned to my room and given another shot, which helped. Then Dave entered the room and checked my vital signs.

"What happened?" I asked, thickly.

"I don't know, but you seem to be stable now. Just get some rest."

Several hours later I was awake but still groggy from the hypo. Phil entered the room and stood at the foot of the bed.

"A couple of hours ago, I would have sworn that by now you'd be in surgery, and we'd be operating on you for a raging peritoneal infection."

He examined me briefly, and after he left the room I became aware that someone else was in the room.

"How are you feeling?" a soft voice asked. It was one of the nurses.

"Much better."

She stood up and fluffed the pillow behind my head.

"Before, when your pain started, I was at the other end of the hall. I heard you scream."

Her hand trembled as she brushed the hair off my forehead.

"It scared me," she said simply. "I was afraid for you."

I was touched by her sincerity and honesty. Someone was concerned for me and wished me well. I drifted off to sleep, thankful for her presence.

No one could explain why the pain had persisted since surgery, nor why it had flared up so violently. From then on, it gradually receded. There were times during the next three weeks when I was uncomfortable, but it no longer presented any problem.

One other thing became apparent during that second week. Even with no food in the stomach to stimulate it, the pancreas was producing digestive enzymes and pouring them into my abdominal cavity. Ascites was beginning to develop.

"We'll get your weight every morning," Dave told me. "And I'm also going to have the nurses measure your girth."

The third week brought an end to the radiation therapy and the ALG treatments. The insulin-infusion pump had been disconnected earlier and even with the added calories of the hyperalimentation, my blood sugars continued to be right where Dave wanted them to be. We were both elated. I was following pretty much a standard course of anti-rejection medication: 175 mg of Imuran, high doses of prednisone that were tapered back every third day, and Gantrisin to prevent any bladder infections which occur often in people who are on high doses of immunosuppressant drugs.

Because immunosuppressant drugs also can inhibit the healing process, the stitches in the incision were not removed until more than sufficient time had lapsed for it to heal.

"All ready for the unveiling?" One of the residents said as he removed the bandage over the incision.

"I'm ready," I remarked to him, "as long as the unveiling doesn't turn into a grand opening."

I touched the area, expecting to find stitches tied in the usual tight little knots.

"What's this?" I asked in complete amazement. "What'd you guys do to me?"

For marching in a long unbroken line that swerved only to detour past my navel were a host of metal staples bridging the incision.

"What do you use to get these things out? A pliers?"

"Just about," he said whistling, as he proceeded to remove them.

I could follow the course of his progress down the incision by the stings I felt as each staple was removed quickly and neatly.

Without meals, the pattern of the day had lost some of its significance, and I was genuinely surprised when Dave entered the room and said, "It's lunchtime. Are you hungry?"

"I suppose so."

"Well, you're not going to get much at first. I've ordered clear liquids for today and tomorrow."

"What do you mean by clear liquids?"

Dave laughed.

"Anything the dietician can see through she'll let you have, like apple juice, tea, and jello."

Then, on a serious note, he continued, "The pancreas has been functioning perfectly as far as the endocrine function goes. Your blood sugars lately have been normal."

Several days before, when Dave had first informed me of those blood-sugar levels, it had been hard for me to contain my enthusiasm. I had shared it with Judy, but we both knew that the possibility of rejection was far from over. I tried to temper my enthusiasm with that knowledge, but it wasn't easy.

"When you start eating," Dave continued, "we're going to see what happens to the exocrine function of the gland. If that function of the pancreas is unimpaired, it's going to start kicking out more and more digestive enzymes, and the ascites could get worse."

It was with a greal deal of trepidation that I ate that first meal and the following ones the next day. But once the transition was made, several things combined to make mealtime an event I looked forward to. The high levels of prednisone that I was taking made me ravenously hungry. I don't know what it is about that drug, but even with a full stomach I looked forward to the next meal. But that wasn't the most important thing. I was eating on my own, and, for the first time in twenty-two years, without taking insulin, my blood sugars remained in a completely normal range— no matter what I ate or how much I ate. It was a completely new experience for me. I ate cake and pie and all kinds of desserts without any feelings of guilt. My meal tray was loaded to the hilt.

"Good night, Al! Are you going to eat all this?" One of the nurses laughed. "Carrying your meal tray is enough to give me a double hernia."

But the initial success of the transplant, the incredible wonder that Dave and his surgical team had wrought, wasn't brought home to me until a week later when the dietician came to my room.

"Good morning, Mr. Beckler," she said pleasantly. "Let's see if we can fill out your menu."

I hadn't talked to her for quite a while, and I waited expectantly as I heard her rustle through her menus looking for mine.

"I better check on this. There must be a mistake," she said, a puzzled tone in her voice as she headed toward the door. "I thought you were on a diabetic diet, but they've got you on a general diet."

I explained to the dietician that I had had a pancreas transplant and that the general diet was correct. She was dumbfounded. She was only vaguely aware of the pioneering attempts being made at the university to cure diabetes, and what she had encountered this morning could only have happened to a handful of dieticians in the entire world.

"I'm probably only the fifth or sixth person in the world to have received a working pancreas," I told her.

And then it came home to me. I was free. Free from the daily insulin injections and free from observing a rigid diet. But those freedoms were secondary. The insulin injections had only been a nuisance, and I could have lived with them. And the thrill of eating previously forbidden foods would pass and become commonplace. The greatest freedom was that now, at last, after twenty-two years, after a kidney transplant, after blindness, after two pancreas transplants, I had beaten diabetes. I had undergone countless tests and procedures. I had been subordinate to other men as they practiced their medical skills on me. I was not a good patient. I questioned every procedure every step of the way. I chafed under the yoke of submitting myself to the will of others. It was difficult for me to be active in my pursuit of a cure for diabetes and then, once in my hospital bed, to assume a passive role. But I had presevered. I had done something positive. I had done something for myself, and it felt good.

Complications

December 17, 1979 to March 1980

The ascites continued to grow worse. By December 17, a month after the transplant, on the day I was transferred from Station 22 to the Clinical Research Center, my stomach was very distended. There wasn't any sharp pain, but there was a persistent low-grade discomfort. The effects of major surgery, too many hypos for pain, and a month's inactivity, most of it bedrest, had taken their toll, and I was very weak. But the pancreas was doing a marvelous job in controlling my blood-sugar levels, and I was in high spirits.

"You look pregnant," Heidi laughed as I stepped from the wheelchair to my bed at the Clinical Research Center. "What are you going to have? Twins?"

"Yes," I grinned at her. "And when I'm delivered, I'm going to call them amilase and lipase." This was in reference to two of the digestive enzymes that the pancreas produces. It had become my stock answer for the good-natured ribbing that occasionally came my way.

"What kind of tests will they be running while you're here?" she asked.

"I'm slated for a glucose-tolerance (GTT) test and a 24-hour profile."

The GTT would measure the ability of the pancreas to handle a large amount of glucose taken orally. After that test was completed, the 24-hour profile would show blood-sugar levels in samples drawn around the clock. For this stay on CRC, as well as every future stay, I would be on a 300-gram carbohydrate diet.

"In that way," Dave told me, "we will be able to see how the pancreas responds over the years to the same amount of calories."

Four days later the tests were completed. I was waiting to be discharged when Dave came into the room with the results. He was excited.

"The results of both tests are absolutely great. They're perfect. We couldn't ask for anything better."

Both of us were enthusiastic, but Dave cautioned, "The main problem we need to be concerned about is the same thing that's bothered us in previous transplants. That's rejection. If you can get past six months without a rejection episode, your chances of keeping the pancreas improve dramatically. Once you've gone a year post-transplant without a rejection episode, it's unlikely that one will occur. We'll have to keep our fingers crossed and hope for the best."

"Can't you treat a rejection episode of the pancreas like you can a kidney?"

"In the transplants that we've done so far, we haven't been successful in reversing rejection episodes. It's possible that the pancreas may not react to treatment in the same way a kidney does. Let's not borrow trouble, but if your blood sugars suddenly skyrocket, be sure to get hold of me immediately."

"What about the ascites, Dave? When do you think the pancreas will stop kicking out those enzymes?"

"Generally, it occurs somewhere in from four to six weeks, but in your case it looks like it may take longer. So far you've traded diabetes for ascites. The only way we have of stopping the ascites is to remove the pancreas, and I don't think you want to do that, do you?"

"No. Of course not," I told him emphatically.

"If the ascites continues to worsen, we may have to go in and do a peritoneal tap. We'll open you up, insert a tube, and remove the fluid."

"When would you consider doing it?" I asked.

"That would be up to you, Al. When the intra-abdominal

pressure becomes too much for you to handle, that's when we'll do the tap."

Dave shook my hand and said, "I'll send a discharge summary to Bill Landis. Good luck, Al. Have a nice flight home." And then he remembered something.

"But wait just a minute. I want to get your picture."

"My picture! What have you got goin'? A rogues' gallery?"

"No," he laughed. "It helps me keep track of my patients. It's important to me."

Dave took my picture in the hallway of CRC. Then I caught a cab and flew from Minneapolis to Omaha. Judy met me at the airport.

The airport was full of travelers scurrying to reach destinations before the Christmas holidays.

"It's so good to see you again. But you look so pale. Do you feel alright?" Judy asked.

"I'm fine," I said. "Just a little weak."

"You really do have a tummy. Does it still hurt?"

"A little bit. Not much." We walked slowly and carefully to pick up my baggage.

Judy had lowered the second seat of the station wagon and put a foam mattress in the back. It was there that I spent the three-hour trip from Omaha to Grand Island.

"It's sure going to be good to get home."

"It's great to have you home. Having you home is the best Christmas present the boys and I could have asked for."

The holiday season was spent quietly. The ascites was continuing to worsen, and with snow and ice on the ground, I ventured outside with extreme caution. The skin on my stomach was stretched so tight that it felt like a drum. I was afraid if I fell, I would really be injured.

After the holidays I made daily appearances at the office, staying most of the day, but by now the ascites was so bad that my rib cage area was swollen and I found it hard to draw a full breath. At the end of the first week in January 1980, I called Dave to tell him that something would have to be done.

On January 10 I found myself in surgery. The peritoneal tap

would be done under a local anesthetic, and all I felt was the sharp pinpricks of the needle as the novocaine deadened a three-inch strip of the transplant incision below my navel. I had been given Valium intravenously, but I lay tense and rigid as Dave opened the area and inserted the tube, probing gently and pushing it between the intenstines, deep in the abdominal cavity.

"How's it going, Dave?" I grunted through the towels and surgical drapes around my head.

"We're aspirating the fluid now."

"How much have you taken off?"

"I'll let you know in a minute."

He withdrew the tube.

"How much did we take?" he asked a nurse.

"4,300 cc, Dr. Sutherland," she said.

"4,300 cc," I exclaimed. "There's a thousand cubic centimeters in a quart, so that means you have removed over a gallon of fluid."

After the dressing was in place, Dave said, "Okay, reach down and feel your nice, flat belly."

I did, and he was right. It was flat. But after I had patted and pinched it, I grinned to myself. Even lying flat on my back I could pinch an inch of fat. My unchecked eating habits were bearing the expected fruit.

That evening I wore the nurses out walking the corridors and the hallways.

"You don't know how good this feels," I said, patting my stomach. "With all that weight gone, it's a real joy to get some exercise."

But before I went home three days later, it was apparent that the ascites was beginning to redevelop.

"If the ascites gets worse, I'll put in a LeVeen shunt," Dave said. "It's a device mostly used for alcoholics who have cirrhosis of the liver and develop ascites from that condition. A LeVeen shunt is made of three parts. A perforated tube would extend down into the abdominal cavity. A valve or cap would be placed on top of the wall of the abdominal cavity, but under the skin. From the valve a tube would run under the skin to your neck, and the distal end of that tube would be inserted into the jugular vein. Since the pressure in the vein is lower than the pressure in the abdominal cavity, fluid would flow into the vein, be collected by the kidneys, and excreted as urine. In that way we can control the ascites until the pancreas decides to stop producing those enzymes."

I returned home, hoping and praying that the ascites would subside. It didn't, and on January 22 I was again in surgery, this time for the insertion of a LeVeen shunt. Neither the hypo given to me in my room nor the IV with Valium did much to relax me, and I lay on the operating table, flat as a board and just as rigid.

"We'll have to be careful when we go in here," Dave said a few minutes later, talking to his assistant. "With as many surgeries as Al has had, there's liable to be all kinds of adhesions. The intestines could be adhered to each other or even to the peritoneum."

Some minutes later I felt the tugging, probing, and lifting stop. Dave said, "Wait a minute. I want to see that."

To one of the nurses he said, "Send this to the lab and have it analyzed."

"What's the matter?" I asked.

"The small intenstine may have been perforated," Dave said, and all activity in the surgical room stopped as we waited for the lab to report.

I heard the report on the intercom.

"That's a piece of small intestine, doctor."

Dave and his assistant spent some time cleaning the area and then closed the incision.

"I'm not going to bother with the LeVeen shunt," Dave said. "But while you're here, I'm going to do another tap."

He reopened the site of the original tap and withdrew 1500 cc of fluid that had accumulated in twelve days. It was not until I was back in my room that I became aware of the seriousness of the situation.

"What we want to avoid," Dave told me, "is a peritoneal infection. When the small intenstine was perforated, it's possible that bacteria from inside the intestinal tract leaked into the abdominal cavity. The abdominal cavity is warm and wet, and provides a perfect medium for bacteria to grow in. However, the incision into the gut was small, and we were able to clean the area very well. I don't think we're going to have a problem, but we still have to play it safe."

Dave's voice sounded tired as he continued, "We'll have to withdraw you from food for about ten days. We don't want to stimulate the bacteria in the intestinal tract. We'll also have to put down a naso-gastro tube to keep the stomach empty, and we're going to start you on a heavy dose of Keflex, an antibiotic. We'll also give you some IV's to feed you."

The words peritoneal infection jolted me. I knew only too well the implications of that type of infection. A peritoneal infection had caused one death in the pancreas-transplant program and had directly contributed to another.

I was upset and concerned, and after the naso-gastro tube and the IV were in place, I called Judy. I explained what had happened, and she was very worried.

"Dave feels that we shouldn't have a problem. I feel good about that. We'll just both do a lot of praying and take it one day at a time."

"All right, I'll do that. I'll tell the boys that you won't be home for a while."

Dave had been right, and as the week passed, no sign of an infection appeared. However, the problem of ascites continued unabated, and after a short stay at home, I was readmitted to Station 22 on February 5. The next day I was again in surgery— this time for the insertion of the LeVeen shunt.

I croaked through the muffler of surgical drapes around my head, "Dave, we've got to quit meeting like this."

The procedure went smoothly enough, and there was little discomfort, although the thought of the tube bent downward into the jugular vein made my stomach queasy.

"It's working," Dave said. "I can see some of the fluid flowing through the tube into your vein. It's kind of sluggish, though."

After he sutured the incision and placed a bandage over it, I touched the dressing and felt the curve of the tube as it bent 180 degrees and disappeared deep in my neck.

A close watch was maintained on my weight and girth over the next four days. However, both continued to increase. And the amilase level in the urine, which should have risen if the shunt were working, did not rise. On the fourth day I was again back in surgery. This time Dave opened the skin over the valve.

"It's just as I suspected," he told me. "The digestive enzymes are too thick to pass through the valve. I'll clean it out this time and leave the shunt in place."

I returned home the next day and over the next week I noted with apprehension that my weight and girth continued to increase steadily. I called Dave.

"The shunt isn't working and what's more, it's beginning to really irritate me."

"All right," he said, with a somewhat dejected tone in his voice. "We'll have to take it out."

"Can't I have it done here? The flights to Minneapolis are killing me."

"Yes, that's all right with me. I'll call Landis and talk to him about it. You'll have to be hospitalized for a few days, though."

That afternoon the shunt was removed and when the procedure was finished I lay limp and weak on the operating table.

I knew that continued peritoneal taps increased the likelihood of an infection spreading into the peritoneal cavity. I was between a rock and a hard place. Peritoneal taps were unacceptable. Prolonged ascites was unacceptable. And most of all, removal of the pancreas was unacceptable.

Bill discharged me from the hospital and on the following Sunday morning, the problem of ascites was eliminated, but another, more serious one took its place.

"Do you think you should go to church this morning?" Judy asked.

She was worried. I wasn't feeling well at all. I was full of fluid again and breathing was becoming difficult. Deep breaths were impossible.

"Yes. I think I'll try," I said as I pushed off the bed and

lumbered slowly to the bathroom. "I'm going to wash my hair."

The angry incision in my stomach was too fresh to immerse in water. I knelt on the floor by the bathtub and leaned over the side to wash my hair. Then, as I leaned forward to get the bottle of shampoo and leaned back on my heels, I felt my legs become wet. When I investigated, I felt a steady stream of warm fluid flowing from the incision. Weakened by repeated entry and suturing, a portion had given way. I stood up, grabbed a towel and, bending double, walked back to the bedroom and sank in a chair.

"What's the matter? What's happened?" Judy asked.

"The incision gave way. The fluid is just pouring out."

"I'll get another towel," she said, hurrying to the bathroom. "What else can I do for you?"

"Bring the phone. I'm going to see if I can get hold of Bill."

"I was afraid this might happen," Bill said when I got through to him. "The peritoneum was weakened by all those surgeries, and the pressure of the ascites has made it give way."

"Can you close it off?"

"No, I don't think so. What's happened is that a track has been established to the outside, and it's going to stay there until the pancreas stops making enzymes."

"You mean that it will continue to drain until then?"

"I'm afraid so. You better get to the hospital."

I was quiet for a moment, considering.

"Why?" I finally asked.

"Because now you've got a direct opening in the gut. We've got to be damned careful that no infection sets in."

"Bill, it's going to drain whether I'm in a hospital or at home, right?"

"Yes," he said slowly.

"What can you do for it in a hospital that I can't do for it at home?"

"We'll apply sterile bandages over the area to collect the drainage. The important thing is to keep the area as clean as possible. If we don't, we might give an infection a chance to start, and once it starts it's a straight shot—"

I didn't give him a chance to finish.

"I know. It's a straight shot into the peritoneal cavity."

And there it was. The same problem that had been present in a previous pancreas transplant, and one I had faced in late January. I felt as if a sword were hanging over my head by a thread.

"Bill, who knows when the pancreas is going to shut down? It might be next week, and it might not be for six months. I can't spend that much time in the hospital. I've got a family I want to be with, and I've got a business to run. I want to try to handle this at home. Does that make sense?"

There was a pause at the other end of the line.

"All right. Here's what we'll do. Most of the drainage will take place today, but there'll continue to be a small daily amount. You're going to have to keep that area clean, and you'll have to practice the best hygiene you know. Get a large supply of sterile gauze pads and place them over the incision. They'll collect the drainage, but you'll have to change them often. The best place for any bacteria to grow is where it's warm and wet. Use paper tape and remember that the most important thing is to keep the area clean. Don't bring anything in contact with the incision unless it's been sterilized. Can you get in to see me tomorrow?"

"Yes. I'll make it first thing in the morning."

"If you have any problems, be sure to call."

I contacted Dave next and told him what had taken place and what I planned to do.

"That sounds fine. How much prednisone are you on now?"

"Twenty five milligrams," I said.

"Cut that back to ten. That should help reduce the chances of any infection. It may jeopardize the pancreas, but that's a chance we'll have to take."

"Anything else?" I asked.

"Yes, take your temperature four times a day and keep a close watch on your blood count. I want you to call me three times a week."

"All right."

"How are your blood sugars doing?" He asked.

"They're absolutely perfect."

"That's terrific. The endocrine function of the pancreas is doing everything we wanted it to do."

"But I wish we could do something about the exocrine function," I grumbled. "It's really been giving me fits."

I bid Dave goodbye. Slumping back in the chair, I readjusted the towel.

"I had already violated the cardinal principle of keeping the area clean. I cleaned it with hydrogen peroxide, and for the rest of the day was careful to keep the towels below and away from the opening in the incision.

The weeks passed into March and still the pancreas poured out copious quantities of digestive enzymes. I was constantly aware of the threat of infection, and the thought nagged at me incessantly. The skin around the opening became irritated from the abrasive effects of the digestive enzymes. The constant application of paper tape left those areas raw and sometimes bleeding. It was a painful procedure to change the dressings, but I had to do it four or five times a day.

Changing the bandages during the day meant several trips home from the office, and there was one occasion when I didn't make it in time. Karen had ushered some insurance clients in to my office and they were seated in front of my desk. The conversation with them had been time consuming but was worth it. After I closed the sale and the clients were about to leave, I stood up and shook hands with them. I was wearing a light-colored suit. As the people left I heard the voice of a small child say to his father, "Daddy, daddy, that man has wet his pants."

However, there was one benefit to be gained from all this. The ascites was no longer a problem. As fast as the pancreas produced the enzymes, they were expelled, and now the fluid seemed to be moving through the lower left quadrant of the abdominal cavity. I asked Bill about it.

"You're probably developing a pancreatic pseudo-cyst. Fibrous tissues are being formed, probably from the pancreas to the opening in the abdomen. Most likely the enzymes are being contained in this area. These cysts are not uncommon. We see them in other people experiencing problems with the pancreas."

With the ascites gone I regained my mobility, and I went back to a reduced schedule of walks with Judy and the boys. My blood sugars and white blood-cell counts remained normal and, with the exception of a low-grade fever that remained consistently at 99° to 99.5° (which no one could explain), things seemed to be stable. Then another problem presented itself.

The incision opening, or fistula, as Dave now called it, began to seal off, and the enzymes that the pancreas was still producing were becoming trapped in the now fully mature cyst, with no place to go. As a result, pressure in the lower abdomen began to build.

"That needs to be drained," Dave said. "It will have to be kept open until the pancreas shuts down the enzymes."

On March 25 I was in Minneapolis in the ambulatory-patient care area of the hospital. Dave, using a catheter, probed the fistula and reopened the tract. He drained approximately 250 cc from the cyst.

"Send this to the lab for cultures," he said, handing the small vial to one of the nurses.

I returned home the next day and was completely unprepared for Dave's phone call later in the week.

"The culture we took from the fluid showed a candidia infection present."

"Is that the same as a candida infection?"

"It's sometimes called that."

I knew about candida infections. They are fungal in nature and are mean, ugly things, and now I had one in the fluid in my abdominal cavity.

"We'll have to get you started on some medication right away," Dave said, giving me a prescription.

"This medicine can be taken orally. If the candida is resistant to this medicine, the only other one we have left is a medicine called Amphotericin B, but it will have to be given by IV. In the meantime start taking this prescription immediately."

I hung up and sat in my chair, stunned. I leaned forward and placed my hands on the desk and my head on top of them. I had traded diabetes for ascites, and now the ascites was gone, but in its place I was carrying around a potential killer.

Dave was terribly worried. I could tell by the tone in his voice.

A cold sweat gripped me. What if the candida infection was resistant to this medication? What if the Amphotericin B wasn't effective in stopping the candida? What if?

I prayed hard and long. I went home and told Judy. She cried. We sat close for a long time, both of us silent, thinking.

Rejection

✧✦✧✦✧

April to August 1980

"I'll call over to St. Francis and tell them you're coming. Get there as soon as you can," Bill said. "Dave just called to tell me the results of the lab tests."

"You'll have to go on Amphotericin B. The other medicine isn't touching the infection."

Judy packed a suitcase and we drove to the hospital. When Bill arrived, concern was etched in his voice. The good-natured verbal sparring, the laughter that generally characterized our greetings, was absent.

"We'll get the Amphotericin B started. I've ordered an IV. It's vitally important now that we keep the fistula open and draining. We're going to insert a catheter in it once a day to keep the track free, irrigating the cyst with the Amphotericin B solution."

"For how long?"

"You'll need to take it once a day for three to four weeks. It can be toxic to the kidneys so we'll watch kidney values closely. If they stray too far from normal, we'll have to skip a day and try it again the next."

I was afraid to ask the question that was on my mind, but I had to.

"How will we know if the Amphotericin B is effective against the candida?"

"That's going to be tough," Bill said slowly. "Any culture of the fluid taken after we've started irrigating the area should be negative. But we don't know if the candida has spread into other areas. We'll have to give you the full-course treatment and hope that it is sufficient to kill any lingering remnants of the candida."

"Will I have to stay here for three or four weeks?"

"No. I talked to Dave about it. We want to keep you here for five days to see how you react to the IVs and watch your kidney function closely."

"But what about the IVs?"

"Dave thought that at the end of the week if things go well, we could put in a Hickman catheter."

"Oh, great," I groaned. "Another one of those things."

"Well, I agree with Dave. With a Hickman in place it's a simple matter to give you the treatment."

For the next five days the IVs and irrigation went without a hitch, and on April 10 I was once more in a hospital operating room.

"Dr. Cronk will begin in a few minutes," the nurse said. She finished scrubbing my left shoulder and chest and placed a drape over it.

"How come you're not having a general anesthetic?"

"I don't know," I laughed. "I'm not that tough, so I must be stupid."

"What was it like when you had your other one put in?"

"I don't know. They put it in while I was having the pancreas transplant. I was out like a light then. Anyway, Dr. Cronk said it's a relatively minor surgery."

Dr. Cronk crossed the room and stood beside the operating table. "Hello, Al."

"Hello."

"I'm ready," he said in his deep voice, "if you are."

While he worked, I talked to him, lying tense and rigid.

"Al, are you relaxed at all?"

"Why?" I asked through clenched teeth. "Am I talking too much?"

"No. It's just that I want to make this procedure as comfortable for you as possible.

"How much Valium has he been given?" he asked a nurse.
"Ten milligrams."

"It takes a lot to put you down, doesn't it? Give him ten more, slowly."

The additional Valium helped, and an hour later I was once again in my room, the Hickman in place, a swathe of bandages over the incision in my shoulder, and a smaller one on my chest where the catheter exited. It lay coiled up over my chest, held in place by paper tape.

The catheter worked like a charm, and several days later, with my blood chemistries still showing no ill effects from the Amphotericin B, I left the hospital. For the next four weeks I spent an hour each morning either at Bill's office or at the hospital receiving the treatment and having the fistula irrigated.

I resumed my full activities at the office. I felt physically strong, but the mental strain of wondering whether the treatment was working against the candida infection was at times hard to bear. At night, I would lie on my back for many hours, listening to the sounds of the night.

Toward the end of the month the persistent low-grade fever that had been troubling me disappeared. The fever was probably caused by the candida infection, Bill told me.

"The fact that you don't have it now is a good sign."

We were both encouraged.

The drainage from the fistula was also diminishing, and the fistula opening was narrowing and would have sealed over were it not for the daily insertion of the irrigation catheter.

"It's really slowing down," Bill said enthusiastically. "When we stop irrigating, it'll seal over, and you'll probably be left with a small cyst. But it shouldn't bother you."

On May 2 the Hickman catheter was removed. The dacron flaps on the end of the tube were anchored deeply and firmly in the subcutaneous tissue, and Dr. Cronk worked for almost an hour to free the tube.

"This will really be sore when the shots wear off."

I left the hospital, and Judy drove me home. I was nervous

and filled with anxiety. With the Hickman gone, my body was on its own in the fight against the candida infection. It had become my panacea, and without it I felt uneasy.

A week later the fistula sealed for good, and on the same day it closed the doctor removed the stitches from my shoulder.

"Hooray," I shouted exuberantly to Judy. "For the first time in six months, I don't have a bandage anywhere on my body. I never want to feel another doggone piece of paper tape."

No further sign of the candida infection manifested itself, and I breathed a deep sigh of relief and, with it, a fervent prayer of thanks. It had been a close call, a tightrope act, and it could have been disastrous, but I had come through it unscathed. On the six-month anniversary of the transplant, my oral glucose-tolerance test was again completely normal. I shook my head in wonder at the events of the past 180 days.

As May drew to a close, my attention was focused more and more toward Seward, Nebraska, and the convention of the Nebraska District of the Lutheran Church, Missouri Synod, to be held there May 30 through June 1. Earlier in the month I had received a call at the office.

"President Meyer from the district office is on the phone," Karen said in the intercom.

I took the call. "Hello, Pastor Meyer, what can I do for you?"

Then I caught myself and added, "Old habits are hard to break. I can't get used to calling you President Meyer. Is Pastor still all right?"

"Yes, of course it's all right," he laughed.

President Meyer, strong in the pulpit and even stronger administratively, had left Trinity two years before when he had been elected president of the Nebraska District. In the two years of his presidency he had given the District clear, dynamic leadership.

"There's something I want to talk to you about," he continued. "The Social Ministries Committee of the district is going to present a resolution to the convention asking that the church encourage its membership to use the universal organ-donor card and donate their usable organs at death or, if a need arises in their family, to become a living organ-donor."

"That's really great," I responded. "There's a crying need for organs, especially kidneys. If the church can get members in Nebraska behind the program, it would alleviate the pain and suffering of a lot of people."

"I agree with you, but the resolution is twofold. The first part speaks to the membership here in Nebraska. The second part would have the Nebraska District sponsor and offer the same type of resolution to the full church body at its national convention next summer at St. Louis."

I was excited.

"How many members do we have in our church body?"

"Almost three million."

I whistled softly. That many potential donors could be of tremendous benefit to an organ-transplant program.

"Are there any other church denominations on record supporting the organ-transplant program?"

"No. The Lutheran Church, Missouri Synod, would be the first, and the Nebraska District would be in a position of pioneering a truly worthwhile social ministry."

"Who put the resolution together?"

"Rev. Jack Thiesen authored it. He's one of the pastors in northeast Nebraska. Jack has had two unsuccessful kidney transplants and is presently undergoing dialysis treatments several times each week. Anyway, here's the reason for the call. The committee would like you to address the convention in support of the resolution. You've had both types of transplants, living-donor and cadaver, and the delegates could see firsthand the benefits of organ transplantation."

I jumped at the chance.

"Certainly, Pastor Meyer, I'd be pleased to speak at the convention."

That conversation was very much on my mind as Judy and I drove through the campus of Concordia College in Seward. The last day of May had dawned clear and sultry, and the mid-morning sun was hot and bright on our faces as we walked toward the gymnasium. We met Pastor Thiesen and his wife in the lobby.

"We have a little while before we're due on the rostrum," he said. "The National Kidney Foundation has a booth in the basement, and they're serving coffee and cookies."

Judy and I found a seat in the corner.

"Do you have your speech ready?" she asked, handing me a fresh cup of coffee.

"Yes, I believe so."

"Nervous?"

"Yes, a little."

I was nervous. Not because I would be speaking to around seven hundred people, but because I had completely changed the text of the speech that I generally use when speaking about the transplant program. It would not be analytical, full of hard numbers and statistics, but an honest retelling of the story of what had happened to me since just prior to the kidney transplant. At least that's what I hoped it would be.

My worries were obviously in vain, because my speech was received warmly.

Judy and I sat with Pastor Thiesen on the rostrum facing the assembly. President Meyer was at the microphone.

"All in favor of Resolution 201 please say aye."

The chorus of assenting ayes was unified and enthusiastic.

"All opposed?" said President Meyer.

Not one dissenting vote. I was extremely pleased. The district, by its vote, would place the matter in front of the national convention in St. Louis. Would the delegates of this staunchly conservative church denomination respond favorably? I fervently hoped so.

Some days later I heard from President Meyer again. He told me that the National Kidney Foundation booth had distributed over thirty-eight thousand organ-donor cards to the pastors, teachers, directors of Christian education, and delegates, to be distributed in their home congregations. Over one hundred organ-donor cards were signed at the convention. The program had gotten off to a good start in Nebraska.

The month of June, however, couldn't have gotten off to a worse start. On the evening of the third a slow-moving thunderstorm cell stalled over the city and spawned seven tornados that ravaged Grand Island, killing five people. In some areas, whole blocks were flattened. Incredibly, the damage was in excess of one hundred million dollars. The news coverage was nationwide. Later, President Carter toured the city, viewing firsthand the total desolation in some areas.

"There are trees down all over our neighborhood. The street in front of the house is blocked by several," Judy said, her voice hushed.

We stepped outside and picked our way over tornado debris and tree limbs. We had a few broken windows, and the roof, steel siding, and garage had been damaged. Our large ash in the backyard was one-third gone.

"I've got to get down to the office," I told Judy. "Our insurance clients will be calling to report claims. They're going to need help."

We were without electricity at the office, but our telephone still worked with outgoing calls. I purchased a small portable generator and put it by the back door. Its unmuffled noise was with us for a week. We offered office space to one of the insurance companies we represented, and their clerical help and adjusters ere with us for six weeks, handling the flood of incoming claims.

But the storm wasn't the only blow that came my way in June. One Sunday afternoon as I reclined on the couch in the living room, I felt that something was wrong.

"You know," I told Judy apprehensively, "I feel as if my blood sugar is high."

I left a urine sample in the bathroom and stood nervously by as Judy checked it for sugar. I heard the Clinitest tablet clink in the test tube. If sugar were present, the fluid would change color from a dark blue, which indicated no sugar, through distinct color phases to orange, which would indicate 4 percent sugar present. I heard the faint boiling of the chemical reaction and waited while Judy compared it to a color chart.

"It shows 3 percent," she said slowly.

She repeated the test, with the same results.

Agitatedly I said, "Let's get to the hospital and have blood drawn."

It was 316. Far too high. Dave had warned me that an abrupt rise in blood-sugar levels could indicate the start of a rejection episode.

"Keep checking the urine sugars at home and get a couple more blood sugars drawn this evening," he told me now. "If it's rejecting the levels will stay high, but hopefully they'll start to drop off. Get a fasting blood-sugar reading tomorrow morning and then call me. If it's rejecting, we'll try to combat it with large doses of prednisone, tapering it down just like we did after the transplant."

I ate a light evening meal, and, during the course of the evening, made two trips to the hospital lab. The blood-sugar levels dropped, and the next morning's fasting blood-sugar was normal.

"What do you think happened?" I asked Dave the next morning.

"I don't know," he replied, puzzled. "It's hard to draw a conclusion from this single incident, but I'm not going to start you on an anti-rejection treatment. Continue the way you've been doing. Don't alter your medication at all, but get three or four blood sugars drawn during the week at random times. Monitor your urine, and if you start throwing sugar, or if your blood sugars are out of line, get hold of me right away."

I contacted Bill and let him know what was going on.

"Have you ever had a glycosylated hemoglobin test done while you were in Minneapolis?" he asked.

"Yes, I have. Why?"

"The labs here are starting to perform them. It might be good to have one drawn periodically to see what kind of control the pancreas is maintaining.

"Glycosylated hemoglobin is hemoglobin that is present in the bloodstream in small quantities. The more sugar that is present in the bloodstream, the more glycosylated hemoglobin is also present. The test doesn't measure the highs and the lows," Bill said. "What it does measure is the average, and that's why it can be such a valuable tool in showing the kind of control the pancreas is maintaining."

"All right, Bill. That sounds like a good idea. I'll get the test run."

Several days later, I was pleased to get the results. The level was 7.3 percent, right where it should be.

For the next month, the blood sugars behaved themselves. Then they began to rise, slowly at first, almost imperceptibly. I talked to Dave.

"It's possible that this is a chronic, long-term rejection," he said, "and it may have started when we cut way back on the prednisone dosage when you had the candida infection. Let's continue like we're doing for a while longer. If the blood sugars suddenly get worse, we'll start treating you for a rejection episode."

Now I became preoccupied with the pancreas and the daily blood and urine tests. I cut back on caloric intake, hoping to ease the strain on the pancreas, but it did no good. Even in the face of a restricted diet, my blood sugars continued to rise. I was sick with worry. I wanted so much for the pancreas to work. I would go to the clinic in the morning to have the blood drawn, and an hour later my palms would be sweaty as I called to get the results. They were now consistently high. I would wait in tortured silence, pacing the hallway while Judy, in the bathroom, performed the urine analysis. Occasionally in the morning it would be negative, but by mid-afternoon and evening, readings of 3 or 4 percent or more were the rule.

One afternoon while at the office, I noticed my eyes watering, and my mouth and tongue became thick and coated. I knew what was wrong. I went to the clinic to have blood drawn.

Pat Enck, who was in charge of the lab, said softly, "It's 700."

I was shocked. Not even when I was diagnosed a diabetic had my blood sugars been that high. Again I called Dave.

"Something's really wrong, Dave. None of this is making sense. My blood sugar this afternoon was 700."

"What did you eat?"

"That's what's so queer. It was 190 before breakfast, and I ate a peach at the office. At eleven o'clock it was 412. I had a bowl of soup for lunch, and then this afternoon it's 700. I didn't take in enough calories to make the blood sugars rise to anywhere near those levels."

I caught a flight to Minneapolis the next morning and checked into the Clinical Research Center. Dave immediately started the high dose of prednisone.

"This dosage itself will cause high blood sugars," Dave said, "but if the pancreas starts working, they should remain reasonable. I'm also concerned about the ketones now showing in your urine. We can't let that go on for too long."

Ketones are produced in diabetics when the body, faced with consistently high blood sugars, becomes unable to metabolize sugar. If left unchecked, the situation worsens, and a coma may develop. At the end of the week, my blood sugars remained much too high, and large amounts of ketones were present in the urine. The pancreas wasn't working.

"We've got to do something," Dave said.

"I know, I know, but let's give it a couple more days," I pleaded. "Maybe it'll kick in by then."

But by the second day, the elevated ketone levels had become a real threat, and it was apparent that something had to be done. I heard Dave walking into my room. He was tired. I could tell by his footsteps. He sank wearily in a chair.

"I've been in surgery all day. I'm bushed," he said.

I heard him flip the pages of the chart. The room was silent, and we both knew that the time had come.

"I'm sorry. I've written orders for you to go back on insulin. The nurse will be here to give you ten units of regular. Tomorrow we'll start the old routines of shots twice daily. You'll discontinue the prednisone and you'll go back to the immunosuppressant levels that you were on when you had the kidney transplant. Four milligrams of Medrol plus the Imuran is all you need to keep your kidney safe."

I didn't argue. I knew it had to be done. The pancreas wasn't working, and the insulin was needed to eliminate the ketones and reduce the blood-sugar levels.

After Dave left I bared my arm for Heidi. The insulin she gave me seemed to represent the death knell of the pancreas and, with it, the end of something I had dreamed and worked for for five long years. It didn't make sense. All the operations and suffering. I was sick inside, sore at heart, and I hurt deeply. I sat, my arms on the sill, my head on my hands. I listened to the sounds of students in the dormitories across the street. The deep hurt, the overwhelming disappointment welled up, and tears flowed down my cheeks in torrents I could not stop.

"My God, my God," I thought, "how much will you require of me?"

It Works!

✿✦✿✦✿

September 1980 to February 1981

It was fall again, my favorite time of year. Gone are the lazy heat-filled days of summer. The crisp night air, laden with its promise of frost, seems to me to herald a change, a beginning.

This year was no different. I returned from Minneapolis in late August, and, as September worked its magic on me, the disappointment of summer receded. I spent long hours at the office. The economy was beginning to spiral downward, and activity in the real-estate market was getting slower and slower. We were busy seeking ways to improve our sales.

Back on insulin again, I adjusted my life-style to accommodate regular meals and dietary restrictions. I found I had to raise the amount of insulin I took each day. A blood sugar drawn during the first week in October was still too high.

I was taking 75 units per day, more than I had ever taken in my life. I was worried about insulin reactions, but during that period of time I never experienced one. In early November the increased insulin seemed to have achieved the desired effect.

"What's my fasting blood sugar this morning?" I asked Pat at the clinic.

"It's normal, 92."

"I seem to be stuck on 92. It's been that the last three times."

I was pleased. I felt that I had achieved the right balance between insulin intake and diet.

Later that month Bill called me at the office with the results of a glycosylated hemoglobin test.

"Are you having any reactions?" he queried.

"No. I haven't been having any. Why?"

"Your glycosylated hemoglobin is 3.9. Normal levels are 5.5 to 8.5. You're way below that. I expected you to be 12 to 14 percent. How much insulin did you say you were taking?"

"Seventy-five units per day, split dose."

"And you say you're not having any insulin reactions? That's strange. With a glycosylated hemoglobin of 3.9, you'd think that you would be taking too much insulin. That doesn't seem right either, because if you were taking too much insulin, you'd be having repeated insulin reactions."

"Do you think the pancreas is functioning?"

"No, I don't think so. If the pancreas were functioning and producing insulin, you would require less of it by injection, but you're taking more. Have you talked to Dave about it?"

"No, I haven't."

"Why don't you call and give him this reading. I'd be interested to hear what he thinks."

Later in the week I reached Dave and I filled him in.

"What do you think?" I asked him.

He agreed with Bill that if the pancreas were functioning, I would require less insulin, not more.

"Maybe something has happened since the transplant, making your body more resistant to the injected insulin so that now you require more. It's safe to continue those levels of insulin as long as you're not having reactions. One thing is for sure, you're doing something right. Your blood sugars and glycosylated hemoglobins show tremendous control."

The remaining six weeks of the year passed quickly, and it seemed as though the holiday season had ended almost before it began. The Christmas Eve service was beautiful and inspiring. I reviewed the past year's events as I did each year at this service.

"Ups and downs," I thought ruefully. "The pattern hasn't changed any. Maybe that's the way my life's supposed to be."

Early in the year I experienced some minor irritation with my stomach. Dr. Cronk inserted a tube called an endoscope down my throat to see into the stomach. The pyloris, the outlet of the stomach, seemed scarred and narrowed, he told me.

"It's closing down, and the food isn't passing through it normally."

"What has to be done?"

"If it gets worse, the muscle that controls the outlet will have to be cut."

"No thanks," I groaned. "I've had enough surgery. It'll have to get a lot worse before I'll do that."

In January it did get worse, and late that month I called Dave.

"Yes, we'll do the surgery here, but before we do, I want Dr. Goodale to take a look at it. He's had a lot of experience with cases like yours."

"Dave, there's one other thing. I've been thinking about putting my name down to have another pancreas transplant."

"Al, you've been through an awful lot. Are you sure you want to try again?"

"I think so, but I'm not going to jump into it right away. Are you still having as many problems with ascites?"

"No, we've changed our technique. Now, instead of letting the digestive enzymes flow freely in the abdomen, we seal the pancreatic duct. It completely eliminates the ascites."

"That's great. I wish you could have done that with me," I laughed.

"At the time when you had your transplant, we felt that ligating the duct would create serious problems for the pancreas, but now we're doing it differently, and it doesn't seem to affect the gland adversely. But you're right. I sure wish we could have done it with you."

"If I had another transplant, where would you put it?"

"We'd put it in the same place as the other one."

"Then you'd have to remove the one I've got now."

"Yes. We could do it at the time of the transplant, or we could do it now while I'm operating on the stomach. In fact, if you're seriously contemplating another transplant, now would be the time to do it, when I'm in the peritoneal cavity anyway."

On February 1, 1981, I left a cold, blustery Nebraska for an even more frigid Minnesota.

That evening the nurse said, "Don't take anything by mouth after midnight. We want your stomach to be completely empty for the test tomorrow morning."

The next morning an IV of 5 percent dextrose was started in my right arm.

I flexed my fingers, adjusting them to the board lying under the wrist and palm.

"Are you going to give me insulin now?" I asked.

"No. We'll check your blood sugars later today and adjust the dose to cover it. You'll be on an IV from now on."

Several hours later, I was taken to an examination room, where Dr. Goodale greeted me.

"Have you had an endoscopy before?"

"I'm afraid so," I said, shrinking from the thought of having to swallow the thumb-sized tube.

"All right then," he said, cheerfully, "you know what to expect. Let's get started."

His assistants sprayed some foul-tasting mixture in my mouth to stop the saliva from flowing and to lubricate the throat. I was given some Valium through the IV, and I managed to swallow the endoscope. It was almost noon before I was back in my room. I felt no discomfort, but the Valium had made me drowsy, and so I slept away the early part of the afternoon. Dave entered the room at two, and I came groggily awake.

"Dr. Goodale told me that the endoscopy didn't show anything wrong with the outlet of the stomach. In fact, he was able to enter the pylorus and go through into the duodenum. How has your stomach been this last week or ten days?"

I thought for a minute. "It hasn't been as bad as it was the first part of January."

"It's possible that what you have is an intermittent gastric-outlet obstruction. Sometimes it's better and sometimes it's worse."

"If the pylorus is now open, then you won't have to do surgery?"

"Not yet. We'll run an upper gastro-intestinal series tomorrow.

In the meantime, I'm going to keep you on IVs. You can have some liquids for dinner tonight, though."

At dinner I sipped my way through several courses of soup, juice, and sugared tea.

"There's always room for jello," I told the nurse. She got me another bowl.

It was seven-thirty and I had a vague, uneasy feeling that I had forgotten something. Then I put my finger on it. I rang for the nurse. "I wasn't given any insulin before dinner. Are there any orders on the chart?"

"I'll check." She left the room and came back in a few minutes with news that electrified me.

"There aren't any orders. Your blood sugar at four o'clock was 92."

"What?" I exclaimed. "Did you say 92? You don't mean 192, do you?"

"No, nine, two, ninety-two."

"Thank you," I said as she left the room.

This didn't make sense. I hadn't had insulin all day and since early morning had been on an IV of 5 percent dextrose. My blood sugar should have been considerably higher than that. I rang the nurse again and explained the situation to her.

"I'll call the intern and get an order for another blood sugar at nine."

This blood sugar would be crucial. I had ingested a large amount of carbohydrates in the fluid at dinner. That plus the dextrose in the IV should send the blood sugars skyrocketing in the absence of injected insulin. "That is," I thought, "if the pancreas isn't working."

At nine o'clock the blood sugar was drawn, and I wore the nurses out asking every five minutes if the report was back from the lab. The nurses caught my excitement and were aware of the importance of that reading.

"Al," one of them said, bursting in the room, "it was 108. It's perfectly normal."

I tried unsuccessfully to reach Dave that evening. The next morning when he entered the room, he had the results of the blood sugars drawn the day before and the one drawn that morning.

"Your fasting blood sugar this morning was 89. It's too early to draw any conclusions from this. It's obvious that the pancreas has kicked out some insulin, otherwise your sugars would be much higher. We'll have to wait and see if the pancreas can sustain those levels."

He was being cautious, but still I caught the note of excitement in his voice.

The upper GI series and other tests on my esophagus and stomach were inconclusive.

All week long, the pancreas kept blood sugars completely normal. As the days passed, I became more and more jubilant. I was scheduled to leave shortly after noon on Friday. Early that morning the phone rang. It was Dave.

"Al, I've got some bad news. Your blood sugar this morning was 265."

I was thunderstruck.

"That doesn't make any sense at all. My urine sugar this morning was negative. If I had a blood sugar of 265, I'd be spilling sugar in the urine."

Dave was in a hurry to be in surgery.

"I'll order another one for later this morning, and I'll talk to you before you leave."

I was baffled and beginning to feel depressed. "That can't be. Something is wrong," I thought. I grabbed my robe and walked to the nurses' station.

"Good morning. What can we do for you?" The nurse said.

"What was my blood sugar this morning?"

"Which bed are you?"

"Four."

"Let's see," she muttered as she paged through that morning's lab results. "Here you are. Beckler, bed four. Your blood sugar was 85."

"Hah," I said, crashing my hand down on the desk, dislodging a bell and a stack of papers. "I knew it."

The nurse jumped and asked, "You knew what?"

"I'm sorry," I apologized. "Dr. Sutherland just called me and said that someone here told him my blood sugar was 265."

"I can see where the mistake came from. Bed three's blood sugar was 265."

I again apologized for startling her and making a mess on the counter top. Whistling loudly and cheerfully, I walked back to the room. Dave had already left his office, and I busied myself showering and packing the suitcase. Later that morning I talked to Dave and gave him the good news.

"That's great!" he said enthusiastically. "Keep a close eye on it while you're home. We'll want you back in May, and we'll do another oral glucose-tolerance test and a 24-hour profile."

"What do you think happened during all that time I was on insulin?"

"I just don't know. It's possible that the injected insulin sublimated the pancreas's need to produce insulin. It just produced enough to give you good control. Then when you were withdrawn from insulin, it began to produce all you needed."

Then he voiced something that had been on my mind all week.

"You know, if the endoscopy Monday morning had shown that you had a problem with your stomach, I'd have operated, and we would have removed a healthy, functioning pancreas."

"I know, Dave," I said wonderingly. "Oh yes, how I know."

A New Beginning

✿✿✿✿

March to July 7, 1981

The months passed and the pancreas continued to work. On April 26, the seventh anniversary of the kidney transplant, the results of the blood tests drawn that day showed everything completely normal.

"That kidney Vic gave you is doing a really great job," Bill told me in his office. "And so is the pancreas. You," he said, leaning back in his chair and handing me a cigar, "are an absolute medical marvel."

"I wouldn't be if it weren't for Vic and Sarah and the parents of that child in Minneapolis."

More and more I began to think about the church's national convention to be held in St. Louis in July. I hoped the convention would adopt a resolution placed there by the Nebraska District, encouraging organ donations. During the spring months I spoke at different congregations in the area urging support of this resolution and encouraging the members to make use of the universal organ-donor cards. One day in late spring, President Meyer called.

"The Social Ministries Committee of the district would like you to meet with the floor committee in St. Louis on Memorial Day weekend. The floor committee is responsible for presenting Resolution 8-05 to the delegates at the convention. We passed this resolution last summer at our district convention in Seward."

"What kind of presentation do I give the floor committee?"

"That'll be up to you. Dr. Karl Barth from Wisconsin is chairman of the Social Services Committee of the Synod. We'd like you to meet with him and help to plan the presentation of Resolution 8-05 to the convention."

"All right. You know that I really feel strongly about this, and, if you feel I can do the job, then I want to help."

Friday of Memorial Day weekend found me arriving in St. Louis in the evening. I checked into my hotel room in time to hear the phone ringing. It was Dr. Leslie Weber, Executive Secretary of the church's Social Services Ministry. We introduced ourselves and talked briefly about the meeting on Saturday morning.

"If you're not too tired, I'd like to stop in. Would that be all right?"

"Certainly. I'd look forward to meeting you in person."

"Good. I'll be up a while later."

I called room service and ordered a sandwich and salad. I found that the water tasted terrible, so I called room service again.

"Send along a couple of bottles of beer."

I had just begun to eat when I heard a knock. I thought perhaps the bellboy had forgotten something.

"Yes," I said, opening the door.

"Hello, Al. I'm Dr. Weber."

I wasn't expecting him for at least an hour. I stood in my stocking feet, sleeves rolled up, tie off, and collar undone. Then I groaned inwardly. "Oh, no," I thought, "there are two bottles of beer on the tray. What's he going to think?"

We sat down at the table in the corner.

"You just go ahead and finish your meal. We can visit while you eat," Dr. Weber said.

"And drink," I thought ruefully to myself.

"Uh, the water here is really lousy," I said lamely, pouring beer in the glass and moving the bottle to what I hoped was a more inconspicuous spot.

"It does take some getting used to," he said, and then I heard a suppressed chuckle.

In the course of the evening I found Dr. Weber to be a gracious, extremely likable gentleman.

"We'll come by for you in the morning," he said as he left the room. "The meeting's at nine o'clock."

I entered the meeting room shortly before nine the next morning. I met Dr. Barth, and he introduced me to the other members of the committee.

"You're first on the agenda, Mr. Beckler," he said.

Resolution 8-05 was read. I took a deep breath and addressed my remarks to the committee. When I finished there was silence in the room.

"Are there any questions?" I asked the group.

There were only a few, but I was unable to read any reaction from the committee. We adjourned for a coffee break, and I stood in the hallway. Dr. Barth joined me.

"Al," he said in his deep, rich voice. "Your talk was a beautiful testimony. I've talked to members of the committee, and we feel that the best way to present Resolution 8-05 is for you to speak in its behalf at the convention in July. Will you do it?"

"Yes, I'll be happy to."

Once home, I started working on the speech I would give to the convention, but as Tuesday, July 7, 1981, dawned, the day I was to deliver the speech, I wasn't pleased with it.

"All ready for tonight?" Judy asked, when we boarded the plane to St. Louis.

"I don't know," I said, going over the Braille notes I had made on the index cards. "I'm not happy with this. It's too stiff. I'm not comfortable with it."

"I'm sure you'll do fine, you always do."

I went over my notes again, trying to memorize the speech, but my mind wandered. Busy as I had been since February, I had occasionally experienced a vague uneasiness, a gnawing feeling that there was something I had left undone, but I couldn't put my finger on it. At times in the office, my mind's eye would form a picture, but the elusive image was never completed. However, now wasn't the time to think about that. I pulled myself back to the present and my upcoming speech. I tried to memorize the statistics, the cold facts about organ donation, but I knew that that wasn't the kind of speech I wanted to give. Why not, I thought, tell them the same story that I had told in Seward last year about how a transplant can transform a life, make it rich and abundant and full of joy?

Impulsively, I tore the cards in two and put them in my pocket. I felt better. This speech might not be as polished as the other, but it was the one I wanted to give.

There were some members of the family in attendance at the convention. Bern, Sarah's husband, was a delegate from the Minnesota District, and they were both there. Gordon, now president of St. John's College, was also in attendance. We met them in the hotel for dinner and afterwards walked to the convention center.

"Judy, is it all right if Sarah takes me to the podium? I'm going to mention her in my speech."

"Yes. That would really be nice."

We found seats close to the convention floor, and as we sat, the tension inside me mounted. Gordon came over. "You'd better get set. They're almost ready for you."

"All right," I said, standing up. "Sarah, are you ready?"

"Gosh," she said laughing a little nervously. "Are you sure you want me to take you?"

"Yes I am," I said, squeezing her arm gently. "You'll do just fine."

We walked with Gordon to an area below the rostrum.

"Just a second. I want you to meet somebody," Gordon said.

"Al and Sarah, this is Dr. Jacob Preus, President of the Lutheran Church, Missouri Synod."

He greeted us cordially.

"There's someone else I'd like you to meet," Gordon continued. "This is Dr. Robert Sauer, Vice-President of the church and administrative assistant to Dr. Preus."

Earlier in the year I had talked with Dr. Sauer on the phone, and I found him now as then to be a thoughtful and considerate gentleman.

The five of us chatted briefly.

"You'll have to excuse us. We're wanted on the rostrum," Dr. Preus said.

He and Dr. Sauer went up the steps. The three of us stood, waiting.

"Nervous?" Sarah asked.

"Yes, a little."

Then it was our turn, and she and I ascended the steps to the rostrum and took our seats.

Leaning close, Sarah whispered, "You should see the crowd. Bern said there would be about three thousand people here."

I heard the buzz from the convention floor, the hum of voices that filled the large hall. And I hoped that my speech would be good enough to get through to them.

Before I could even begin to try to persuade them to vote for 8-05, I would need their undivided attention.

The session began, and Resolution 8-05 was read to the delegates.

WHEREAS, We accept and believe that our Lord Jesus came to give life and give it abundantly (John 10:10), and

WHEREAS, Through advances in medical science we are aware at the time of death, some of our organs can be transplanted to alleviate pain and suffering of afflicted human beings (Gal. 6:10), and

WHEREAS, Our heavenly Father has created us so that we can adequately and safely live with one kidney and can express our love and relieve the unnecessary prolonged suffering of our relatives, and

WHEREAS, We have an opportunity to help others out of love for Christ, through the donation of organs, therefore be it

RESOLVED, That our pastors, teachers, and DCEs be encouraged to inform the members of the Lutheran Church, Missouri Synod, of the opportunity to sign the Universal Organ Donor Card (which is to authorize the use of our

needed organs at the time of death in order to relieve the
suffering of individuals requiring organ transplants), and be
it further

RESOLVED, That we encourage family members to
become living kidney donors, and be it further

RESOLVED, That the program committees of pastors'
and teachers' conferences be encouraged to include 'organ
and tissue transplants' as a topic on their agendas, and be
it finally

RESOLVED, That the Board for Social Ministry and
World Relief seek ways to implement this program so that
the entire Synod may join in this opportunity to express
Christian concern.

Dr. Barth took the microphone.

"Mr. President, we think that this is an extremely significant
moment in our church body and I would like to call on Dr.
Weber to make a special introduction concerning the discussion
of this resolution."

Dr. Weber approached the microphone and addressed the delegates.

Slowly he said, "This resolution places before us an opportunity to share parts of our bodies with people in need. To indicate
the importance of this issue, we are happy to have with us this
evening Mr. Alfred Beckler of Grand Island, Nebraska. He has
been the recipient of three transplants and will speak to us at this
time. Mr. Beckler."

Sarah and I stood up and walked to the podium. She stood
slightly behind me and to my right. I took the microphone, and
before I began, I heard again the sounds of the convention, of
low voices, of people milling together.

I prayed silently. "Oh, God, please help me get through to
them."

I told them my story, about the days of early sickness, the
kidney transplant, the blindness, and my interest in the work
that Dave Sutherland was doing on laboratory animals, trying

to find a cure for diabetes. I told them of the time when I considered the transplant with Sarah.

"Sarah, that lovely young lady who brought me to the podium," I said, inclining my head toward her, "loves me very much, but she also knows me very well."

"She told me that 'if this procedure will work on rats—it's a lead-pipe cinch to work on you.'"

The convention laughed, and I heard Sarah behind me shuffle her feet in embarrassment. But when I told of its failure, Sarah's presence and the old ache of that memory caught at my throat, and I had to stop for a few seconds to regain my composure.

The auditorium was absolutely still. I didn't hear a sound.

I told them about the child that was killed in Minneapolis, and how the parents of that child responded in love and donated the child's organs. I told of my third transplant and its success. Finally, I spoke of Resolution 8-05: "We feel that this resolution is scripturally sound and is in complete accord with the mandates that our Lord has given us, that we should be concerned for, and loving and sharing to, our fellowman. We feel that if Missouri adopts this resolution and encourages her members to make use of the universal organ-donor cards, thousands of people will have their lives changed. We feel that if Missouri places her weight behind this resolution, other major church denominations will follow her lead, and tens of thousands of people may have their lives changed in a very dramatic and beneficial way. The Nebraska District of the Lutheran Church, Missouri Synod, urges you as delegates here in convention gathered to prayerfully consider this resolution, and we further urge its adoption. Thank you. Thank you all very much."

I stepped back and took Sarah's arm, and we walked to our seats. I stood with her, acknowledging the loud, prolonged applause, and then sat down.

"Al, Al," Sarah said urgently, pulling at my arm, "you can't sit down. They're giving you a standing ovation."

I stood beside my sister, that person who was so dear, so close to me, and smiled out at the audience. I knew what the vote would be.

"Oh, God, thank you," I prayed silently. "Thank you."

Dr. Preus came to the microphone. Slowly he said, "Would it be all right with the convention to let that applause be the vote on this subject?"

As the applause rang out again, he added, "I can't believe there would be any debate." But parliamentary procedures had to be followed and he opened the floor for discussion. The delegates were almost unanimous in voicing their support for the resolution. As I listened to them, waiting for Dr. Preus to call for the vote, I suddenly felt very good.

I thought of Vic and Sarah and what they had undergone with me. I thought of my blindness. I thought of my perseverance in fighting against diabetes. I thought of my friends and my family, and I thought of the parents of that child in Minneapolis, unknown to me and I to them. Then the uneasiness, the gnawing feeling that something was left undone, came over me. What was it?

I thought of Judy waiting for me on the convention floor and I thought of our boys, Kevin, Scott, and Russell. Suddenly, desperately I wished my sons were here. I wanted them to have heard my speech. I wanted them to know what had happened to me in the last eight years. I wanted them to know why I had done what I had done, what had prompted, motivated, and compelled me. I wanted them to know me. Now I knew what was left undone.

"Some day, some day," I had told Judy years before, "I want to tell the boys. Maybe I'll write a book."

And as the realization of what I had left undone came to me, so also came the determination, will, and desire to see it through. I would tell my sons. I would write a book. I was eager, vibrant, and alive. It lay there before me, waiting, and I was anxious to begin.

Dr. Preus called for the vote. "All in favor of the resolution will please raise your hand and say aye."

The vote was overwhelming, enthusiastic in its unified assent. I rose from the chair. Sarah stood close to me, and as I took her arm, she squeezed my hand fiercely to her side.

"Oh, Al," she said, and I heard the sudden catch, the emotion stirring in her voice. "We all love you very much."

"I know," I said, and a tear creased my cheek. "I've always known."

We turned, crossed the rostrum, and descended the steps.